Brett Beemyn
Erich Steinman
Editors

Bisexuality in the Lives of Men: Facts and Fictions

Bisexuality in the Lives of Men: Facts and Fictions has been co-published simultaneously as *Journal of Bisexuality*, Volume 1, Numbers 2/3 2001.

Pre-publication
REVIEWS,
COMMENTARIES,
EVALUATIONS . . .

"**A**t last, a source book which *ex-plains* male-centered bisexual desires, practices and identities in a language which *all of us* can under-stand!

This is informative reading for a general audience, and will be especially valuable for discussions in gender studies, sexuality studies, and Men's studies courses."

William L. Leap, PhD
Professor, Department of Anthropology,
American University, Washington DC

Harrington Park Press

Bisexuality in the Lives of Men: Facts and Fictions

Bisexuality in the Lives of Men: Facts and Fictions has been co-published simultaneously as *Journal of Bisexuality,* Volume 1, Numbers 2/3 2001.

Bisexuality
in the Lives of Men:
Facts and Fictions

Brett Beemyn
Erich Steinman
Editors

Bisexuality in the Lives of Men: Facts and Fictions has been co-published simultaneously as *Journal of Bisexuality,* Volume 1, Numbers 2/3 2001.

Harrington Park Press
An Imprint of
The Haworth Press, Inc.
New York • London • Oxford

Published by

Harrington Park Press®, 10 Alice Street, Binghamton, NY 13904-1580 USA

Harrington Park Press® is an Imprint of the Haworth Press, Inc., 10 Alice Street, Binghamton, Ny 13904-1580 USA.

Bisexuality in the Lives of Men: Facts and Fictions has been co-published simultaneously as *Journal of Bisexuality,* Volume 1, Numbers 2/3 2001.

Cover image by Gary H. Brown.
Cover design by Jennifer M. Gaska.

Library of Congress Cataloging-in-Publication Data

Bisexuality in the lives of men : facts and fictions / Brett Beemyn, Erich Steinman, editors.
     p. cm.
    Includes bibliographical references and index.
    ISBN 1-56023-147-5 (alk. paper)–ISBN 1-56023-148-3 (alk. paper)
      1. Bisexual men–United States–Social conditions. 2. Bisexual men–United States–Attitudes. 3. Bisexuality–United States–Public opinion. 4. Public opinion–United States. I. Beemyn, Brett, 1966- II. Steinman, Erich W.
   HQ74.2.U5 B53 2000
   305.38'9663'0973–dc21   00-047243

Indexing, Abstracting & Website/Internet Coverage

This section provides you with a list of major indexing & abstracting services. That is to say, each service began covering this periodical during the year noted in the right column. Most Websites which are listed below have indicated that they will either post, disseminate, compile, archive, cite or alert their own Website users with research-based content from this work. (This list is as current as the copyright date of this publication.)

Abstracting, Website/Indexing Coverage ...... Year When Coverage Began

- **CNPIEC Reference Guide: Chinese National Directory**
  of Foreign Periodicals 2000

- **FINDEX <www.publist.com>** 2000

- **GenderWatch <www.slinfo.com>** 2000

- **Linguistics and Language Behavior Abstracts (LLBA)**
  <www.csa.com> 2000

- **OCLC Public Affairs Information Service**
  <www.pais.org> 2000

- **Social Services Abstracts <www.csa.com>** 2000

- **Sociological Abstracts (SA) <www.csa.com>** 2000

Special Bibliographic Notes related to special journal issues
(separates) and indexing/abstracting:

- indexing/abstracting services in this list will also cover material in any "separate" that is co-published simultaneously with Haworth's special thematic journal issue or DocuSerial. Indexing/abstracting usually covers material at the article/chapter level.
- monographic co-editions are intended for either non-subscribers or libraries which intend to purchase a second copy for their circulating collections.
- monographic co-editions are reported to all jobbers/wholesalers/approval plans. The source journal is listed as the "series" to assist the prevention of duplicate purchasing in the same manner utilized for books-in-series.
- to facilitate user/access services all indexing/abstracting services are encouraged to utilize the co-indexing entry note indicated at the bottom of the first page of each article/chapter/contribution.
- this is intended to assist a library user of any reference tool (whether print, electronic, online, or CD-ROM) to locate the monographic version if the library has purchased this version but not a subscription to the source journal.
- individual articles/chapters in any Haworth publication are also available through the Haworth Document Delivery Service (HDDS).

Bisexuality in the Lives of Men: Facts and Fictions

CONTENTS

ABOUT THE EDITORS

Brett Beemyn, PhD, co-edited *Queer Studies: A Lesbian, Gay, Bisexual, and Transgender Anthology* (1996) with Mickey Eliason and edited *Creating a Place for Ourselves: Lesbian, Gay, and Bisexual Community Histories* (1997). He is currently working in higher education at the University of Rochester and writing a history of LGBT life in Washington, D.C. during the twentieth century.

Erich Steinman is a PhD student in sociology at the University of Washington in Seattle. He has organized, presented at, and participated in a variety of conferences and other events for bisexuals and the bisexual community in the last 10 years. He is currently working with the Makah Nation of northwestern Washington to develop a course examining interracial conflict and Native American treaty rights. He also teaches leadership and team-building skills for "learning communities," and a class on ethics and identity that examines modern and post-modern contexts of contemporary selfhood.

About the Contributors

Brett Beemyn, PhD, co-edited *Queer Studies: A Lesbian, Gay, Bisexual, and Transgender Anthology* (1996) with Mickey Eliason and edited *Creating a Place for Ourselves: Lesbian, Gay, and Bisexual Community Histories* (1997). He is currently working in higher education at the University of Rochester and writing a history of LGBT life in Washington, D.C. during the twentieth century.

Cover artist **Gary H. Brown** is Professor of painting and drawing in the Department of Art Studio at the University of California-Santa Barbara. During the last decade, his art work has centered on issues of life, love, and loss, and his inspiration has been Thomas Eakins, particularly Eakins's role as an American artist and teacher.

Amity Pierce Buxton, PhD, is a researcher, educator, and author. Her writings include *The Other Side of the Closet: The Coming-Out Crisis for Straight Spouses and Families* and "The Best Interest of Children of Gay and Lesbian Parents" (in *The Scientific Basis of Child Custody Decisions*). Director of the international Straight Spouse Network, she counsels spouses in mixed-orientation marriages and lectures across the country and abroad. She also leads a support group in the San Francisco Bay Area and serves on the board of the Family Pride Coalition.

Lynda S. Doll is Senior Behavioral Scientist in the Office of Prevention Research in the Centers for Disease Control and Prevention's Office of the Director. Prior to accepting this position, Dr. Doll was Chief of the Behavioral Intervention Research Branch and Associate Director for Behavioral and Social Science in the Division of HIV/AIDS Prevention. Dr. Doll has a PhD in developmental psychology, and during her 13 years at CDC, has been responsible for developing and managing HIV-related behavioral and social science research, most recently in the area of evaluating behavioral interventions and synthesizing and disseminating data on effective behavioral interventions. She has published extensively, with a particular focus on determinants of HIV-risk behaviors among men who have sex with men, bisexuality and HIV risk, and blood donation by HIV-seropositive persons.

Mickey Eliason is an associate professor of nursing and the director of the sexuality studies program at the University of Iowa. Her research has focused on issues of identity formation and homo-negativity.

Meaghan Kennedy, MPH, formerly an epidemiologist with the Division of HIV/AIDS Prevention at the Centers for Disease Control and Prevention in Atlanta, Georgia, has written on issues of sexuality and HIV/AIDS for several years. She is currently a writer and student.

Larry W. Peterson is Professor of Music at the University of Delaware. His publications include an analysis of the Surrealist poetry of the composer Olivier Messiaen, a study of the laments in Handel's operas and oratorios, and numerous articles on using technology to teach music. His multimedia work has won four national awards and is currently featured on a CD ROM, *Technology Tools for Today's Campuses*, funded by Microsoft. He founded three listservs and managed a fourth devoted either to music instruction or married bisexual/gay men.

Paula C. Rust, PhD, is Associate Professor of Sociology at the State University of New York at Geneseo. She is the author of *Bisexuality and the Challenge to Lesbian Politics: Sex, Loyalty, and Revolution* and *Bisexuality in the United States: A Social Science Reader.* Her research focuses on the development of bisexual identity and community. She lives with her partner and three children in Rochester, New York.

Erich Steinman has been active in local and regional bisexual organizations in the West and Midwest and presented at numerous bisexual and LGBT conferences. He currently is a graduate student in sociology at the University of Washington in Seattle, and has plans to research how relations between gay and bisexual men impact on HIV education and safer-sex behavior.

Introduction

Erich Steinman
Brett Beemyn

[Haworth co-indexing entry note]: "Introduction." Steinman, Erich and Brett Beemyn. Co-published simultaneously in *Journal of Bisexuality* (Harrington Park Press, an imprint of The Haworth Press, Inc.) Vol. 1, No. 2/3, 2001, pp. 1-14; and: *Bisexuality in the Lives of Men: Facts and Fictions* (ed: Brett Beemyn and Erich Steinman) Harrington Park Press, an imprint of The Haworth Press, Inc., 2001, pp. 1-14. Single or multiple copies of this article are available for a fee from The Haworth Document Delivery Service [1-800-342-9678, 9:00 a.m. - 5:00 p.m. (EST). E-mail address: getinfo@haworthpressinc.com].

What do we know about male bisexuality, and about men who understand themselves as bisexual? How can we conceptualize the relationship between sexual desire, behavior, and identity for men who are not exclusively involved with "same-sex" or "opposite-sex" partners? How can we understand the social and cultural dimensions of bisexuality in relation to men? The relative paucity of empirical studies and cultural critiques regarding bisexual men and male bisexuality makes trying to answer these questions difficult and requires patching together information, much of it dated, from a wide variety of sources. This lack of "facts," along with the corresponding prevalence of numerous myths or "fictions," motivated the publication of *Bisexuality in the Lives of Men: Facts and Fictions*, as well as our forthcoming work, *Bisexual Men in Culture and Society*.

All told, we know strikingly little about male bisexuality in the U.S. in terms of social scientific research. We lack basic information about "bisexual" behavior and the prevalence of self-identified bisexual men, as well as interpretations of the meaning and impact of such behaviors and identities on these men's lives. We do not have a clear picture of how they see themselves in relation to the world and to various conceptualizations of sexuality. A number of important studies and publications have placed bisexuality on the research map in the last 25 years, and these works offer various insights into the questions raised above.[1] Generally, however, these studies merely include bisexual men, rather than focusing specifically on their lives and experiences (public health research has been the primary exception).[2] In contrast, a number of book-length studies have considered bi women, often in relation to lesbians, such as Paula Rust's *Bisexuality and the Challenge to Lesbian Politics: Sex, Loyalty, and Revolution* (1995) and Kristin Esterberg's *Lesbian and Bisexual Identities: Constructing Communities, Constructing Selves* (1997).

Not only do we know little empirically about bisexuality and men, we still have minimal knowledge about the various ways that male bisexuality is popularly understood, evaluated, and represented in cultural production and social discourse. Through a conceptualization of bisexuals as having a "gay" and "straight" side, it is often believed that cultural attitudes toward and representations of gay men can also be understood as largely applying to bi men. This "sameness of effect" assumption appears frequently in research on many aspects of bisexuality–witness the ubiquitous phrase "gay and bisexual men" in the titles of countless journal articles which do not actually differentiate between the two.[3] Yet, as many of the essays in *Bisexuality in the Lives of Men* make clear, this assumption is simplistic, incomplete, and sometimes clearly inaccurate even regarding the aspects most seemingly shared by gay and bisexual men. For example, Mickey Eliason demonstrates that negative attitudes toward bisexuals are somewhat distinct from homophobic attitudes, suggesting that "bi-negativity" is not simply homophobia directed against the "gay side" of bisexuals. In her study, a group of heterosexual respondents were more accepting of gay than bi men, and lesbians than bi women, respectively, on a number of different survey items. The highest levels of disapproval and disgust were directed at bisexual men. These findings suggest that to be a self-identified bisexual man is to be the recipient of substantial social stigma.

While bisexuality has rarely received careful, serious consideration in the news media, literature, and film, three recent books make important contributions to our understanding of how bisexuals are represented in popular culture. Supplementing and going beyond identity-based anthologies,[4] Marjorie Garber's *Vice Versa: Bisexuality and the Eroticism of Everyday Life* (1995), Donald Hall and Maria Pramaggiore's *RePresenting Bisexualities: Subjects and Cultures of Fluid Desire* (1995), and the Bi Academic Intervention's *The Bisexual Imaginary: Representation, Identity and Desire* (1997) examine some of the ways that bisexuality is commonly constructed and interpreted. But, while these texts offer specific analyses of the representations of bisexual women, they provide little discussion of the treatment of male bisexuality and bisexual men in popular fiction, television, and movies; narratives of safer-sex education; and the language used to discuss sexuality and sexual orientation in general. The essays by Traci Carroll and Chris Cagle in *RePresenting Bisexualities* are notable exceptions here, and serve as an important beginning for the creation of a substantial, wide-ranging body of work on bisexual men. Analyzing representations of male bisexuality is crucial, for beyond shaping societal perceptions, these explicit and implicit cultural messages greatly influence bisexual men's self-images and behavior.

Our interest in addressing both empirical research and cultural and discursive studies led us to edit two separate collections; we felt that with so little published on male bisexuality, one text with a single perspective would be wholly inadequate. Thus these works take a wide variety of methodological and analytical approaches, from nuanced readings of how male bisexuality is posited by contemporary theory, to empirical studies of the lives of self-identified bisexual men, to critiques of the treatment of bisexual men in different cultural contexts.[5]

Our primary goal in producing both *Bisexuality in the Lives of Men: Facts and Fictions* and *Bisexual Men in Culture and Society* is to offer researchers, theorists, and more general readers new information and perspectives about male bisexuality through rigorously analytical, yet accessible, essays. We imagine these works as sites where bisexual men can engage theories about bisexuality that often remain in remote, sometimes uninviting, academic environs. We also want to make the experiences and viewpoints of bisexual men available to scholars interested in sexuality and gay and lesbian studies, and imagine these collections as sites where academics who are deeply embedded in particular disciplinary frameworks can be exposed to new ideas and approaches. These aims set forth a challenging task, but we feel accountable both to bisexual individuals and communities who lack information with which to make sense of their lives, and to analysts of various disciplines for whom these works can provide understanding and lead to further insight, theory, and research. Toward that end, almost all of the essays were written specifically for these volumes.

Our motivation is also personal. We each began to identify as bisexual about 10-15 years ago after having felt increasingly at odds with the existing possibilities for understanding our gender and sexual selves. Critical to both of us was becoming active in BiNet USA, the leading national bisexual organization, in 1992, where we learned about the concept of bisexuality and met a group of out, self-assured bisexuals. Encountering the idea of bisexuality expanded our thinking about gender and sexuality and suggested new interpretations for our experiences and desires. Later, developing a bisexual social network enabled us to overcome a host of negative myths about bisexuality and to claim that identity proudly.

Yet, despite our personal experience, we have found that the hostility toward bisexual men (when they are acknowledged or imagined at all), combined with the stigmatization of all expressions of male-male emotional, sensual, and sexual intimacy, continue to warp and distort the self-images of men who identify as bisexual. We are also painfully aware that cultural assumptions, such as the omnivorous sexual behavior ascribed to bi men (parodied in the bisexual magazine title *Anything That Moves*),[6] have had a detrimental impact on how others interact with self-identified bisexual men. While social theory has moved far beyond a relatively simplistic "good versus bad images" perspective for conceptualizing the politics of representation, the pervasively negative treatment of bisexual men calls for direct and sustained critique. It is painfully obvious and urgent to us that, along with challenging the stigmatization of homo-eroticism, we must identify and debunk stereotypes of male bisexuality.

By providing important information about bisexual men's images of community, their relationships, and other aspects of their lives, the essays in *Bisexuality in the Lives of Men* offer just such a counter to the myths about male bisexuality. Meaghan Kennedy and Lynda S. Doll review and evaluate public health research on bisexual men and HIV transmission, examining both the findings of different studies and the assumptions that researchers make about bisexuality. They conclude that the fear that bisexual men would provide a substantial "HIV bridge" from homosexual to heterosexual populations, which contributed to the stigmatization of bisexuality, was largely unfounded. Kennedy and Doll are critical but also appreciative of public health research paradigms and discourses, and their work presents the most current data on the relationship between bisexual male behavior and HIV transmission.

Drawing upon years of experience as Director of the Straight Spouse Network to enrich her interpretation of survey data, Amity Pierce Buxton discusses both the marital consequences of a husband's bisexual identity and how groups of married bi men and the heterosexual wives of bisexual men have worked successfully to maintain their relationships after disclosure. While these mixed-orientation marriages are similar in many ways to gay-heterosexual marriages, the former couples often devote more energy to the relationship to try to work out difficulties. Such partnerships are a challenge, but as Buxton's study demonstrates, many can be successful through extensive communication, honesty, and love.

First-hand experience also informs Larry W. Peterson's analysis of over a thousand postings to an electronic mail list that he moderated. His essay documents the profound effects that a virtual community can have on its members; for example, such lists help alleviate isolation, provide peers and role models, and facilitate the extensive sharing of personal experiences. Among the main themes that Peterson identifies in these exchanges are discussions about self-image, coming out, relationships with wives and other men, and the nature of marriage. Taken together, Buxton's and Peterson's essays provide a rich sense of the contemporary struggles, strategies, and successes of married bisexual men. Still, as with research on male bisexuality in general, we need many more empirical studies, along with discursive and representational analyses, in order to have a clearer understanding of their lives.

One very basic difference among bisexual men that needs to be more closely examined is the fact that not all bi men conceptualize the world in terms of gay, straight, and bisexual. Some wish to make bisexuality central to a broader liberation movement based on eliminating the focus on sexual identities (Board, 1995), while others want to use the ways that both bisexuality and transgenderism resist dichotomies to develop a radical gender/sexuality framework (Martin-Damon, 1995; Sunfrog, 1995). Many of these and other proposals for reframing sexuality present compelling analytical and political arguments, and hint at the inability of bisexuality as a descriptive category to capture all of the complexities that characterize the relationships between sexual desire, behavior, and identity in the lives of contemporary bisexual men. They also touch on ways in which many bisexuals feel somewhat uncertain about a bisexual identity. Among those who identify themselves as bisexual, there is tremendous variation in relative attraction to men and women, the frequency and gender mix of romantic and sexual relationships, the primacy of each gender in terms of organizing one's life and commitments, and other social and sexual differences (see Klein, 1993, for one multidimensional scale for conceptualizing sexual orientation). Thus we are aware that using the word "bisexual" to describe certain emotional, sensual, and erotic sensibilities and attractions (as not "gay" or "straight") may be taken to suggest a set of understandings that significantly misrepresent aspects of some people's sexual selves.

Even the simplest definition of bisexuality–emotional, sensual, and sexual involvement with or attraction to both men and women–is premised on notions that are not reflective of some bisexuals' experiences and sensibilities. The conventional understanding of sexual orientation, in which the biological gender of one's partner(s) indicates one's sexual type, is a serious oversimplification. Some bisexuals, for example, do not consider gender to be a primary factor in attraction, while others try to dispense with gender categories altogether. Even bisexuals who see gender as a critical component of their romantic and sexual relationships can interpret the meaning and source of this gendered attraction quite differently. Such differences remind us that there are "bisexualities" rather than "bisexuality" per se.

The essays included here also make specific contributions to a broadening or changing of the frameworks for discussing bisexuality. Paula C. Rust, for example, uses the words and elaborate maps of bi men to understand how they envision the bisexual community and its relationships to gay, lesbian, and straight communities. The fact that many respondents described the bisexual community as relatively small and lacking the organization of lesbian and gay communities suggests the importance of factors beyond desire and behavior in shaping one's sexual and social identity. Moreover, their very different comments and maps raise the question of what even self-identified bisexual men have in common, other than not being gay or straight.

Bisexuality in the Lives of Men is not simply about a discrete category of men–bisexuals–and their experiences, but about how a range of behaviors and identities are enacted, understood, and represented, and the effects of these interrelated phenomena upon various aspects of life. It is also about how straight, gay, and bisexual individuals are constructed within specific historical contexts. Individuals are enmeshed in historical processes through which personal identities and group boundaries are produced, challenged, negotiated, and transformed, and which in turn have important social, psychological, and political consequences. One hundred and fifty years ago, the concept of the homosexual as a category of persons did not exist, much less the concepts of bisexual and heterosexual.[7] This history helps ground the ambiguity regarding bisexuality in a continuously evolving sexual order. It also suggests that not only should claims about bisexual men be carefully examined, but also sexual categories in general need to be approached with caution. All are fundamentally fictions, stories of our sexual selves that orient our engagement with the world.

These stories keep changing, and in doing so, bring new anxieties and confrontations. Amidst this unstable sexual landscape, bisexuality has come to be a contentious, openly-hidden identity at the turn of the millennium. Drawing on these themes, Erich Steinman's essay addresses sexual identity and gay-bi male relations through an examination of bisexual men's relative invisibility in comparison to bisexual women. He suggests that while gay men may have negative attitudes about bisexual men, these have generally been much more concealed in the U.S. than have lesbians' negative reactions to bi women, widely considered to have spurred bi women's visibility. Bi men have not valorized or publicly asserted their sexual identities as widely as bi women because, he proposes, they have been less excluded from and stigmatized by their broader homo-erotic community. In making this argument, Erich links social scientific "constructionist" theory and humanities-based "queer theory" to develop a nuanced explanation of how discomfort shared by many gays and lesbians regarding bisexuals may generate dissimilar levels of conflict among men than among women.

The prevalence and intricacies of identity politics, at the core of Erich's essay, help explain why bisexuality, although an ambiguous identity, is nonetheless emerging today as a significant position from which to raise challenges to the dominant sexual order. For people who are bisexual, either in terms of behavior or identity, access to many sexuality-related rights has historically come only through non-disclosure. They have thus often been faced with a dismal choice between silencing or concealing aspects of their sexualities on the one hand, and diminished political access, unchallenged cultural assumptions, and lower social acceptance on the other. Some bisexuals have not been concerned by these limited options, but others have resisted such demands or found them impossible to live up to. While straight and lesbian/gay people have often reacted negatively when confronted with how they have forced bisexuals to remain in the closet, the fact that bisexuals responded to this silencing by emphatically asserting their sexual identities is an understandable, though not inevitable, consequence of the current sexual order.

These dynamics have driven the emerging bisexual socio-political movement and made its activities increasingly important. Within and alongside lesbian and gay institutions, campaigns, and projects, bisexual political efforts have supported and mobilized thousands of individuals across the U.S. and beyond. Today, more than 300 specifically bisexual organizations exist in at least 17 countries (Ochs, 1999). BiNet USA marked its tenth anniversary in 2000, and since 1995, the annual International Bisexual Conference has been held in Amsterdam, London, New York, Berlin, and Boston. Yet, despite these accomplishments, bisexual activists often feel isolated, and even with frequent references to the "bisexual community," it is not clear that there actually is such a thing. Bisexuals like the men in Paula C. Rust's study are imagining the bisexual community within the context of a still-emerging social movement. But, as shown by their comments, the bisexual community, even if only a concept, clearly has meaning and importance for many men, helping them find support and develop a sense of belonging.

FUTURE RESEARCH NEEDS

While the essays in *Bisexuality in the Lives of Men* primarily address research and theorizing about sexuality, the relationships between bisexuality and masculinity serve as a critical context for this work, and issues of gender need to be examined in greater depth in future studies. According to masculinities scholar R. W. Connell, the dominant gender system is in the midst of a crisis, as the relationships between men and women, as well as between hegemonic and subordinate masculinities, are being challenged, defended, and negotiated (Connell, 1995). A growing body of scholarship on men and masculinities insists that all men have an unstable relationship to dominant masculinity; for self-identified and behaviorally gay and bisexual men, this relationship is particularly volatile. Existing and newly emerging forms of masculinity both subvert and emulate dominant expressions of masculinity through exposing, employing, and transforming them (Levine, 1998; Nardi, 2000). Among the most important questions for future research to address include: Is there something distinctive about bisexual men's engagement with masculinity? How do masculinity-related dynamics shape and affect bisexual behavior and identity in the current sexual and gender (dis)order? How do bisexuals perceive their masculinities, and how are their masculinities perceived by the non-bisexuals around them?

Another important direction for future research is the need for more studies on the lives of men of color and white, working-class men, and for issues of race and class to be incorporated into all critical analyses of male bisexuality. As feminist theorists such as Patricia Hill Collins and bell hooks have eloquently argued, a unidimensional social analysis fails to capture the multidimensionality of any individual and their social locations (Collins, 1989; hooks, 1981). Building upon this work, June Jordan (1991) and Orna Izakson (1995) make similar arguments regarding approaches to bisexuality, the latter in her appropriately titled essay, "If Half of You Dodges a Bullet, All of You Ends Up Dead." The beliefs and behaviors of bisexual men are shaped simultaneously by their class, race, and other social positions; therefore, considering any aspect in isolation will be inadequate to understanding their lives. The solution is not simply one of adding more studies about men of color and other male subpopulations. Instead, conscious attention to members of dominant as well as historically marginalized groups is called for; rather than making dominant group members the supposed norm, such assumptions need to be explicitly analyzed. Underlying this argument is the idea that on dimensions like race, gender, and sexual orientation, members of various groups can only be understood in relation to one another. Male bisexuality thus cannot be interpreted simply as its own category, but must be recognized in relation to gay and straight; one cannot exist and take on meanings without the reality of the other(s).

Research therefore needs to address both how bisexuality is in a dynamic relationship with homosexuality and heterosexuality and how conceptions like race and class may be complexly interwoven in the ways that bisexuals envision their communities and understand their masculinities. For instance, do themes of choice and subversion, which are often articulated in bisexual activist writing, reflect notions and experiences of independence and mobility, and a fundamental communal rootlessness, that are largely specific to white, middle-class individuals and their socio-cultural locations? Does the tone of superiority, conviction, and revolutionary zeal with which bisexuality is occasionally presented, in its transcendence of sexual and gender categories and norms, sometimes have masculinist, vanguard connotations–its grand, visionary mission contrasted with supposedly unthinking, regressive, trapped "monosexuals" who unwittingly support the current sexual order? While these questions are offered here only as examples, grappling with such complexity and multidimensionality needs to occur much more frequently in sexuality research and theorizing than is currently the case.

A final suggestion for future research relates to methodology, and is much more basic: researchers must begin to listen to bisexual men and consider their experiences, perceptions, and desires. As each of the essays included here illustrates, bi men's voices need to be heard not only to understand the specificity of their lives, but also to recognize how their lives differ from those of gay and heterosexual men on the one hand and bisexual women on the other. We hope that this collection can serve as one starting point, and will help end the silence around male bisexuality.

ACKNOWLEDGMENTS

Many people have contributed to this volume, often from afar and sometimes without their knowledge. Foremost, we thank Fritz Klein and The Haworth Press for believing in the project and giving us the opportunity to publish not just one but two works, when other presses felt that *any* book about male bisexuality was unmarketable, if not unworthy. All of the authors have written groundbreaking essays, and we thank them for supporting us even when it seemed that these volumes would never be completed. We also greatly appreciate the sustenance, inspiration, and support provided by long-time bisexual activists, including Stephanie Berger, Elias Farajajé-Jones, Alexei Guren, Loraine Hutchins, Lani Ka'ahumanu, and Naomi Tucker. To them and to the many other individuals we have failed to name here, we are greatly indebted, and hope that the final product constitutes partial repayment for their assistance.

These collections began as Brett Beemyn's vision, and initially they were his solo project. Erich would like to thank Brett for his invitation to join him in editing the volumes. He would also like to recognize the support of faculty and colleagues at the University of Washington, especially Julie Brines, Stephanie Burkhalter, Judy Howard, and Davis Patterson. Brett would like to acknowledge Erich's willingness to come on board part-way into the process to make these collections a reality, and the important social scientific perspective he has brought to the project. He would also like to thank Michele

Spring-Moore for her editing advice, and for bringing greater personal meaning to these volumes and his life.

In closing, we hope that these essays not only add to current research and our collective knowledge, but also serve as a resource to help men of all sexual behaviors and identities, but especially bisexual men, experience more affirmation and understanding, and individually and collectively build more satisfying lives. It will require substantial changes in both individual attitudes and the society at large for the day to come when, as a matter of course, people will embrace rather than stigmatize such desires and sensibilities in themselves and others. Bisexual men can move us closer to that day by supporting and celebrating each other's bodies, desires, and relationships and by developing a positive sense of themselves as bisexuals.

NOTES

1. Some of the groundbreaking studies of bisexuality include: Pepper Schwartz and Philip Blumstein's interview-based research (1976, 1977); Fritz Klein and Timothy Wolf's *Two Lives to Lead: Bisexuality in Men and Women* (1985); Klein's *The Bisexual Option* (1993); Gilbert Herdt's *Ritualized Homosexuality in Melanesia* (1984); Martin Weinberg, Colin Williams, and Douglas Pryor's *Dual Attraction: Understanding Bisexuality* (1994) and their recent extension of these findings (1999); Beth Firestein's *Bisexuality: The Psychology and Politics of an Invisible Minority* (1996); and Erwin Haeberle and Rolf Gindorf's *Bisexualities: The Ideology and Practice of Sexual Contact with Both Men and Women* (1998). This last work contains two chapters focusing on bisexual men.

2. Among the groundbreaking public health studies of bisexual men are Aggleton, 1996; Boulton, Hart, and Fitzpatrick, 1992; Doll and Beeker, 1996; McKirnan, Stokes, Doll, and Burzette, 1995; Stokes, McKirnan, and Burzette. Most of this research, though, reduces bisexuality to those men who have sex with both men and women in a certain time frame. While this approach has an instinctive appeal and internal consistency, it is highly dependent on the time period used for the study, and creates social categories that may be misleadingly reified in a study's findings. Moreover, although the public health field has generated more research on the lives of bisexual men than any other discipline, it still sometimes fails to differentiate bisexual men from gay men.

3. In some cases, though, the research frameworks of these articles offer the best possible solutions to the challenging problems of categorization and analysis, and demonstrate an acknowledgement of bisexuality.

4. Such analyses are most evident in Loraine Hutchins and Lani Kaahumanu's *Bi Any Other Name: Bisexual People Speak Out* (1991), Elizabeth Reba Weise's *Closer to Home: Bisexuality and Feminism* (1992), and Sharon Rose, Cris Stevens et al.'s *Bisexual Horizons: Politics, Histories, Lives* (1996).

5. The existing general bisexual anthologies have predominantly reflected perspectives from literary and social theory/cultural studies (Bi Academic Intervention,

1997; Hall and Pramaggiore, 1995), the social sciences (Haeberle and Gindorf, 1998), psychology (Firestein, 1996; Klein and Wolf, 1985), or public health (Aggleton, 1996). To date, the only general bisexual anthology that brings together these different disciplines is Merl Storr's collection of previously published work, *Bisexuality: A Critical Reader* (1999).

6. The mission statement of *Anything That Moves* reads in part: "We will write, print, or say *anything that moves* us beyond the limiting stereotypes that are displaced onto us."

7. John D'Emilio and Estelle Freedman's *Intimate Matters: A History of Sexuality in America* (1988) is an excellent starting point here. Michel Foucault's *The History of Sexuality* (1980), Jonathan Ned Katz's *The Invention of Heterosexuality* (1995), and Jeffrey Weeks's *Sexuality and Its Discontents* (1985) more broadly address historical changes in conceptions of sexuality.

REFERENCES

Aggleton, Peter, ed. 1996. *Bisexualities and AIDS: International Perspectives.* Bristol, PA: Taylor and Francis.

Bi Academic Intervention (Phoebe Davidson et al.), eds. 1997. *The Bisexual Imaginary: Representation, Identity and Desire.* London: Cassell.

Blumstein, Philip W., and Pepper S. Schwartz. 1976. Bisexuality in Men. *Urban Life* 5 (3): 339-58.

_____. 1977. Bisexuality: Some Psychological Issues. *Journal of Social Issues* 33 (2): 30-45.

Board, Mykel. 1995. Pimple No More. In *Bisexual Politics: Theories, Queries, and Visions,* ed. Naomi Tucker, 281-87. Binghamton, NY: Harrington Park Press.

Boulton, Mary, Graham Hart, and Ray Fitzpatrick. 1992. The Sexual Behavior of Bisexual Men in Relation to HIV Transmission. *AIDS CARE* 4 (2): 165-75.

Collins, Patricia Hill. 1990. *Black Feminist Thought: Knowledge, Consciousness, and the Politics of Empowerment.* Boston: Unwin Hyman.

Connell, R. W. 1995. *Masculinities.* Berkeley: University of California Press.

D'Emilio, John, and Estelle B. Freedman. 1988. *Intimate Matters: A History of Sexuality in America.* New York: Harper and Row.

Doll, Lynda, and Carolyn Beeker. 1996. Male Bisexual Behavior and HIV Risk in the United States: Synthesis of Research with Implications for Behavioral Interventions. *AIDS Education and Prevention* 8 (3): 205-25.

Esterberg, Kristin G. 1997. *Lesbian and Bisexual Identities: Constructing Communities, Constructing Selves.* Philadelphia: Temple University Press.

Firestein, Beth A., ed. 1996. *Bisexuality: The Psychology and Politics of an Invisible Minority.* Thousand Oaks, CA: Sage Publications.

Foucault, Michel. 1980. *The History of Sexuality, Volume 1.* New York: Vintage.

Garber, Marjorie. 1995. *Vice Versa: Bisexuality and the Eroticism of Everyday Life.* New York: Simon and Schuster.

Haeberle, Erwin J., and Rolf Gindorf, eds. 1998. *Bisexualities: The Ideology and Practice of Sexual Contact with Both Men and Women.* New York: Continuum.

Hall, Donald E., and Maria Pramaggiore, eds. 1995. *RePresenting Bisexualities*: *Subjects and Cultures of Fluid Desire*. New York: New York University Press.

Herdt, Gilbert. 1984. *Ritualized Homosexuality in Melanesia*. Berkeley: University of California Press.

hooks, bell. 1981. *Ain't I a Woman*: *Black Women and Feminism*. Boston: South End Press, 1981.

Hutchins, Loraine, and Lani Kaahumanu, eds. 1991. *Bi Any Other Name*: *Bisexual People Speak Out*. Boston: Alyson.

Jordan, June. 1991. A New Politics of Sexuality. *The Progressive* (July): 13.

Katz, Jonathan Ned. 1995. *The Invention of Heterosexuality*. New York: Dutton.

Klein, Fritz. 1993. *The Bisexual Option*. Binghamton, NY: Harrington Park Press.

Klein, Fritz, and Timothy J. Wolf, eds. 1985. *Two Lives to Lead*: *Bisexuality in Men and Women*. Binghamton, NY: Harrington Park Press (the book was also published by Haworth Press under the title *Bisexualities*: *Theory and Research*).

Levine, Martin P. 1998. *Gay Macho*: *Life and Death of the Homosexual Clone*. New York: New York University Press.

Martin-Damon, Kory. 1995. Essay for the Inclusion of Transsexuals. In *Bisexual Politics*: *Theories, Queries, and Visions*, ed. Naomi Tucker, 241-50. Binghamton, NY: Harrington Park Press.

McKirnan, David J., Joseph Stokes, Lynda Doll, and Rebecca G. Burzette. 1995. Bisexually Active Men: Social Characteristics and Sexual Behavior. *Journal of Sex Research* 32 (1): 65-76.

Nardi, Peter M., ed. 2000. *Gay Masculinities*. Thousand Oaks, CA: Sage Publications.

Ochs, Robyn, ed. 1999. *Bisexual Resource Guide, 2000*. Cambridge, MA: Bisexual Resource Center.

Rose, Sharon, Cris Stevens et al., eds. 1996. *Bisexual Horizons*: *Politics, Histories, Lives*. London: Lawrence and Wishart.

Rust, Paula. 1995. *Bisexuality and the Challenge to Lesbian Politics*: *Sex, Loyalty, and Revolution*. New York: New York University Press.

Stokes, Joseph P., David J. McKirnan, and Rebecca G. Burzette. 1993. Sexual Behavior, Condom Use, Disclosure of Sexuality, and Stability of Sexual Orientation in Bisexual Men. *Journal of Sex Research* 30 (3): 203-13.

Storr, Merl, ed. 1999. *Bisexuality*: *A Critical Reader*. New York: Routledge.

Sunfrog. 1995. Pansies Against Patriarchy: Gender Blur, Bisexual Men, and Queer Liberation. In *Bisexual Politics*: *Theories, Queries, and Visions*, ed. Naomi Tucker, 319-24. Binghamton, NY: Harrington Park Press.

Weeks, Jeffrey. 1985. *Sexuality and Its Discontents*. London: Routledge.

Weinberg, Martin S., Colin J. Williams, and Douglas W. Pryor. 1994. *Dual Attraction*: *Understanding Bisexuality*. New York: Oxford University Press.

_____ 1999. Bisexuals at Midlife. Paper presented at the American Sociological Association Annual Meeting, Chicago, August 8, 1999.

Weise, Elizabeth Reba, ed. 1992. *Closer to Home*: *Bisexuality and Feminism*. Seattle: Seal.

Interpreting the Invisibility of Male Bisexuality

Theories, Interactions, Politics

Erich Steinman

[Haworth co-indexing entry note]: "Interpreting the Invisibility of Male Bisexuality: Theories, Inter-actions, Politics." Steinman, Erich. Co-published simultaneously in *Journal of Bisexuality* (Harrington Park Press, an imprint of The Haworth Press, Inc.) Vol. 1, No. 2/3, 2001, pp. 15-45; and: *Bisexuality in the Lives of Men: Facts and Fictions* (ed: Brett Beemyn and Erich Steinman) Harrington Park Press, an imprint of The Haworth Press, Inc., 2001, pp. 15-45. Single or multiple copies of this article are available for a fee from The Haworth Document Delivery Service [1-800-342-9678, 9:00 a.m. - 5:00 p.m. (EST). E-mail address: getinfo@haworthpressinc.com].

SUMMARY. Bisexuality has come to be a contentious, openly-hidden identity amidst evolving sexual identities and contested sexual politics. A number of specific dynamics characterize engagements involving bisexuality, including definitional controversies, border disputes among gay, lesbian, and bisexual communities, and debates over minority group rights that have both reflected and produced gay and lesbian investments in identity. This article draws on these themes and addresses sexual identity and gay-bi male relations through an examination of bisexual men's relative invisibility in comparison to bisexual women. I bring together social scientific "constructionist" theory and humanities-based "queer theory" to develop a nuanced explanation of how discomfort shared by many gays and lesbians regarding bisexuals may generate dissimilar levels of conflict among men than among women. I suggest that while gay men may have negative attitudes about bisexual men, these have generally been much more concealed in the U.S. than have lesbians' negative reactions to bi women, widely considered to have spurred bi women's visibility. Bi men have not valorized or publicly asserted their sexual identities as widely as bi women because, I propose, they have been less excluded from and stigmatized by their broader homoerotic community. Implications for analysis and sexual politics are considered. *[Article copies available for a fee from The Haworth Document Delivery Service: 1-800-342-9678. E-mail address: <getinfo@ haworthpressinc.com> Website: <http://www.HaworthPress.com>]*

KEYWORDS. Bisexual men, bisexuality, gay, identity politics, lesbian, masculinity, queer, queer theory, social constructionism, social movements

. People who have been on the lookout for "bisexual" men in the 1990s–AIDS educators, heterosexual women, gay men, and women-led bisexual groups–have had a hard time finding them. Bisexual men are not easily identified, and have had a distinctively low public profile. Particularly since visibility has been a central strategy of gay and lesbian social movements, the low public profile of bisexual men constitutes a notable absence. Inverting a common Gay Pride chant, one might ask, "Are they here?" With the gay and lesbian movement increasingly enjoying astounding institutional and attitudinal advances (albeit with significant setbacks), the elusive, (non)public nature of male bisexuality seems surprising. Shouldn't men who have relations with or attractions to both men and women have relative freedom today to disclose what they do? Now that men can more often find affirmative or tolerant responses from therapists, school counselors, and employers to the knowledge that they have sex with other men (sex with women, of course, has always been received favorably), might not one expect to see greater public enactment of a "bisexual" identity?

In this essay, I consider several possible explanations for the minimal public presence of "bisexual" men, developing a thesis which synthesizes queer theory and social constructionist theory. Through a historical account of the development of the 1980s bisexual movement, I illuminate the *divergent* experiences of behaviorally bisexual men and women in gay and lesbian communities, respectively, and suggest how these experiences generated distinct and unequal motivations to affirm bisexual identities and build visible bisexual communities. I then discuss the political implications of this analysis and consider possibilities for sexual politics as we enter the new millennium.

BISEXUAL WOMEN AND MEN

Several stereotypical images of bisexual men have recently become prevalent in the U.S. Bi men have been designated a high-risk category for HIV/AIDS (see Marshall Miller's essay in this volume) and both male and female bisexuality has been portrayed as a strange, yet trendy lifestyle in the mainstream press, coverage which eerily echoes stories on bisexuality run by *Newsweek* and *Time* in 1974 (Leland, 1995; Toufexis, 1992). Beyond these representations, male bisexuality has largely lacked a public profile in the U.S., and even within lesbian, gay, bisexual, and transgender communities, bisexual men are much less visible than bisexual women.

An illustrative anecdote: at the 1999 Seattle Gay Pride festival, the Seattle Bisexual Women's Network had a well-staffed booth to publicize the frequent activities of the roughly 35-member group, including their nationally distributed newsletter. In contrast, the Seattle Bisexual Men's Union, which meets monthly with an average group of 6-8, was nowhere in sight. While the visibility of bi women in comparison to bi men may be different elsewhere in the country, this situation is not atypical, and is most striking in three public activities which I will consider below: published personal writings about bisexuality, grassroots community group formation, and social and political leadership.

In the last eight years, there have been three bisexual anthologies combining analytical and personal essays published in the U.S., and all three have been individually or collectively edited by women (Hutchins & Kaahumanu, 1991; Tucker, 1995; Weise, 1992). One of these focused on bisexuality and feminism, and had only female contributors. The other two contained mostly women writers: 51 women to 25 men in one, and 27 to 6 in the other. In addition, a women's bisexual anthology was published by a group of Canadian women (Bisexual Anthology Collective, 1995), and a recent mixed-gender international anthology from the U.K. included 34 female and 22 male contributors, among them five women and no men from the U.S. (Rose, Stevens et al., 1996). In bookstores and magazines, on search engines, and virtually anywhere else you look, women are reporting, digesting, and analyzing their experiences of bisexuality much more than men.

As suggested by the Seattle story above, there are more bi women's groups than men's, and they are more active and public. Characterizing local bisexual social group activity in 1991, Elizabeth Reba Weise stated: "These days you can go to most major cities in the U.S. and find a group of bisexuals to meet with, especially if you're a woman" (Weise, 1996: 306). Bi women's groups have fueled the revival of bisexual organizing since the mid-1980s, and in many large cities, active bi women's groups often exist alongside mixed-gender groups, and occasionally bi men's groups.[1] While all bisexual groups fluctuate in size and organizing ability, bi women's groups have consistently had a more significant presence than men's groups (Udis-Kessler, 1996).

Beyond gender-specific groups, a similar pattern holds. Bisexual activists in mixed-gender organizing projects (such as national organizations; regional, national, and international conferences; and specific activities) have noted the relative absence of men in their ranks, particularly in leadership positions, for a number of years. "One major difference between the movements of the 1970s and early 1990s," according to long-time bisexual activist Stephen Donaldson, "is the noticeable preponderance of men in the 1970s, whereas women now outnumber men by far both at the leadership and grass roots levels" (Donaldson, 1995: 37). Another activist, Gary North, agrees; writing in the early 1990s, he stated that "in my research, I kept running into women who were taking leadership roles or leading the movement–or a bi movement–and men were few and far between" (North, 1990: 40). A similar sentiment has been expressed in numerous articles in *Anything That Moves*, a national bisexual magazine, and *BiNet News*, the newsletter of the leading national bisexual political organization (see, for example, Berger, 1995; Silver, 1998). Activists are clearly asking, "Where are the bi men?" Even behaviorally and self-identified bisexual men have difficulty finding other bisexually active men, at least in bisexual organizations.[2]

THEORIES OF BIOLOGICAL
AND BEHAVIORAL DIFFERENCE

One explanation for the lower visibility of bi-identified men considers whether this absence may result from a lower level of bisexual sexual activity by men than women. Are there simply more "behaviorally bisexual" women than men in the U.S.? This "behavioral difference" approach reflects a traditional understanding of sexuality; the focus is on the individual, and the key question is "what attribute causes a certain behavior." Historically, this perspective has pathologized same-sex sexuality, as researchers commonly saw almost any non-normative personal characteristics as signs of sexual deviancy.

Nevertheless, the behavioral difference perspective underlies some academic arguments and "folk" perceptions, in which it is held that because women can often be more physically intimate together (i.e., that they can more easily deviate from the assumed norm of opposite-sex relations), "women are more bisexual than men." This belief in the greater "natural" bisexuality of women has had some famous advocates; Sigmund Freud, for example, claimed that "there can be no doubt that the bisexuality, which is present, as we believe, in the innate disposition of human beings, comes to the fore much more clearly in women than in men" (Freud, 1964: 227-28). Freud based his assertion not on socialization, though, but on his conception of psycho-sexual development–the notion that same-sex intimacy for women develops before opposite-sex desire, and thus women's heightened bisexuality results from erotic attachments originally generated toward the mother that remain even after a socialized re-orientation toward men.

Such perceptions implicitly suggest that there is an inner sexual essence and that sexual identity inevitably reflects sexual behavior. Freud's proposition of a developmental polymorphous sexuality notwithstanding, the concept of some sort of individual sexual essence, understood in terms of the gender of one's partners, has become an inescapable social concept and personal attribute in twentieth-century U.S. society. Essence is seen as informing behavior and identity, which can then be either closeted or "out" for the public to see.

The search for a "gay gene" (Hamer & Copeland, 1994) is premised on the "unity" of these elements, for it attempts to explain gay identity and behavior by finding some specific underlying biological cause. In the future, it could conceivably offer some posited difference between the bisexual behavior of men and women, thereby potentially explaining the comparative invisibility of bisexually-identified men. But biological approaches that attempt to account for non-heterosexual sexual behaviors have been severely challenged by both historical research and cross-cultural anthropological evidence that documents a dizzying variety of sexual practices (Blackwood, 1986; Herdt, 1984; Mead, 1935; Williams, 1986).

Even if there are gender-based differences in bisexual behavior, might not these possible differences reflect socially learned behaviors and attitudes? One prominent theory of individual sexual behavior, William Simon and John Gagnon's social scripting approach, argues that all sexual behavior reflects three levels of social understanding: cultural, interpersonal, and intrapsychic (Simon & Gagnon, 1987). Using this perspective, the sexual rules that women learn could be applied to behavioral patterns that include both sexes. For example, women's "scripting" in terms of emotional intimacy may lead some women to develop more satisfying, albeit deviant, sexual relationships with other women rather than with men, for whom the scripting of sex is more focused on conquest and intercourse.

While there are plausible arguments to be made using a differential social scripting analysis, and conceivable biological explanations as well, empirical sexuality research provides some strong evidence against the main premise such views must rest on: that bisexual male (in)visibility stems from lower levels of "bisexual" behavior. Numerous sexuality surveys report rates of male bisexual behavior that are very comparable to those of women (see Fox, 1996, for an excellent summary). For example, two large-scale sexuality studies conducted in 1994, the National Health and Social Life Survey and the National Opinion Research Center General Social Survey, together revealed that "of the 4.1% of the men and the 2.2% of the women who reported homosexual experiences in the preceding 5 years, 51% of the men and 64% of the women had sexual experiences with both women and men" (Fox, 1996: 16). While such studies use different measures for sexual activity (within the last year, since age 18, etc.), virtually all show similar levels of "bisexual" behavior among the men and women who report same-sex experiences. Furthermore, summarizing their review of a number of national studies conducted between 1970 and 1990, Susan Rogers and Charles Turner conclude that "the total percentage of men reporting such mixed sexual histories is greater than the percentage reporting exclusively male-male sexual contacts during their adult life or in the last year" (Rogers & Turner, 1991: 509). While such surveys yield purely descriptive information and can tell us little about how someone identifies, it seems reasonable to conclude that a significant number of men engage in same- and opposite-sex behavior, and that this figure is comparable to the number of behaviorally bisexual women. Thus the relative invisibility of bisexual men most likely does not result from the level of male bisexual behavior either in absolute terms or in comparison to women.

SOCIAL CONSTRUCTIONIST THEORIES

Beyond these empirical findings, the most direct challenge to biological and behavioral approaches to sexual identity is offered by social construc-tionism, which in the last 10-15 years has become the leading social science perspective for considering issues of sexuality. This approach combines a variety of theoretical perspectives that challenge the classic "antithesis of sex and society" (Seidman, 1996: 8). In contrast to the once-dominant idea that sexuality, sexual orientation, and other sexual characteristics are uniform, distinct, and innate across time and place, and that it is merely their expres-sion that varies due to social constraints, constructionism highlights the changing nature of sexual sensibilities, behaviors, and identities. Rather than controlling or merely shaping some innate sexual desire, society is seen as constructing sexual desires, behaviors, and subjects in a historically specific and evolving social process. The "natural" is no longer considered the root of sexual behavior, because the natural–i.e., the body–is thoroughly infused by society (Turner, 1996). Identities do not simply follow from behaviors; rather, as each varies historically, so too does the relationship between the two, reflecting the many different social forces at work.

Inspired in part by Michel Foucault's *The History of Sexuality*, in which he argued that the homosexual as a type of person arose as a result of late nineteenth century discourses (Foucault, 1980), other scholars developed analyses of the material and cultural forces shaping "gay" and "lesbian" individuals and communities (D'Emilio, 1983; Faderman, 1981; Katz, 1976; Weeks, 1985). Applying a social constructionist approach to the question of bi male invisibility is limited, however, by the gay and lesbian focus of research and theory, and highlights one of the tensions of social construction-ist sexuality research (Storr, 1999). Until very recently, bisexuals had barely made it onto the constructionist map in the social sciences. Furthermore, almost no empirical or theoretical sociological, anthropological, or historical work has yet focused specifically on bisexual men; the limited published research primarily reflects cultural studies, public health, and sexological perspectives (see note 1 in the introduction to this volume for a quick summary of this literature). Bisexual men often appear as add-ons, and their experiences are seen as synonymous with those of gay men (a general trend in sexuality research) or bisexual women (who have frequently been ignored themselves). This reflects one of the problematic characteristics of constructionist theory: it develops a historically and socially coherent account of gay history, community, and identity by erasing differences and ignoring experiences that do not easily or necessarily fit into such narratives. In commenting on four formative gay and lesbian constructionist texts, Scott Bravmann states that "though revealed as internally differentiated, the 'modern' category homosexuality nonetheless provides the thread that sutures together the diverse, unstable, contradictory, shifting histories recounted within each book" (Bravmann, 1996: 346).

Even authors who are well aware of these issues can appear to be contributing to a naturalization of "gay" by implying that gay identities have a certain coherency that is theoretically and empirically questionable. For example, in *Telling Sexual Stories*, sociologist Kenneth Plummer provides a detailed analysis of how the gay community elicits and facilitates an individual's utilization of the "coming out" narrative and highlights how some of the most widely circulated stories now include people not represented in previous versions. "The stories," Plummer writes, "have snowballed. Not just white gay men and lesbians 'coming out,' but black men, black lesbians, Hispanic lesbians, Hispanic men, Asian men, Jewish women, elderly gays, aging lesbians, deaf gays and lesbians" (Plummer, 1995: 96). Noticeably absent is any consideration of bisexual identity formation or how emergent bisexual coming out stories diversify the "gay" coming out story.

Plummer's focus on gay identity is understandable, though, for legitimating and celebrating homosexuality has clearly been instrumental in facilitating sustained resistance to enforced heterosexuality. One theme of this affirmation has been that homosexuality is "just as natural" as heterosexuality, a view that conflicts with constructionist sensibilities (which see neither as "natural"). Deeply informed by this legitimating project, research that focuses on gay identity often overlooks how the gay community may also *discourage* the consideration of other identity possibilities that are struggling to be articulated amidst the terrain dominated by heterosexual and homosexual narratives. Similarly, this type of approach precludes analysis of how the adoption of "gay" identities may require ignoring or devaluing dissonant behaviors and desires.

Above I said that Plummer *appears* to naturalize "gay," because these are dynamics of which Plummer is critically aware, having identified some of these issues himself almost fifteen years earlier. In *The Making of the Modern Homosexual* (1981), Plummer wrote that with all sexual categorizations comes "the paradox: they *control, restrict* and *inhibit* whilst simultaneously providing comfort, security and assuredness" (p. 29, my emphasis). However, it would be easy to read the more recent work without perceiving this more critical and complex perspective; in my reading of *Telling Sexual Stories*, I found no hint that such *restrictions* could be one of the effects of a gay community.

I do not mean to single out Plummer; his status as a leading social constructionist in the area of sexuality simply offers a high-profile example of a pattern found in constructionist research: even as it is widely understood that gay identities "control, restrict and inhibit," there is often a subtle naturalizing of the social process by which gay and other identities are constructed through researchers' omission of or inattention to the social control functions of contemporary gay narratives and communities in relation to other, non-heterosexual possibilities. Given that individuals interpret their sexual selves "by scanning their past lives (their bodies, group involvements, feelings and behaviors) and connecting these to 'accounts' available in their contemporary worlds" (as discussed by Plummer, 1981: 69), the degree to which bisexuality is experienced as a plausible option is shaped by gay community discourses and constructions of identity. Thus the gay community's advancement of gay and lesbian interpretations of non-heterosexual attractions and actions may function to restrict bisexual self-interpretations. While a single research project cannot address all related material, in a research area that highlights the social factors shaping sexual self-understanding and socio-sexual identification, the possible social control effects of gay communities should seemingly be more centrally and consistently acknowledged, even if they are not a focus.

Studies of bisexual women offer the most useful constructionist insights into the question of bi male visibility. Particularly suggestive is Amber Ault's research into the processes through which lesbian feminists have constructed boundaries around their identities, and in doing so, excluded others (Ault, 1994, 1996). She analyzes the ways in which lesbian feminists have constructed a "hegemonic discourse" which stigmatizes bisexual women, making them "doubly deviant," and discusses how this stigmatization has prompted bisexual women to become more visible and organize themselves politically.

The discourse analysis Ault employs, with the focus on boundary construction by lesbians, suggests the need to examine whether there has been similar boundary construction between gay and bisexual men, and whether similar exclusionary practices have acted to generate a distinctive and strongly held bisexual identity among men. Before I further develop this constructionist thesis, though, I will discuss the related and influential theoretical framework of queer theory to demonstrate how it adds useful elements to this analysis.

QUEER THEORY

Queer theory is fundamentally opposed to the individual, causal, and bio-behavioral "theories of difference" approach, and is similar to but distinct from social constructionist approaches. Generated primarily by humanities and literary studies scholars (though employing longstanding sociological notions, as well as textual interpretations and psychoanalytic analyses), queer theory insists on shifting the terms of inquiry from explaining the behavior of gays, lesbians, and other sexual minorities to examining the dominant "discourses" of knowledge that are built on sets of binary oppositions, such as man/woman, heterosexual/homosexual, and other pairs (Butler, 1993; Sedgwick, 1990). Sexuality is seen as a domain of power in which heterosexuality is privileged and valorized, while homosexuality is pervasively denigrated. Power is also manifested through sexuality, for conceptions of sexuality organize how we experience and understand ourselves; sexual regimes *constitute* individuals. One of the most influential queer theorists, Judith Butler, draws on "post-structuralist" theories (centrally associated with Derrida, 1976; Foucault, 1969, 1980) in insisting that in the contemporary West, people can only truly be "subjects"–agents who, because they are recognizable to themselves and others as stable, coherent entities, have "standing" and can act in the world–through culturally available categories, in this case sexualized self-identities (heterosexual or homosexual). In other words, you cannot exist psychically or socially in Western consciousness without a sexual orientation, and the two that we recognize, albeit unequally, are homosexual and heterosexual.

Queer theory centrally asserts that this binary framework for understanding sexuality, and the categories it employs (including the notion that sexual self-understanding should be organized around the gender of our real or desired partners, i.e., "sexual orientation"), are inherently unstable. In the last one hundred years, people have generally understood themselves as being within one of these two categories, but it is not a perfect fit. Conceptions of fixed or essentialist sexual identities are disputed by queer theory, and seen as products of a "heteronormative" cultural system. Even gay identities that were once seen as expressing a universal and transhistorical homoerotic sexual nature are understood within queer theory as reflecting this system of control and regulation. The logic of the heterosexual power/ knowledge system requires a marked "outside" gay position to naturalize heterosexuality's unmarked "inside" status; heterosexuality requires homosexuality against which to compare and thus define itself as the standard (Fuss, 1991).

Using and extending the psychoanalytic approach developed by Jacques Lacan, Butler emphasizes that these identities are not simply instilled by "outside" forces, nor maintained by purely external pressure (Butler, 1993). Rather, people who come to understand themselves as heterosexual or homosexual have a deep investment in these identities. A sexual self-understanding *outside* of these categories is looked at with dread and even repulsion. Moreover, each of us also desires to have a unity and coherency between our actions, desires, and identities (Lacan, 1977).

This framework for conceptualizing sexuality and sexual identity suggests that bisexuality is an extremely loaded, deeply confusing, and potentially critical issue for both individuals' sexualities and the modern sexual order. Indeed, bisexuality has been heralded as a transgression by both heterosexuals and homosexuals–considered "not only as the most politically radical of all sexual minorities, but provocatively postmodern as well" (Dollimore, 1997: 250). Butler uses the term "abject" to refer to those sexual elements which are not allowable within the heteronormative binary order. Though generally not directly stated, this is where queer theory positions bisexuality. According to Butler, the abject exists only in "uninhabitable zones; their very humanness" is questioned by the dichotomous sexual order (Butler, 1993: 3, 8).

While queer theory is insightful in understanding the relationships of various sexual subject positions to one another and to cultural narratives of sexuality, it has been criticized for failing to address the actual lives of bisexuals, who are trying to forge an existence in this "uninhabitable" terrain of the abject (du Plessis, 1996; Namaste, 1996). Collectively, albeit unintentionally, activists and writers in gay and lesbian politics, gay and lesbian studies, and sexuality and queer studies have issued conflicting demands to bisexuals and to individuals studying bisexuality. As U.K. bi theorist Clare Hemmings has observed, a definition of bisexuality and a substantial social presence sometimes seem to be prerequisites for taking bisexuals and bisexuality seriously (Hemmings, 1993). However, the demand that bisexuals be able to demonstrate the "reality" of bisexuality through a shared, definitive understanding of themselves conflicts with the queer emphasis on destabilizing identities. Conversely, underlying many other critiques of bisexuality is the notion that bisexuals want to create an "essentialist" bi identity, which is considered highly outmoded because of the queer subversion of fixed identities (Gamson, 1995; Solomon, 1991). For example, noted sex researchers John Gagnon, Cathy Stein Greenblat, and Michael Kimmel dismissively claim that "most scientists who study bisexuality and many of the better-educated persons who have sex with both men and women aspire to give bisexuality an essentialist status coequal with that of 'gay men,' 'lesbians,' and 'heterosexuals'" (Gagnon, Greenblat, & Kimmel, 1998: 88).

These critiques are often made against straw figures (Gagnon, Greenblat, and Kimmel do not refer to any specific claims or individuals), indicating that not much attention has been paid to how bisexual activists articulate their self-perceptions. For example, the existing bi anthologies have a substantial *anti-essentialist* sensibility, and their accounts of derisive and stigmatizing treatment support the notion that it can be daunting trying to articulate a sexual identity outside of the hetero-homo binary, due to conceptual unintelligibility and personal and institutional hostility. This space is not, however, truly uninhabitable; men and women have been identifying as bisexual, and gathering in regional, national, and international conferences, in increasing numbers over the last 15 years (see Ochs, 1999, for more detailed information).

Emergent bisexual identities could be understood through queer theory as one indicator that some of the latent instability of the binary system is exposed and cannot be effectively contained. According to Butler, the discourse of hetero-homo opposition continues to have power not because it is imposed by an outside force, but rather because it is "cited" over and over again and utilized repeatedly by individuals to understand themselves and the world. While never realized completely, categories like heterosexual and homosexual are invoked and stabilized over time to produce apparently natural sexual beings. Butler applies the term "citationality" to the process by which seemingly coherent and stable sexualities are produced by repetition. As she states, sexualities are "sedimented effect[s] of a reiterative or ritual practice," which accumulate an authoritative status over time and which are mistakenly seen as "real" and "essential" (Butler, 1993: 10).

The dynamic element in Butler's analysis is that such categories are always incomplete and generate elements that do not fit into the dominant sexual schema. There is inevitable excess; gaps and fissures, and potential for instability, are always near at hand. But what queer theory cannot do is explain how such potential instability is manifested. How does the abject, such as bisexuality, develop in the face of its cultural incoherence and institutional prohibition? Why does this occur? How are crises addressed, and who participates in efforts to sustain this order?

These questions highlight the need to study both discursive conceptualizations *and* social relations and to develop historical, contextual, and social analyses of how sexual dynamics work in specific settings, where instability is revealed, negotiated, hidden, contained, etc. As Susan Bordo, Steven Seidman, Steven Epstein, Barry Adam, Rosemary Hennessy, and others have emphasized, analyses which focus on the power of discourse sometimes disregard the other social forces which "discipline" and produce sexualized bodies. Bordo (1993), for example, points out that in Foucault's groundbreaking work on the discursive production of the modern subject, he also discusses institutional monitoring, "normalizing" examinations, the spatial and temporal organization of schools and prisons, "confessional" relations between physicians and patients, and other institutional and everyday practices.

This is why sociological analyses and theories of interaction are crucial to understanding the greater visibility of bisexuality and the relative invisibility of bisexual men. Only by integrating the discursive insights of queer theory with a social, particularly an *interactional*, constructionist analysis can we fully assess the dynamics of agency and change at work here. In an attempt to begin this type of integration, I will consider some of the events leading up to the emergence of bisexual communities in the early 1980s, and propose a synthetic analysis explaining their emergence.

DIVERGENT DISCLOSURES AND CONCEPTUALIZATIONS: AN INTERACTIONAL HYPOTHESIS

One common analysis of bi male invisibility, which can be heard among many bisexual activists, goes something like this: some women who were involved in "women-centered" lesbian-feminist communities in the late 1970s and early 1980s found themselves attracted to or involved with men. When they shared this within the community, or it somehow became known, they were heavily criticized for "sleeping with the enemy" and seeking heterosexual privilege, thus demonstrating their untrustworthiness and lack of "true" political commitment (Armstrong, 1995; Udis-Kessler, 1996;

Young, 1992). Even if these women identified as lesbian, they were made to feel unwelcome in their lesbian-feminist communities, and eventually left or were expelled. From this experience, they developed a politicized bisexual identity and went on to lead in the creation of both a mixed-gender bisexual movement and distinctively feminist bi women's communities.

This story also includes a negative perception of bi men as bisexuals, but the primary stigmatization is seen as directed toward bi women and fueled by lesbian-feminist ideology. Gay men, while sometimes perceived as being in denial that bisexuals really exist, are implicitly posited as not having much bi-negativity and are rarely seen as generating the active hostility toward bi men that lesbians have expressed toward bi women. For example, they do not construct bisexual men as double agents or traitors, and there is no fundamental, explicit exclusion of bi men from the gay community. Consequently, there is not a pool of men who are motivated to create a visible bi men's community.

The problem with this narrative is that no one knows whether it is actually true. It fits some of the evidence, but other information challenges it. For example, according to David Lourea, one of the founders of San Francisco's Bisexual Center in the mid 1970s, it was established in part because of the "biphobic notions" and "anti-bi" feelings of gay men, as well as lesbians and heterosexuals (Paul, 1998: 134). Likewise, in recalling the sometimes-explosive discussions among early post-Stonewall gay academics, John D'Emilio writes that some of the most heated debates involved bisexuality: "I can't forget the atmosphere–emotions boiling over, veins on necks standing out as individuals strained to be heard above the din. . . . It was as if the room were suddenly crowded by a trainload of former lovers who had betrayed each of us by crossing back to 'the other side'" (D'Emilio, 1992: xxx).

More recent reports from the U.S. and U.K., by Linda Garnets and Douglas Kimmel and Jo Eadie and Peter Tatchell, respectively, confirm that both lesbians and gay men are frequently hostile toward bisexuals (Eadie, 1996; Garnets & Kimmel, 1991; Tatchell, 1996). Moreover, it is not uncommon to hear of gay men who sleep with women, but who remain silent about these relationships, seemingly because of the stigma against bisexuality. While some of these reports can be categorized as third-hand hearsay, it is obvious from the weight of the evidence that negativity toward bisexuals and bisexuality cannot only be attributed to lesbians.

Clearly, an approach to bi male invisibility is needed which is not based on the premise that bisexual women and men face different levels of stigma. The theory that I will use to develop such a framework reflects the sociological perspective of "symbolic interactionism," which understands meaning as being generated by the dynamic process through which we define ourselves in relation to concepts, objects, actions, and other individuals (see Blumer, 1969; Goffman, 1959). In particular, my analysis draws upon the cognitive aspect of this process and emphasizes how different conceptualizations of ourselves and others are enacted, depending on the social contexts structuring specific interactions.

There are two key elements to my approach: the particular "social markings" of sexualities utilized by gays and lesbians, and the interactional requirements central to the socio-sexual engagements of gay-bi men and lesbians-bi women. Differences in how these factors shape gay-bi male and lesbian-bi female relations, respectively, have resulted in less direct conflict and exclusion between men than between women, and this in turn has made bi men less visible than bi women. Social marking, as discussed by sociologist Wayne Brekhus (but with roots in linguistic theory), is a "rigid, asymmetrical classification process that accents one side of a contrast as unnatural, thereby naturalizing the unmarked side" (Brekhus, 1996: 497; Trubetzkoy, 1975). Through social marking, individuals place others into a particular identity based on a certain dimension of self–in this case, sexual orientation. Such markings may be binary (see Figure 1), in which a dichotomous conceptualization draws attention to the marked identity as "socially perverse." In essence, this is the mental structuring queer theorists suggest is generated by social interactions occurring in the context of heteronormativity.

In as much as the challenge facing gay, lesbian, and queer studies is to "develop analyses of sufficient, *interdisciplinary* complexity" regarding the "discursive, structural, and socio-historical aspects" of heterosexist social power, as Barry Adam recently suggested (Adam, 1998: 398-99, my emphasis), I attempt in my thesis to relate discursive and social analyses to one another and to combine their strengths. In doing so, I hope to address other issues that, according to Adam, must be considered by social theory: "how already constituted actors deploy discourse" and "a sense of the historically

FIGURE 1. Binary Model of Markedness

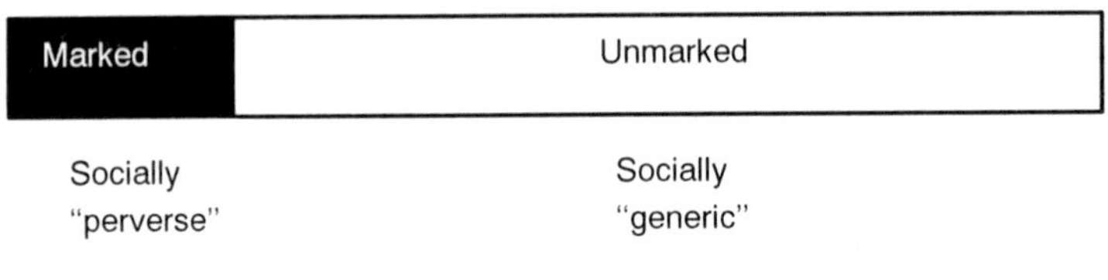

Marked	Unmarked
Socially "perverse"	Socially "generic"

moving structure of opportunities and consequences that lead to the adoption of some discourses and the discrediting of others" (Adam, 1998: 401).

Under the marking system, the social values of categories may be inverted by members of marked or stigmatized groups, resulting in a "reverse markedness" that homogenizes and lumps together elements which normally remain unnamed. It is in this spirit that the expressions "gay is good" and "gay pride" developed as political and theoretical assertions of the truly positive values of the stigmatized group, while also serving as a means to expose the "unmarked" status of its opposite (heterosexuality).

I propose that while both gay men and lesbians may mark bisexuality in similar ways, the markings which predominate and have greater influence differ between the two groups. The key dimension that separates them is the use of what Brekhus identifies as the "one drop rule" or the "entire ocean rule" (1996: 514). One of the most influential lesbian-feminist perspectives of the 1970s, referred to earlier, made political commitment to women the defining element of lesbianism. This "woman-centeredness" was expected to rule out sex with men, the patriarchal enemy, and was seen as within the reach of every (politically conscious) woman. Lesbianism and a commitment to feminist liberation were thus co-defined; one necessarily invoked the other, and one's absence negated claims to the other. In terms of social marking, this framework constitutes a reversed binary model in which "women-centered women/lesbians" are the unmarked category, the true non-patriarchal norm, and those complicit with the patriarchy are the marked, stigmatized category. This also coincides with the "one drop" rule model, in that it "assumes deviance" from the (lesbian) norm "with [only] the slightest hint of evidence" (Brekhus, 1996: 514; see Figure 2). Women whose sexual and intimate relations included men were simultaneously coded as bisexual and as not "committed to women." Lesbian feminists thus employed a "vigilant framework" to "avoid ambiguities . . . in-between identities" and guard against even a "traceable amount of perversion" (Brekhus, 1996: 515; for historical accounts of lesbian feminism, see Rust, 1995; Weise, 1992).

FIGURE 2. Reversed Binary Model of Mental One-Drop Rule

Marked	Unmarked

| Heterosexual and bisexual women as "deviants." | Women-centered women/lesbians as "norm." |

Significant numbers of gay men in the 1970s and 1980s, particularly those in New York, San Francisco, and other centers of gay culture, put a different twist on the social constructionist sensibilities of both lesbian feminists and gay male liberationists. While the markings used by gay men are diverse, one of the common perceptions is that there is a potential homoerotic partner lurking behind every "straight-appearing" man. This suspicion, supported by the "purposive perceptivity" of being alert for sexual and romantic partners, constructs a reversed marking model that coincides with the "entire ocean" rule (see Figure 3). In this framework, an individual must display "an entire ocean" of deviant attributes (in this case, complete and unambiguous heterosexuality) before they are mentally excluded from the unmarked norm. Men are thought to have homoerotic potential–active or latent, out or closeted–unless they thoroughly disqualify themselves from consideration. The possibility that a homoerotic man might also sleep with women (i.e., exhibit "bisexual" behavior) is not seen as a highly salient feature that would discourage engagement. On the contrary, it may result in *increased* interest due to a fetishization of straight men by some gay men.

If correct, these notions add clarity to the "differential bi-negativity" narrative explaining bi male invisibility. Lesbian feminists categorized women as political and sexual "others" (i.e., *not* like themselves), where "one drop" of male involvement existed, while gay men saw other men as potential partners as long as this was a plausible interpretation and they were not confronted with an "ocean" of contradictory information. This analysis also emphasizes the importance of conceptual/discursive binary oppositions, especially how seemingly similar structural relationships (bi-gay and bi-lesbian) can be utilized in disparate ways. Analyzing the language and concepts of bisexuality is especially needed. As of now, there is no widely recognizable symbol, dress code, or "performance" that denotes bisexuality or a bisexual (although a bisexual flag was recently developed). Generally, an observer cannot tell if someone is bisexual based on clues available at any one given time, whereas specific indicators are often taken to suggest "gay"

FIGURE 3. Reversed Binary Model of the Mental Entire-Ocean Rule

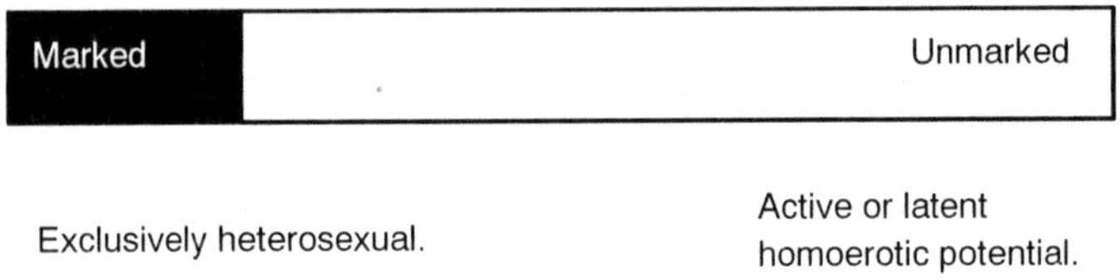

Marked	Unmarked

Exclusively heterosexual.   Active or latent homoerotic potential.

or "straight" identities. Thus language and individuals' perceptual frameworks play a central role in how bisexuality and bisexuals are understood and treated. The differential "markings" which I suggest exerted strong influences over gay and lesbian communities both reflect and produce particular interactions.

Much of the conflict between lesbians and bi women in the late 1970s and early 1980s arose within the "consciousness-raising" groups, planning meetings, and other "women's spaces" where lesbian-identified women extensively discussed their lives, particularly their relationships, in order to create women-centered communities. Such disclosure was critical to the process of group formation, but it could also lead to tensions, as Susan Krieger discovered in her study of a women's community in the late 1970s. For example, one woman told Krieger that "in this community, in order to know anybody pretty much at all, or to define yourself and become known, you had to give a considerable amount of what in other communities could be kept private." It was "a way for everyone to relate vicariously to everyone else. It was what was in common" (Krieger, 1983: 17-18). Another woman agreed, suggesting that "at first you didn't want everyone to know your business. Then you found out it wasn't possible, or it wasn't the norm in the community" (p. 25). The basic rule was that "unless you stated specifically that you didn't want information passed, it got passed pretty quickly" (p. 35). These and similar reports (Rust, 1995; Stein, 1997) suggest a social environment in which sharing deeply about oneself was not only valued, but expected.

· This extensive disclosure brought to light the fact that some women also found themselves attracted to men–that there were, in fact, behavioral or self-identified bisexuals within these "safe spaces" and communities. It is precisely because of these interactional expectations within the confines of close-knit social networks, combined with the reversed "one drop" social marking model, that bisexuality became so strikingly salient when some members had relationships with men. Given the common conceptualization of sexuality and identity within groups, it is easy to see how such disclosures would lead to exclusionary practices aimed at bisexual women.

While gay men and behavioral or self-identified bisexual men interacted within some similar contexts in the 1970s, the expectations for disclosure were starkly different than for lesbian-identified women. A host of venues existed for participating in gay community life and gaining sexual access to other men which did not require disclosure of one's sexual partners or sexual identity. In a gay culture in which "promiscuity was seen as a form of personal liberation and social revolt and a vehicle for change" (Bronski,

1998: 69), and in which sexual freedom was a central goal of gay liberation, ready access to male sexual partners was considered crucial. Thus the men who gathered in sex clubs, cruising spots, and other locations to meet each other were relatively uninterested in an individual's identity or outside sexual behaviors.[3] Clearly, the interactional requirements of such settings, whether in relation to sex or other interests, did not force the issue of who might be bisexual. Instead, someone who frequented such sites would be included in the functionally salient "ocean" of homoerotic men. If "bisexual" individuals sought a greater level of integration between their lives and the lives and community organizations of gay men, this would likely entail more disclosure. However, one could be very involved without being asked or expected to disclose such information, and if one did, it likely did not "follow" the person in the same way as it did in women's communities.

CONTEMPORARY DYNAMICS: BISEXUALITY IN THE '90s AND BEYOND

These comparisons are most germane to the late 1970s and early 1980s, when the conflict between lesbians and bi women first emerged. To what extent do they continue today? Certainly evidence suggests that such differences remain pertinent, even if the importance and centrality of these issues may have decreased somewhat over time. For example, in her study of a northeastern lesbian community in the late 1980s and early 1990s, Kristin Esterberg found that bisexual women were still marginalized. As one bisexual woman commented: "It's who you sleep with that is really important. Not anything else. And bisexuals are not going to be accepted because they're sleeping with men" (Esterberg, 1997: 162). Likewise, male-male sexual encounters in which sexual identity and outside female sexual partners are irrelevant continue to be made possible by bars, baths, and known cruising spots (see, for example, the recent study by Goldbaum et al., 1998).[4]

Depending on the interactional contexts, one (or more) of many cultural conceptualizations of sexuality may be in use. Certain binary oppositions may be created, forgotten, or remain unspoken, and individuals identified as "abject" may, by their presence, demand new frameworks. Queer theory offers insights into the power of binary oppositions which normalize heterosexuality. Adding a sociological analysis enables a greater understanding of more specific, local operations of power–not all of which are directly heteronormative. In most gay and lesbian contexts, discourses are "homo-normative," but bisexuality is still often interpreted through a binary framework. In order to explore this concept of "local power" and to trace its effects on the continuation of binary notions of sexuality, I will offer a reading of "Gay/ Lesbian Sex Crosstalk," a discussion held at the National Gay and Lesbian Task Force's annual Creating Change Conference. This analysis will demonstrate how the crisis posed by bisexuality continues today.

In its seventh incarnation at the 1995 conference, the workshop's content had morphed from its original purpose–gays and lesbians hearing about one another's sex lives and cultures–to include a considerable focus on participants' sexual experiences with and desires for members of the opposite sex. Gay men related stories of sexual involvement with lesbians, a lesbian told of using her brother's gay porn and sex toys, and both men and women recounted various opposite-sex attractions, fantasies, and curiosities. While the workshop structure was set up for personal disclosure rather than general dialogue, some discussion and overall reflection did occur.

With a number of notable radical and very queer gay and lesbian activists and theorists in the room, I imagined that this would be a site where binary categories could be questioned in celebration of queer sensibilities. But what the participants demonstrated was a strong willingness to interpret a great variety of behaviors within a gay and lesbian context, an indication of how much meaning is carried by these identities. Correspondingly, there was a notable absence of the "b word." This silence, I suggest, held much meaning too, and I will return to Butler's concept of "citationality" to flesh out its implications.

The identities "gay" and "lesbian" are relatively known. Due to their continued usage, they have developed an authoritative status and can be "cited" or invoked to present oneself as a member of an intelligible category of persons. Part of that intelligibility involves perceptions about how that person will act, to whom they will be attracted, and so on. The discussion in this session revealed that, contrary to common sense notions, behaviors and desires of gay and lesbian individuals do not always match expectations associated with gay and lesbian identities.[5] The implications here for personal and collective identities are immense. If the categories "gay" and "straight" are so encompassing that their coherence becomes questionable, then how are individuals to understand themselves as gay or straight? If the categories are dubious, then who are the gay "we"? What are "our" bonds, and on what grounds can "we" find common interests? That such a discussion occurred indicates some degree of comfort and interest in probing the links that exist between these identities, even when behavior is not in simple "alignment" with them.

In contrast to the relative stability of "gay" and "lesbian," "bisexual" is an ambiguous identity. It might *appear* to have some legitimacy and refer to a known quality or person–and thus be "citable" in Butler's terms–by virtue of its growing inclusion in organization names, conferences, publications, etc. But such a conclusion is quite premature; bisexuality remains "abject" and "uncitable" due to the many different meanings attached to it. To what does it refer? Is it a mix of "straight" and "gay," a blurring of these identities and types? Is it a new addition, something distinct and identifiable, thus leading to a new "triad" of stable sexual orientations? Or, is it the "residual" or "catch-all" category, referring to identities, desires, and sexual practices that do not match gay or straight, but which themselves have no necessary common link?

Given this historical ambiguity, the lack of a shared meaning would make some gay and lesbian session participants wary, and the mere mention of bisexuality would likely raise a host of negative stereotypes, such as the common perceptions that bisexuals are "double agents," "fence-sitters," and "hetero-privileged" (see, for example, Armstrong, 1995; Young, 1997; for an earlier perspective, Myron & Bunch, 1975). Even though individuals could have attached a particular meaning to bisexuality when introducing it into the discussion, and could have assured the audience of their personal "queerness," they could not control the participants' own interpretations and associations, which could easily be linked to the speaker. As a site magnify-ing the symbolic importance of gay and lesbian identities, yet hinting at their instability, the "Gay/Lesbian Sex Crosstalk" workshop restricted the ways in which "bisexuality" could be used by raising the stakes about its likely meaning. With ambiguity about the relationship between gay and lesbian identity and behavior already on the table, discourses suggesting even greater ambiguity and potential disloyalty would be especially problematic. It is hardly surprising then that bisexuality did not enter into the discussion; the only thing it could lead to in such an interactional context was "trouble"–in-cluding a reminder of the abjectness of "gay" and "lesbian" when they are not partially legitimated by narratives of stable identities and genetic origins. Stacey Young has raised this same point, persuasively arguing that concerns about the instability of gay and lesbian identities, and the associated crises of legitimacy, are (still) displaced onto bisexuality, which is then seen as the only unstable identity (Young, 1997). From this analysis, it is clear how the historical tensions surrounding bisexuality continue to operate in the mid-1990s, and how local instances of "homonormativity" can shape the contours of bisexuality's abject, uncitable invisibility, which serves as a foil to the stability of "gay" and "lesbian" (and "heterosexual").

In gay and lesbian communities, the perceived threat that bisexuality poses to lesbian and gay identities and the set of "goods" associated with these identities is inextricably linked to concerns about political action: either bisexuals' politics are considered untrustworthy or bisexual identity is seen as diverting energy and legitimacy from needed gay minority group, or "identity," politics. While I have suggested above that a bisexual identity has not become as widely politicized for men as it has for women, gay political sensibilities regarding bisexuality impact self-identified and behaviorally bisexual men in a number of ways. The most obvious effect is the pressure exerted on them *not* to identify, especially publicly, as bisexual. Whatever negativity that gay men may feel toward bisexual men is likely greater toward publicly self-identified bisexual men. This is paradoxical, because many of the negative myths about bisexual men presume that they are closeted (some of whom may actually be more "gay" than "bi"). Expressions of difference on the part of bisexual men disrupt their implicit inclusion in the aforementioned unmarked binary category "homoerotic men." While gay and bi men can be interactively indistinguishable, signs of bisexuality, such as "bi pride" t-shirts, emphasize the message "I am different from you. I am not gay."

This lack of unity is troubling for those who think a claim to minority group status is the best, or only, option currently available for oppositional U.S. sexual politics. Some scholars in gay and queer studies emphasize the need for collective action; for example, sociologist Josh Gamson, in discussing relations between bi and gay men, asserts that for effective political action, "secure boundaries and stabilized identities are necessary not in general, but in the specific" (Gamson, 1996: 412). However, Butler and many other queer theorists stress the need to maintain "tension" between identity politics and the uses of these identities, for they recognize that essentialized homosexual identities stabilize heterosexual identities and reinforce homophobic politics.

While these arguments provide useful insights, such views expose a "have it both ways" approach; gays and lesbians may rely on identity politics, but johnny-come-lately bisexuals are considered essentialists for doing so. Beyond this inconsistency, these views also have substantial unexamined costs. The process of achieving "clarity" for the gay movement naturalizes the gay "us" and the bisexual "them" and silences both bi- and gay-identified men (and women) who may be at odds in some way with the dominant gay political subjectivity. "Unruly sexual fantasies, desires, pleasures and practices," argues Biddy Martin, "are sacrificed to investments in identity" (cited in Young, 1997: 60). The rationales for omitting or downplaying bisexuality and bisexuals present exclusionary actions and attitudes as more rational and politically motivated than they may actually be. Consequently, unquestioned acceptance of such reasoning supports the anti-bisexual prejudices which may underlie these political choices.

This perspective also assumes that political action must be based on identities, rather than political values. The limits of this type of thinking were shown by the Human Rights Campaign's support for New York Republican Senator Alphonse D'Amato's re-election campaign in 1998. Widely perceived as indifferent or hostile to women's rights and issues of concern to people of color, D'Amato nevertheless received the official endorsement of the Human Rights Campaign, the largest gay and lesbian advocacy organization, because he was an incumbent and had a relatively good record on gay and lesbian rights issues (although he also received a high approval rating from the virulently anti-gay Christian Coalition). The group's decision highlights how identity politics logically leads to a single issue agenda and to the exclusion of issues of concern to gays and lesbians who are also marginalized in *other* domains (i.e., people of color, women, immigrants, poor people, etc.), even though they constitute the majority of gays and lesbians. Moreover, as Martin points out, "more complex analyses of social realities" are also abandoned by such politics (Young, 1997: 60). While the most effective political strategy is not always clear, it must certainly be both visionary and deftly reactive. Specifically, it needs to reflect a diverse set of agendas; the question is not just "what strategy will be most effective?" but also "effective for what?" Politically-based critiques of bisexuals and bi visibility, I suggest, are not only troubled by inconsistencies and unexamined costs, but also premised on a questionable, albeit still dominant, political strategy.

The analysis I have put forth suggests that gay men may in fact have significant negative views of bisexual men, but that interactions have not made these attitudes salient enough to be publicly displayed. Furthermore, in the absence of explicit exclusionary practices such as those directed against bisexual women, large numbers of behaviorally and self-identified bi men have lacked an urgent motive to construct a community around a valorized bisexual male identity. In contrast, the saliency of bisexuality that resulted from the vigilant "one drop rule" within close-knit, lesbian-feminist communities generated a strong bisexual women's constituency. This constituency has continued to politicize their identity, which has been a central factor in its public visibility. While certainly not silent, bi men have not politicized their identity to an equal degree, nor have they publicly proclaimed it as pointedly as bi women.

These are complex phenomena, and the thesis I have presented is certainly not the whole story. There are other potential factors influencing the relative invisibility of bi men apart from those considered here, such as the effect of feminist social networks in boosting the level of bi women's organizing activity and visibility, the notable feminist influence on many bi organizations, the loss of a significant number of bisexual male activists to the AIDS epidemic, and the restrictive definitions of masculinity facing men who might or do identify as bisexuals. Compared to either gay or straight identities, and the support, sense of belonging, social networks, and cultural intelligibility linked to them, many bisexual men have much to lose, and little to gain, by publicly identifying as bisexual. In addition, as I have demonstrated in this essay, the costs of a bisexual identity are undoubtedly very different for men than for women. I have attempted to provide a comprehensive explanation for the continuing relative invisibility of bisexual men by combining useful elements of social constructionism and queer theory. An interactionist analysis drawn from sociological theory helps account for the particular timing, location, and *gender* of the emergence of publicly bisexual subjects–one configuration of sexuality not successfully contained by the homosexual-heterosexual binary.

Whether more men will adopt bisexual identities and whether male bisexuality will become more visible in the future are difficult to predict. Such factors as the communication possibilities offered by the Internet, the fortunes of identity politics, the political choices made by specific GLBT and Religious Right organizations, and the flexibility or rigidity of cultural expectations for masculinity will play a role in determining the extent to which men will understand themselves as bisexual and how publicly they will disclose and declare such identities.

So what can bisexual men and women do to exert a social and political presence in this milieu? Bi scholars in and outside of academia can theorize from bisexuality and bisexual lives and use it as a starting point for analyzing the whole spectrum of sexual identities and behaviors (see, for example, du Plessis, 1996; Namaste, 1996; Young, 1997). We can also maintain "tension" in our use of bisexuality by acknowledging its indeterminacy as a sexual category, rather than seeing it as an essentialist identity. Accordingly, we should not claim that bisexuality is a superior identity or that it *inherently* transcends gender and sexuality categories (for these are very important for many bisexuals).

Nonetheless, we should affirm our subversive possibility by continuing to "queer" queer politics (the stereotype-parodying magazine title *Anything That Moves* is a good example here) and to reframe sexuality in terms other than the gender of one's partners (such as the concept of monosexuality vs. bisexuality or polysexuality). Bisexual men and women should also support organizations that have worked to understand our issues and to "get real" about diversity (like the National Gay and Lesbian Task Force), as well as make our presence known in countless other organizations that continue to be unsympathetic to bisexuals and bisexuality. While we should challenge biphobia among gay men and lesbians, we must not lose sight of the fact that it is the dominant heterosexual order that systematically maintains fixed sexual identities, enforces compulsory heterosexuality, and reduces all non-normative sexual identities to homosexuality. On an individual level, bisexuals should be allies for one another, as well as for gay men, lesbians, and heterosexuals who are questioning bi-exclusionary practices.

An important part of this support is assisting self-identified and behaviorally bisexual men in navigating the difficult cultural terrain of finding a gendered subjectivity within which they can affirm a bisexual self. Many of these men are unlikely to identify as "queer" or to come out publicly as bisexual, due to the great social and psychic costs they would incur by doing so. Therefore, we should urgently make space for them to find both public and anonymous affirmation and support, while not blaming them for the substantial social pressures that constrain what they see as plausible options. And as we insist on our place at the table–without uncritically accepting the current distribution of various social goods at that table–we must allow others to define who they are, regardless of their behaviors, and thoughtfully consider specific, strategic appeals to minority group politics. Most importantly, we should keep being beautiful, boisterous, and if it fits, bisexual, in any of its possible meanings.

NOTES

1. An earlier wave of mixed-gender bisexual organizing occurred in the 1970s; see the essays by Chuck Mishaan, Maggie Rubenstein and Cynthia Ann Slater, and George Barr in Klein and Wolf, 1985; and Donaldson, 1995.

2. While organizational membership is not necessarily a "public" act, and belonging to a political organization is obviously affected by many factors, involvement in specifically bisexual organizations is nonetheless one of the best indicators of bi male visibility. Indeed, such organizations are often the primary means through which legitimacy and visibility, when sought, are gained by sexual minority groups.

3. Indeed, "public sex" has been vociferously defended in recent politicized debates over bathhouses and HIV-prevention measures (Dangerous Bedfellows, 1996; Rofes, 1999).

4. At the same time, it is widely known that bisexual men are, perhaps increasingly, sought out by gay men for sexual interactions via such venues as phone chat lines and online chat rooms. While a detailed understanding of this dynamic must await a separate analysis, it is clear that the evaluations and interests underlying gay men's attentiveness to sexual orientation are quite distinct from that of lesbians. This fetishization of bi men highlights the complexity of relations between gay and bi men, but I would argue that it does not significantly undercut the narrative I have developed here. Clearly, it is quite possible for a sexual fetishization of a particular group to coexist with the denigration of that group and attributes associated with it.

5. Such a disparity evokes Eve Kosofsky Sedgwick's description of gay "incoherency" (Sedgwick, 1990) and comes perilously close to Judith Butler's claim that the use of binary sexual identities to describe ourselves makes us seem like "imitations" of a norm to which we may not wish to aspire (Butler, 1993).

WORKS CITED

Adam, Barry D. 1987. *The Rise of a Gay and Lesbian Movement.* Boston: Twayne Publishers.

_____ . 1998. Theorizing Homophobia. *Sexualities* 1: 387-404.

Armstrong, Elizabeth. 1995. Traitors to the Cause?: Understanding the Lesbian/Gay "Bisexuality Debates." In *Bisexual Politics: Theories, Queries, and Visions,* ed. Naomi Tucker, 199-217. Binghamton, NY: Harrington Park Press.

Ault, Amber. 1994. Hegemonic Discourse in an Oppositional Community: Lesbian Feminists and Bisexuality. *Critical Sociology* 20 (3): 107-22.

_____ . 1996. The Dilemma of Identity: Bi Women's Negotiations. In *Queer Theory/Sociology,* ed. Steven Seidman, 311-30. London: Blackwell.

Berger, Stephanie. 1995. Women to Women, Men to Men: Shall We Talk? *BiNet News: The Newsletter of the Bisexual Network of the USA* (Summer-Fall): 4-5.

Bi Academic Intervention (Phoebe Davidson et al.), eds. 1997. *The Bisexual Imaginary: Representation, Identity and Desire.* London: Cassell.

Bisexual Anthology Collective (Nancy Acharya et al.), eds. 1995. *Plural Desires: Writing Bisexual Women's Realities.* Toronto: Sister Vision: Black Women and Women of Colour Press.

Blackwood, Evelyn, ed. 1986. *The Many Faces of Homosexuality: Anthropological Approaches to Homosexual Behavior.* Binghamton, NY: Harrington Park Press.

Blumer, Herbert. 1969. *Symbolic Interactionism: Perspective and Method.* Englewood Cliffs, NJ: Prentice Hall.

Bordo, Susan. 1993. *Unbearable Weight: Feminism, Western Culture, and the Body.* Berkeley: University of California Press.

Bravmann, Scott. Postmodernism and Queer Identities. In *Queer Theory/Sociology,* ed. Steven Seidman, 333-61. London: Blackwell.

Brekhus, Wayne. 1996. Social Marking and the Mental Coloring of Identity: Sexual

Identity Construction and Maintenance in the United States. *Sociological Forum* 11 (3): 497-522.

Bronski, Michael. 1998. *The Pleasure Principle: Sex, Backlash, and the Struggle for Gay Freedom.* New York: St. Martin's Press.

Butler, Judith. 1993. *Bodies that Matter: On the Discursive Limits of "Sex."* New York: Routledge.

Clarion, Meg. 1996. The Hasbians. In *Bisexual Horizons: Politics, Histories, Lives,* eds. Sharon Rose, Cris Stevens et al., 122-26. London: Lawrence and Wishart.

Dangerous Bedfellows (Ephen Glenn Colter et al.), eds. 1996. *Policing Public Sex: Queer Politics and the Future of AIDS Activism.* Boston: South End Press.

D'Emilio, John. 1983. *Sexual Politics, Sexual Communities: The Making of a Homosexual Minority in the United States,* 1940-1970. Chicago: University of Chicago Press.

_____. 1992. *Making Trouble: Essays on Gay History, Politics, and the University.* New York: Routledge.

Derrida, Jacques. 1976. *Of Grammatology*, trans. Gayatri Chakravorty Spivak. Baltimore: Johns Hopkins University Press.

Dollimore, Jonathan. 1997. Bisexuality. In *Lesbian and Gay Studies: A Critical Introduction*, eds. Andy Medhurst and Sally R. Munt, 250-60. London: Cassell.

Donaldson, Stephen. 1995. The Bisexual Movement's Beginnings in the 70s: A Personal Retrospective. In *Bisexual Politics: Theories, Queries, and Visions*, ed. Naomi Tucker, 31-45. Binghamton, NY: Harrington Park Press.

du Plessis, Michael. 1996. Blatantly Bisexual; or, Unthinking Queer Theory. In *RePresenting Bisexualities: Subjects and Cultures of Fluid Desire*, eds. Donald E. Hall and Maria Pramaggiore, 19-54. New York: New York University Press.

Eadie, Jo. 1993. Activating Bisexuality: Towards a Bi/Sexual Politics. In *Activating Theory: Lesbian, Gay, Bisexual Politics*, eds. Joseph Bristow and Angelina R. Wilson, 139-70. London: Lawrence and Wishart.

_____. 1996. Indigestion: Diagnosing the Gay Malady. In *Anti-Gay*, ed. Mark Simpson, 66-83. London: Cassell.

Epstein, Steven. 1996. A Queer Encounter: Sociology and the Study of Sexuality. In *Queer Theory/Sociology*, ed. Steven Seidman, 145-67. London: Blackwell.

Esterberg, Kristin G. 1997. *Lesbian and Bisexual Identities: Constructing Communities, Constructing Selves.* Philadelphia: Temple University Press.

Faderman, Lillian. 1981. *Surpassing the Love of Men: Romantic Friendship and Love between Women from the Renaissance to the Present.* New York: Morrow.

Foucault, Michel. 1972. *The Archeology of Knowledge*, trans. A.M. Sheridan Smith. New York: Harper and Row.

____. 1980. *The History of Sexuality, Volume 1.* New York: Vintage.

Fox, Ronald C. 1996. Bisexuality in Perspective: A Review of Theory and Research. In *Bisexuality: The Psychology and Politics of an Invisible Minority*, ed. Beth A. Firestein, 3-50. Thousand Oaks, CA: Sage Publications.

Freud, Sigmund. 1961. *The Standard Edition of the Complete Psychological Works of Sigmund Freud, vol. 21*, trans. James Strachey. London: Hogarth.

Fuss, Diana, ed. 1991. *Inside/Out: Lesbian Theories, Gay Theories.* New York: Routledge.

Gagnon, John H., Cathy Stein Greenblat, and Michael Kimmel. 1998. Bisexuality: A Sociological Perspective. In *Bisexualities: The Ideology and Practice of Sexual Contact with Both Men and Women*, eds. Erwin J. Haeberle and Rolf Gindorf, 81-106. New York: Continuum.

Gamson, Joshua. 1996. Must Identity Movements Self-Destruct? A Queer Dilemma. In *Queer Theory/Sociology*, ed. Steven Seidman, 395-420. London: Blackwell.

Garnets, Linda D., and Douglas C. Kimmel. 1991. Lesbian and Gay Dimensions in the Psychological Study of Human Diversity. Introduction. In *Psychological Perspectives on Lesbian and Gay Male Experiences*, eds. Linda D. Garnets and Douglas C. Kimmel, 1-51. New York: Columbia University Press.

Goffman, Erving. 1959. *The Presentation of Self in Everyday Life*. New York: Doubleday.

Goldbaum, G. et al. 1998. Differences in Risk Behavior and Sources of AIDS Information Among Gay, Bisexual, and Straight-Identified Men Who Have Sex with Men. *AIDS and Behavior* 2 (1): 13-21.

Hamer, Dean, and Peter Copeland. 1994. *The Science of Desire: The Search for the Gay Gene and the Biology of Behavior*. New York: Simon and Schuster.

Hemmings, Clare. 1993. Resituating the Bisexual Body. In *Activating Theory: Lesbian, Gay, Bisexual Politics*, eds. Joseph Bristow and Angelina R. Wilson, 118-38. London: Lawrence and Wishart.

———. 1997. Bisexual Theoretical Perspectives: Emergent and Contingent Relationships. In *The Bisexual Imaginary: Representation, Identity and Desire*, eds. Bi Academic Intervention, 14-37. London: Cassell.

Herdt, Gilbert. 1984. *Ritualized Homosexuality in Melanesia*. Berkeley: University of California Press.

Hutchins, Loraine, and Lani Kaahumanu, eds. 1991. *Bi Any Other Name: Bisexual People Speak Out*. Boston: Alyson.

Katz, Jonathan. 1976. *Gay American History: Lesbians and Gay Men in the U.S.A.* New York: Thomas Y. Crowell.

Klein, Fritz. 1993. *The Bisexual Option*. Binghamton, NY: Harrington Park Press.

Klein, Fritz, and Timothy J. Wolf, eds. 1985. *Two Lives to Lead: Bisexuality in Men and Women*. Binghamton, NY: Harrington Park Press (the book was also published by Haworth Press under the title *Bisexualities: Theory and Research*).

Krieger, Susan. 1983. *The Mirror Dance: Identity in a Woman's Community*. Philadelphia: Temple University Press.

Lacan, Jacques. 1977. *Écrits: A Selection*, trans. Alan Sheridan. New York: Norton.

Leland, John. 1995. Bisexuality: Not Gay. Not Straight. A New Sexual Identity Emerges. *Newsweek* (July 17): 44-50.

Mead, Margaret. 1935. *Sex and Temperament in Three Primitive Societies*. New York: Morrow.

Myron, Nancy, and Charlotte Bunch, eds. 1975. *Lesbianism and the Women's Movement*. Baltimore: Diana Press.

Namaste, Ki. 1996. From Performativity to Interpretation: Toward a Social Semiotic Account of Bisexuality. In *RePresenting Bisexualities: Subjects and Cultures of Fluid Desire*, eds. Donald E. Hall and Maria Pramaggiore, 70-95. New York: New York University Press.

North, Gary. 1990. Where the Boys Aren't: The Shortage of Men in the Bi Movement; An Interview with Robyn Ochs. In *Bisexuality: A Reader and Sourcebook*, ed. Thomas Geller, 40-46. Ojai, CA: Times Change Press.

Ochs, Robyn, ed. 1999. *Bisexual Resource Guide, 2000*. Cambridge, MA: Bisexual Resource Center.

Paul, Jay P. 1998. San Francisco's Bisexual Center and the Emergence of a Bisexual Movement. In *Bisexualities: The Ideology and Practice of Sexual Contact with Both Men and Women*, eds. Erwin J. Haeberle and Rolf Gindorf, 130-39. New York: Continuum.

Phelan, Shane, ed. 1997. *Playing with Fire: Queer Politics, Queer Theories*. New York: Routledge.

Plummer, Kenneth, ed. 1981. *The Making of the Modern Homosexual*. Totwa, NJ: Barnes and Noble Books.

_____. 1995. *Telling Sexual Stories: Power, Change and Social Worlds*. London: Routledge.

Rofes, Eric. 1999. Building a Movement for Sexual Freedom During a Moment of Sex Panic. http://www.geocities.com/~sexpanicnyc/building.htm

Rogers, Susan M., and Charles F. Turner. 1991. Male-Male Sexual Contact in the U.S.A.: Findings from Five Sample Surveys, 1970-1990. *The Journal of Sex Research* 28 (4): 491-519.

Rose, Sharon, Cris Stevens et al., eds. 1996. *Bisexual Horizons: Politics, Histories, Lives*. London: Lawrence and Wishart.

Rust, Paula. 1995. *Bisexuality and the Challenge to Lesbian Politics: Sex, Loyalty, and Revolution*. New York: New York University Press.

Sedgwick, Eve Kosofsky. 1990. *Epistemology of the Closet*. Berkeley: University of California Press.

Seidman, Steven. 1993. Identity and Politics in a "Postmodern" Gay Culture: Some Historical and Conceptual Notes. In *Fear of a Queer Planet: Queer Politics and Social Theory*, ed. Michael Warner, 105-42. Minneapolis: University of Minnesota Press.

_____. 1996. Introduction. In *Queer Theory/Sociology*, ed. Steve Seidman, 1-29. London: Blackwell.

Silver, Mark. 1998. Where Are the Boys? *Anything That Moves* 16: 26-27.

Simon, William, and John Gagnon. 1987. A Sexual Scripts Approach. In *Theories of Human Sexuality*, eds. James H. Geer and William T. O'Donohue, 363-83. New York: Plenum.

Solomon, Alisa. 1991. Strike a Pose. *Village Voice* (November 13-19): 35.

Stein, Arlene. 1997. *Sex and Sensibility: Stories of a Lesbian Generation*. Berkeley: University of California Press.

Storr, Merl. 1999. Postmodern Bisexualities. *Sexualities* 2: 309-25.

Tatchell, Peter. 1996. It's Just A Phase: Why Homosexuality is Doomed. In *Anti-Gay*, ed. Mark Simpson, 35-54. London: Cassell.

Toufexis, Anastasia. 1992. Bisexuality: What Is It? *Time* (August 17): 49-51.

Trubetzkoy, Nikolaj S. 1975. *Letters and Notes*, ed. Roman Jakobson. Paris: Mouton.

Tucker, Naomi, ed. 1995. *Bisexual Politics: Theories, Queries, and Visions*. Binghamton, NY: Harrington Park Press.

Turner, Bryan S. 1996. *The Body and Society: Explorations in Social Theory*. London: Sage Publications.

Udis-Kessler, Amanda. 1996. Identity/Politics: Historical Sources of the Bisexual Movement. In *Queer Studies: A Lesbian, Gay, Bisexual, and Transgender Anthology*, eds. Brett Beemyn and Mickey Eliason, 52-63. New York: New York University Press.

Weeks, Jeffrey. 1985. *Sexuality and Its Discontents*. London: Routledge.

Weise, Elizabeth Reba, ed. 1992. *Closer to Home: Bisexuality and Feminism*. Seattle: Seal.

_____ . 1996. The Bisexual Community: Viable Reality or Revolutionary Pipe Dream? In *Bisexual Horizons: Politics, Histories, Lives*, eds. Sharon Rose, Cris Stevens et al., 303-13. London: Lawrence and Wishart.

Williams, Walter L. 1986. *The Spirit and the Flesh: Sexual Diversity in American Indian Culture*. Boston: Beacon Press.

Young, Stacey. 1992. Breaking Silence About the "B-Word": Bisexual Identity and Lesbian-Feminist Discourse. In *Closer to Home: Bisexuality and Feminism*, ed. Elizabeth Reba Weise, 75-87. Seattle: Seal.

_____ . 1997. Dichotomies and Displacement: Bisexuality in Queer Theory and Politics. In *Playing With Fire: Queer Politics, Queer Theories*, ed. Shane Phelan, 51-74. New York: Routledge.

Make Me a Map

Bisexual Men's Images of Bisexual Community

Paula C. Rust

[Haworth co-indexing entry note]: "Make Me a Map: Bisexual Men's Images of Bisexual Community." Rust, Paula C. Co-published simultaneously in *Journal of Bisexuality* (Harrington Park Press, an imprint of The Haworth Press, Inc.) Vol. 1, No. 2/3, 2001, pp. 47-108; and: *Bisexuality in the Lives of Men: Facts and Fictions* (ed: Brett Beemyn and Erich Steinman) Harrington Park Press, an imprint of The Haworth Press, Inc., 2001, pp. 47-108. Single or multiple copies of this article are available for a fee from The Haworth Document Delivery Service [1-800-342-9678, 9:00 a.m. - 5:00 p.m. (EST). E-mail address: getinfo@ haworthpressinc.com].

SUMMARY. Traditionally, a community is a socially interconnected group of people living and working in close geographic proximity to each other–for example, a small town. However, in contemporary Western societies, high rates of geographic mobility, compartmental-ized relationships, and the replacement of social relationships based on factors of birth with relationships based on common interests have rendered this form of community increasingly scarce. For many individu-als, the sense of belonging once provided by geographically bounded communities is now provided by other social structures, such as membership organizations and Internet connections. "Make Me a Map" explores the questions of whether bisexual men feel that a bisexual community exists and, if so, what makes it a community; whether they derive a sense of belonging from it; and how it is related to other sexual and political communities. The data are drawn from an international study of the psychological, social, and political experiences of over 900 bisexual men and women, in which respondents described their bisexu-al communities (or lack thereof) verbally and drew maps of these communities. These verbal responses and maps reveal feelings of both isolation and belonging among bisexual men, a variety of beliefs about what a community is or should be, and a variety of experiences with and perceptions of this bisexual community. Also explored in "Make Me a Map" are bisexual men's perceptions of racial, political, gender, and sexual diversity within their bisexual communities, issues of visi-bility and self-identification, and the relationships of their bisexual communities to gay and lesbian communities. The analysis concludes with a theoretical consideration of the relationship between individual perceptions of community and the concept of a collective social reality. *[Article copies available for a fee from The Haworth Document Delivery Service: 1-800-342-9678. E-mail address: <getinfo@haworthpressinc.com> Website: <http://www.HaworthPress.com>]*

KEYWORDS. Bisexual men, bisexuality, community, intergroup rela-tions, sexual orientation, sexual politics, social construction of reality

September 1, 1998. Early evening. The back room of a leather store catering to the "gay community." An impressive but silent cappuccino machine overlooks a deserted counter, a remnant of the short-lived coffee shop that closed because of "lack of support" from "the community." To-night, the room is filled to capacity with three dozen men and women who have come to hear a panel discussion about bisexuality. On the panel are one "expert," and four "real people," that is, bisexual men and women. Audi-ence members nod in agreement as first the expert describes how hegemonic Euro-American culture revels in binary categories of sex, gender, and sexuality that deny the existence of bisexuality, and then as the real people tell their stories with an emphasis on dispelling stereotypes and exemplifying the diversity of bisexual experience. The question and answer period had not yet begun, but a hand went up. Caught slightly off guard, panel members looked quizzically at the man in the audience, who said, "All of you keep mentioning the 'bisexual community.' Tell me, where can I find it?"

His question was followed by several seconds of silence. "Well . . ." Each panel member ventured an answer. One of us said, "We are it." The audience member looked unsatisfied; can four people be a community? Apparently that was not the answer he had hoped to hear. Another panel member mentioned a local support group. "How do I get in touch with that group?" "We're not sure, who's running it now?" "Try calling the local Gay Alliance; they can tell you." Another panel member mentioned the national organizations; "membership forms for BiNet are on the display table. Have you seen *Anything That Moves*?" "Do you have a computer? There are lots of bisexual discussion groups on-line. Many people today are finding community in cyberspace."

Is there a bisexual community? Yet? Answering that question requires knowing what a bisexual community would be if it did exist, and therein lies part of the problem. Traditionally, a community consists of a residential area whose inhabitants are connected to each other by dense and overlapping social and economic networks. A small town in which residents live and work lifelong, for example, is clearly a community in this sense. Bisexuals do not have this kind of community. But neither do most other people today. In the individualistic electronic age, people move frequently, choose friends not because of physical proximity but because of common interests, and compartmentalize their relationships with others. Instead of growing into social networks consisting of family and neighbors, most of us build social networks by finding people who share our personal characteristics–our sexualities, for example. "Lifelong friends" are those we stay in touch with over the miles; most other friends are associated with particular time periods or aspects of our lives.

If geographic proximity and overlapping social and economic networks no longer define most people's experiences of community, what are the modern bases of community, and do bisexuals have them? Although social scientists have developed modern scientific concepts of community based on functional rather than geographic criteria, this chapter is less concerned with the ways social scientists define community than the ways in which bisexual people–bisexual men, in particular–define and experience community. Do bisexual men feel there is a bisexual community? If so, of what does that community consist? If not, what is lacking?

METHODS AND SAMPLE

The following discussion of bisexual men's experiences of bisexual community is based on the findings of an international study titled "Sexual/Bisexual Identities, Communities, and Politics." The overall purpose of the study is to explore how individuals who are attracted to both genders or have had sexual contact with members of both genders arrange their psychological and social worlds in the context of a society that is organized to facilitate either exclusive heterosexuality or exclusive lesbianism/gayness. Data were collected via in-depth interviews, participant observation, and self-administered questionnaires distributed with postage-paid envelopes in the United States and with postal coupons in several other countries, including the United Kingdom, France, Germany, Belgium, Canada, Australia, and New Zealand.

The questionnaire was designed to be self-explanatory and anonymous to encourage a wide range of people to participate, including those who are secretive about their sexuality. Because it is impossible to draw a representative sample of any population that is defined by its sexual feelings and behaviors, sampling was focused instead on drawing a diverse sample. Therefore, the questionnaire was distributed by multiple means, including conferences on sexuality, social networks, meetings of bisexual and LesBi-Gay social and political organizations, and advertisements in bisexual newsletters, mainstream "alternative" newspapers, and the Internet. Particular efforts were made to maximize the racial/ethnic, sexual, age, gender, and geographic diversity of the respondents.

The remainder of this chapter is based on 200 questionnaire respondents who were born male, were not post-operative MTF transsexuals or otherwise living full-time as women,[1] and lived in the United States at the time of the study. Of these men, 64% (n = 130) self-identify as bisexual or bi and 10% (n = 21) self-identify as heterosexual-identified bisexuals, gay bisexuals, or bisexual-identified gay men. Most of the remainder identify as queer, gay, homosexual, heterosexual, straight, or choose not to label themselves. Regardless of current identity, all have or have had either sexual attractions to both women and men or sexual experiences with both women and men. Six are crossdressers. Most describe themselves as White or of European descent (87.8%); 4.8% are Latin/Hispanic, 2.7% are of Asian descent, 1.6% are Black or African American, and 1.1% each are of Middle Eastern descent or Native American. At the time of the study, 12% of the sample lived in rural areas or small towns, 33% lived in a large town, suburb, or small city, and 54% lived in medium-sized or large cities. Twenty-nine percent had children, and most were in their 20s (26%), 30s (34%), or 40s (24%), with 15% over 50 years old. The sample is very highly educated; only 6% had no more than a high school education and 71% had finished sixteen or more years of formal education, usually equivalent to four years of college. The median income, however, is only $25,000.

Survey questionnaires usually rely heavily on verbal questions and responses. Even open-ended questions, although allowing more individualized responses than forced choice questions, impose a linguistic logic–including unidimensional linearity–on respondents' answers. Such methods of assessment are not always appropriate because some individuals tend to think in visual or artistic rather than linguistic terms and because some topics are multidimensional and therefore less easily explored via linear strings of words. Therefore, in the current study, respondents' experiences of bisexual community were assessed using questions requiring both verbal and non-verbal responses. Instructions in the questionnaire encouraged only bisexual-identified respondents to complete these questions, although some non-bisexual identified men chose to do so also. The primary verbal question was: "Would you say that there is a 'bisexual community'? Explain why or why not. (That is, what does 'bisexual community' mean to you, and in what ways does it exist or not exist for you?)" The non-verbal question asked respondents to draw maps of their bisexual communities. The questionnaire, which was 22 pages long and consisted of over 150 questions, took most respondents over two hours to complete. The map was the last question, and respondents were told that drawing the map was optional. Nevertheless, of the 200 born males in the United States subsample, 119–including 13 who did not identify themselves as bisexual–chose to do the map, suggesting that the map tapped a dimension of bisexual men's perceptions of bisexual community that had not been tapped by the verbal questions.

To draw their maps of "what your bisexual community is like, and how it looks to *you*," respondents were provided an outlined square space. A footnote instructed respondents that "if you don't feel that there is a bisexual community, please read this question as if it refers to the network of bisexual people and organizations that you know about, even if you don't consider this network a 'community.'" The purpose of providing an outlined space for the map was to ensure that map-makers would have sufficient margin space remaining to follow the next instruction, which was to add the lesbian, gay, and heterosexual communities/societies to the map. Finally, respondents were asked to indicate their position on the map with an "X," and, if possible, to use a dotted line to "trace the path by which you entered the bisexual community and arrived at your current location in it." Despite the detailed instructions and the square outline provided, respondents were encouraged to "think outside the box" by a note that read "if you are not a 'visual thinker' or graphically oriented, this might be difficult. Please try anyway, and do not worry about what 'kind' of map you are expected to draw. Different people draw very different kinds of maps, and the point is to draw your own unique kind of map that reflects the way you see things."

FINDINGS

When asked to draw maps of their communities, many bisexual men drew Venn diagrams showing overlap between the bisexual community and other sexual identity communities. Other men drew islands, bridges, mountains, doors, fences, stick figures, houses, flowers, and amoeba-like and octopus-like structures. Some used multiple colors, others apologized for their lack of artistic ability. Two cautioned that "areas are not to scale" in their maps. Only a book with color reprints of all the maps could possibly do them justice; any verbal description and analysis of the wonderful variety in these maps can only impose the very verbal structure that I sought to avoid by asking respondents to draw maps. Fortunately, I am able to use the men's own verbal answers to open-ended questions about the bisexual community to guide my interpretations and analyses of their maps, and the eighteen maps that are reproduced in this chapter can help convey a sense of the complexity and variety among bisexual men's conceptions of the bisexual community.

The first finding to emerge from the comparison of bisexual men's verbal answers with their maps is that the two often seem to contradict each other. Some men who answered verbally that there is no bisexual community proceeded to draw detailed maps of bisexuals, bisexual groups, and bisexual networks that would appear to constitute a community. Some of these men even labeled parts of their maps "bisexual community." Conversely, some men who answered verbally that there is a bisexual community drew maps in which nothing is labeled "bisexual community"; that the map nevertheless represents a bisexual community can only be inferred from knowledge of their verbal comments. In fact, some of these men drew maps that convey a sense of isolation and total absence of community, belying their verbal comments that a community does exist.

Therefore, in describing these men's experiences and perceptions, the word "community" must be used advisedly. To avoid misrepresenting respondents' experiences and perceptions, and to avoid begging the question of whether there is a bisexual community, I do not use the term "community" in this chapter unless I am referring to the concept of community in the abstract or describing the experiences or perceptions of a respondent who uses the term "community" himself. This leaves the problem of what to call that which is not, or might not be, a community. Possible alternatives to "community" are the terms "population" and "world," and although I use these terms when they accurately reflect the experiences or perceptions of particular respondents, neither of these terms encompasses the entire range of experiences and perceptions I will be discussing as I explore the question of bisexual community. Therefore, to highlight the fact that the problem of defining, creating, or detecting the existence of "community" is not one to be solved, but one to be explored and enjoyed in its complexity, I will coin and use the term "popumunity" whenever a more specific term would be misleading or inaccurate. A "popumunity" might be a community or it might be a population; or, its nature as a community, a population, a world, or some other type of social entity might be unknown. The novelty of this combination of the concepts of "community" and "population" should help both reader and author maintain an appropriate level of self-consciousness regarding the ways in which this essay not only examines, but might contribute to, the construction of a concept of bisexual community. For similar reasons, I will follow the same usage when referring to transgenderists, feminists, sex radicals, and other groups that might or might not constitute communities in bisexual men's minds.

Although similar concerns might be raised about the characterization of lesbian, gay, and heterosexual social worlds as communities, the instructions given in the questionnaire for drawing the map specifically referred to lesbian and gay "communities" and to heterosexual "community" or "society," with no footnote suggesting that the concept of a network might be substituted. The question of whether these constitute communities is not a focus in this essay, and many respondents gave little indication of whether they would use the terms "community" or "society" in reference to lesbians, gay men, and heterosexuals. Hence, to avoid detracting from my focus on bisexual experience, I will generally refer to lesbian, gay, and heterosexual social worlds as communities or societies as if this usage were unproblematic.

When interpreted in light of respondents' verbal comments, several themes emerge from the maps. First, there is the question of whether there is a bisexual community. Some respondents indicated that there is no bisexual community, some know of bisexual groups, networks or populations but don't consider them communities, and others perceive themselves to be members of highly elaborate bisexual communities. Second, there is the question of what the bisexual community, network, or population looks like; who and what are part of this popumunity? Many of the maps provide great detail regarding the occupants of the bisexual popumunity, including the individual members and organizations that comprise it and the significant divisions and connections that exist within it; others depict the bisexual popumunity as a single amorphous blob. Third, the map instructions re-quested that respondents graphically illustrate the relationships between the bisexual "community or network" and the lesbian community, the gay com-munity, and heterosexual society; many did so, and added several other popumunities as well.

All names of respondents used in this chapter are pseudonyms. In some cases, the names of small, local organizations, groups, and individuals men-tioned in respondents' verbal answers or maps have been altered. Terms used to describe respondents' racial and ethnic identities–for example, "Cauca-sian" and "Black"–are those they used to describe themselves, although some respondents' detailed ethnic ancestries were edited to protect their anonymity. Respondents' sexual self-identities are generally mentioned only if they do not identify themselves as bisexual; respondents whose sexual identities are not explicitly stated can be assumed to identify as bisexual.

ISOLATION: LACK OF BISEXUAL COMMUNITY

Feelings of isolation and lack of community are very prevalent among these bisexual men. Among the 171 men who answered the verbal question "Would you say there is a bisexual community?" more than one quarter (28%) said that there is no bisexual community, a few others indicated that they didn't know if there is a bisexual community, and one in ten (10%) said or implied that they think there is a bisexual community, but that they are not part of it either because they haven't been able to find it yet, because it exists elsewhere, or because the community they used to belong to has disappeared. Some feel completely isolated: "There may be a bisexual community, al-though not one that I have seen or been involved with. At this point in my life

I've never even met another person who claimed to be bisexual." Others reported that a few bisexual groups exist in their area, but that they are "sparsely attended," that groups portraying themselves as bisexual or bi-inclusive are really "more gay/lesbian than bisexual," or that the so-called "bisexual community" is merely a "subgroup of the larger LesBiGay community" rather than a community "per se." Others noted that there are popumunities in their areas that some bisexuals might feel part of, but none that represent the entire bisexual population or that they themselves could identify with. For example, a man living in a large southwestern city who is almost 60 years old and describes himself as a "White German" wrote, "There definitely is not a bisexual community. Perhaps some groups of swingers could qualify as being close." A 51-year-old, self-described Caucasian man in Berkeley, California wrote that "polyfi groups are as close as I know," and another Caucasian man, 44 years old and living in a small town in Wisconsin, said, "I think there is a fringe bi community of transsexuals." A Caucasian man living in a small California city and approaching 70 years of age reported that he used to feel he was part of a bisexual community through his involvement in human potential organizations and sex clubs, but that these had died out because of "organization decline, mounting concern over diseases, and ageism."

When they reached the end of the questionnaire, many of these men declined to draw maps of "the bisexual community"; what would they draw? Others, however, used the space provided for their map to reinforce their feelings of isolation or their perceptions that there is no bisexual community. Some left the box blank, explaining that "this empty box is a good depiction of the 'bisexual community.'" A 53-year-old, third-generation White German American man living in a midwestern suburb drew an "X" representing himself in the midst of a blank space, conveying a sense of unconnectedness and isolation. Another White man, who lives in Phoenix, Arizona and identifies himself as gay or homosexual, not bisexual because "I, at one time, had a small amount of sexual desire for women, but no longer," drew a box full of H's representing "Heterosexuals." Among the H's he scattered many small G's and B's, representing gay and bisexual individuals amid the heterosexual majority. A White suburban Californian drew a box full of unconnected dots, writing, "On the map below there are a lot of dots. These represent individuals. Some of them are bisexual, and some may form communities. However, I do not know which ones." A 53-year-old living in a southeastern state drew houses along a suburban street, one labeled "me with my wife and children" and next door, "my male friend with his wife and children," commenting "we are friends and have sex but our wives and no one else knows."

Several men who indicated in their verbal answers that they don't believe a bisexual community exists did, however, draw maps showing something other than isolation. In light of their verbal comments, many of these men's maps can be understood as diagrams of populations or worlds of experience rather than communities. In some maps, this is indicated by reference to "bisexuals" or "bisexuality" or "bisexual groups" rather than to a "bisexual community." See, for example, the map drawn by Herman (Figure 1),[2] a White man living in a large midwestern city who answered the verbal question with "No [there is no bisexual community]. I don't consider a group of social support groups a 'community' in the strict sense of the word." In his map, Herman drew the gay community, the lesbian community, heterosexual society, the cross-gender/transgender community, and *bisexuals*, not the bi-

FIGURE 1

Pseudonym: Herman
Would you say there is a "bisexual community"? No. Bi people are spread throughout society, in all forms of living arrangements and lifestyles (and relationships), and in all stages of coming out. Furthermore, bi people face rejection and stigmatization from straights and gays/lesbians, and bisexuals as yet have not congregated in neighborhoods or "ghettos" as have gays and lesbians in many cities. I don't consider a group of social support groups a "community" in the strict sense of the word.

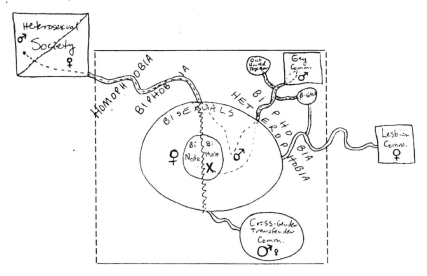

sexual *community*. Some other maps include areas labeled, ambiguously, "bi"; the possibility that this is a reference to a bi community, rather than a bi population or bi experience, can only be ruled out by reading the map-makers' verbal answers. Finally, some men who answered verbally that there is no bisexual community drew maps of the bisexual communities that they wish existed, or that they believe exist elsewhere. For example, Ralph, a 36-year-old living in a small New England city, answered the verbal question with "There may be a bisexual community, although not one that I have seen or been involved with;" nevertheless, he indicated that the dotted lines in his map represent the "bisexual community" (Figure 2). Kevin, a 28-year-old who lives in Phoenix, Arizona, said "No" to the question of whether there is a bisexual community, but indicated in his map that the bisexual community exists in Rhode Island or Maine; only the combination of his map and his

FIGURE 2

Pseudonym: Ralph
Would you say there is a "bisexual community"? There may be a bisexual community, although not one that I have seen or been involved with. At this point in my life I've never even met another person who claimed to be bisexual.

(a) The lesbian and gay communities
(b) The heterosexual community or heterosexual society

(D = BISEXUAL COMMUNITY

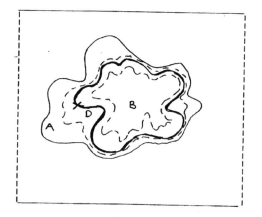

verbal answer reveals a more complete picture of his experience, i.e., that he thinks there is a bisexual community elsewhere, but that he does not feel he belongs to it.

Of course, some men did explicitly indicate in their verbal answers that they think there is a bisexual community but that they are not part of it. These men generally explained that there is no community in their local area but that they had heard or discovered that communities exist in larger cities and nationwide. Knowing that communities exist elsewhere is a source of comfort for some of these men, despite their more immediate experience of isolation. For example, a 22-year-old living in a small southeastern city recalled that "Yes–I met them in D.C.! They're all pretty friendly and casual–just knowing that they're out there is comforting," and another 22-year-old from a small midwestern city noted that "At the moment there is no bisexual community where I live. There is one nationally to work on political issues. And a bisexual community exists in larger cities." Some of these individuals had encountered bisexual communities when they traveled, for example, to the 1993 March on Washington, or found access to bisexual communities in cyberspace; as the aforementioned White suburban Californian wrote, "There probably exist flourishing bisexual communities, but I know nothing about them, except for the internet newsgroup soc.bi, which I occasionally read."

For some men, the lack of bisexual community–or, at least, a bisexual community they feel they belong to–is so profound that they cannot even imagine what a bisexual community would be like. A 35-year-old who describes himself as "Negro" and is now living in a large eastern city explained that "bisexual community means nothing to me. It would be hard for me to say if a bisexual community existed because most [of my] bisexual experiences happened while [I was] incarcerated." However, a few respondents can imagine a bisexual community, and described what that community would look like if it did exist. For a 39-year-old Euro-American living in a medium-sized northwestern city, the criterion for community is a meeting place; "I do not have a sense of a real 'bisexual community'–no identified bi meeting place." For other men, the keys to community are: size ("I have never had any experiences with such a group large enough to be defined as a community"), identifiability ("The bi community is amorphous, indistinct . . . For me a community has to be more identifiable . . . members have to [self identify] as belonging to the group"), geographic proximity ("bisexuals as yet have not congregated in neighborhoods or 'ghettos' as have gays and lesbians in many cities"), public accessibility ("There are extensive networks of friends, but by their nature they tend to be exclusionary"), and scope ("There seems to be a tiny but vocal community of out, proud bisexuals–like drag queens many years ago–but the vast majority of bisexuals are invisible . . . for me, the bisexual community is total community"). For many men, the issue is the variety and wealth of social and cultural resources; they do not believe that a few organizations, especially if they are unconnected to each other and invisible to nonmembers, are enough to constitute a community. For example, Lou, a 47-year-old White man living in New York City, wrote, "No [there is no bisexual community]. There are no places where bi's regularly socialize among themselves, no major bi institutions, no bi ghetto, no newspaper, radio, TV, bars, bookstores, restaurants, etc. Only a few movement groups which are far from representative."

For some men, the isolation of bisexuals lies in contrast to the existence of communities for gay men, lesbians, and heterosexuals. For example, a 64-year-old Caucasian man who identifies himself as queer, gay, or homosexual, not bisexual, drew a large amoeba-like structure representing "straights" (Figure 3). Inside that structure, he drew long, worm-like, interconnected

FIGURE 3

Pseudonym: None
Would you say there is a "bisexual community"? A small number of bisexual people in my area are attempting to form a group with only limited success. It has certain similarities with groups of mixed racial couples: lack of the focus usually required in "agents of change."

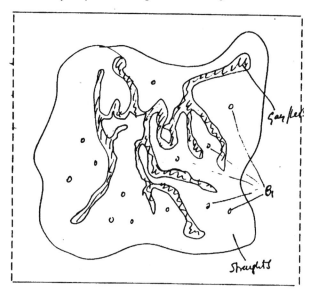

areas labeled "gay/lesbian." He represented bisexual individuals with single tiny circles, scattered throughout the "straights," with no connections among themselves. A Caucasian man living in rural New England, who identifies as gay because "approximately 95% of my sexual/affectional attractions are to males," wrote, "There are small pockets of organized bisexuals, but I would not call this the 'bisexual community' as I would use the term 'gay community.' Gays are more organized."

WE'RE NOT COMPLETELY ISOLATED, BUT ARE WE A COMMUNITY YET?

In addition to the more than one in three respondents (38%) who do not believe that a bisexual community exists at all, at least not for themselves, there is another large group who believe that something does exist but disagree over whether it meets the requirements for a "community." Some conclude that it does, others conclude that it does not, and some debate the issue without drawing a conclusion either way. Although the men who conclude that current bisexual resources do not qualify for the label "community" are similar to the ones described above in that they perceive a lack of community, the tone of their opinion is different. Instead of emphasizing the lack of bisexual resources and offering definitions of community to highlight this lack, these men emphasize the existence of bisexual resources, however inadequate, and use definitions to decide that these resources don't (yet) qualify for the label "community." The sense of isolation conveyed by many of the men described above is absent, replaced by a less desperate–although no less heartfelt–desire for a stronger community and an intellectualized approach focusing on the semantics of the word "community."

Those who conclude that bisexuals do not qualify as a community argued that existing bisexual organizations and networks are too small, weak, or otherwise not well developed or free-standing enough to meet the requirements for a community. Some commented that people are "trying" to form bisexual organizations and community, implying that these efforts had been somewhat less than fully successful. Others described existing bisexual organizations, networks, or events, and shared their reservations about calling these resources a community. For example, George, a 26-year-old White Texan now living in a large California town, wrote, "I am aware of some bisexual groups that are organized through the Gay and Lesbian Resource Center . . . My sense is that there is not so much a bisexual community as a loose population which coalesces around institutions of the lesbian/gay community." Similarly, Warren, a 68-year-old Caucasian man living in a small northeastern city, responded, "Not much of one. There is an international soc.bi group that comes closest to this . . . So long as it is only a computer group, it almost doesn't make it as a 'community.'" Some referred to a bisexual community, but had to qualify the term "community" to make it fit; a 24-year old White, Caucasian man in Chicago, Illinois wrote, "I think there is [a bisexual community] in a sense that there are groups of bisexual people who socialize at least partially on the basis of their sexual orientation." Belying their verbal comments, many of these men did in fact draw maps in which they pictured a "bisexual community." In some cases, this community is minimal, reflecting the map-maker's reservations about calling it a community. For example, in his map, a 46-year old man of British and Native American descent living in a small California city represented the bisexual community with a single, small black dot in a vast expansive space. Others, for example Ricky, a 31-year old White man living in a large California city, drew detailed maps of the collections of individuals and groups that they had verbally said were not communities (Figure 4).

Those who conclude that existing bisexual organizations and networks do qualify as a community made some of the same observations regarding its inadequacies, generally agreeing that the bisexual community is small or underdeveloped. They described the bisexual community as being scattered, weakly connected, unstable, fragile, and focused narrowly on sexual rather than political issues. They commented that it lacks organization, cohesiveness, clear definition, identifiability, visibility and voice, size and strength, distinction as a group, meeting places, variety in social institutions, and outreach efforts. For example, some men observed that bisexual groups are struggling to survive, or that there are not many places that bisexuals can go to meet other bisexuals; a 27-year-old Euro-American in San Francisco wrote, "The word would signify to me that there are places where people meet because they are bisexual. There are a few bi-specific groups here . . . but not many." Others pointed out that large numbers of bisexuals are not part of the bisexual community; a well developed community would involve more, and a broader spectrum, of its members. "Yes [there is a bisexual community]," responded Evan, a White man in Champaign-Urbana, Illinois, "but it doesn't reach out to a big portion of bisexuals and is not completely connected . . . Those who don't know about the support group or who can't access the computer network aren't in the same community. I am and may be completely alone." Sean, a 32-year-old of Irish and Native American descent, commented that a well developed community provides not only resources for its members, but also outreach to non-members; "A community

FIGURE 4

Pseudonym: Rocky
Would you say there is a "bisexual community"? I would say that most of my friends are bi, and that therefore, there is at least that much more community in my own life. In general, though, I don't feel like there is a comm. I look at the g/l community, and : see bars, clubs, cafés, bookstores, political organizations, etc. I don't see that for bi's. It bums me out.

must reach into the populace, we must educate and provide support, we must be out and confident and use every opportunity to debunk Bi myths and misinformation."

Again, for many bisexual men, the deficiencies of the bisexual community are accentuated by comparison to well developed gay and lesbian communities. Several men made explicit comparisons to gay and lesbian communities, noting that bisexuals lack the same level of organization ("There are some loose associations of bi's that I'm familiar with, but in general, they don't have the organizational level that gays [+ lesbians] do, nor neighborhoods or bars devoted to them [us]"), distinction and visibility ("While I'm sure there are more bis whether in groups or as individuals, around Chicago–only a few showed up at our function–certainly nationwide and Chicago-wide they are far less vocal than the Gay and Lesbian community. As a group, they're far less distinctive, even if they are another sub-culture"), structural diversity ("I would say that most of my friends are bi, and that therefore, there is at least that much more community in my own life. In general, though, I don't feel like there is a community. I look at the gay/lesbian community, and see bars, clubs, cafés, bookstores, political organizations, etc. I don't see that for bi's. It bums me out"), autonomy ("Yes, there seems to be a bisexual community, but may be more riding the fringes of gay community in this area"), and political activity ("activities seem to revolve only around sexuality, sexual politics. Not political like the Gay community").

WHY IS THERE NO (STRONG) BISEXUAL COMMUNITY (YET)?

Many men who feel that the bisexual community is small and weak think that this merely reflects its embryonic stage of development. They are very hopeful that a more well developed bisexual community, more deserving of the name "community," will exist in the future. As a Caucasian man living in Rochester, New York stated, "There are more and more support groups starting up all the time."

Others attributed the weakness of the bisexual community to the characteristics of bisexuals themselves, implying that the lack of community is not merely due to its infancy and that time alone might not produce a stronger bisexual community. Some of the reasons that these men gave are that diversity among bisexuals makes unity difficult, that sexuality is not a sufficient basis for community, and that bisexuality itself is not clearly defined enough to form the basis for a clearly defined community. For example, diversity is an inhibiting factor, although not necessarily a problem, for Josh, a 33-year-old Caucasian/Jewish man living in a large California city: "[The bisexual community] is small and sketchy, not well-defined, because bisexuals are a very diverse group and many are very private or not interested in developing community." Josh also feels that sexuality is an insufficient basis for community; "the value [of bisexual community] is limited because sexuality is only one part of life . . . the bisexuals in my bi community and I share little in common." Similarly, Michael, a 46-year-old Anglo-American crossdresser, wrote that "'bisexual' suggests only one's sexuality is the determinant of community identity, and this is insufficient, I think." Others feel that sexual identity in general is an insufficient basis for community. For example, one man stated, "I don't believe in a cohesive gay community either," and another observed, "There's no one monolithic gay 'community' so I don't see bisexuals as having a monolithic single community either."

Several feel that bisexuals tend to gravitate toward, "blend into," or hide within either heterosexual or gay/lesbian communities rather than form their own groups. For example, a Jewish Caucasian man living in Chicago wrote, "[bisexuals are] less distinctive [than gays and lesbians] . . . possibly because some bi's (though not all by any means) at times find it easier to hide their behavior when near heteros." Kevin, the 28-year-old Arizonan, wrote, "Bisexuals (in my opinion) are in the middle. They need to associate with something so they gravitate towards either side. There is too much width and need." Although most of these men seem to feel that the tendency for bisexuals to camouflage themselves within heterosexual, gay, or lesbian communities is a trait inherent to bisexuals or bisexuality, an 83-year-old Caucasian man living in a large northeastern city suggested that it has more to do with a lack of societal approval for bisexuality: "It is very difficult to pull such groups together, since there is so little social recognition for bi-sexuality and other potential identifications for individuals have stronger recognition." This lack of recognition and acceptance might be particularly inhibiting for married men; as a man living in the rural south wrote, "I cannot associate for fear of being 'outed.' [I feel] pressure from others in the group to tell my wife." Some respondents feel that bisexuals are too closeted or "underground" to form a community; as a 23-year-old White man living in the rural midwest put it, "It is like a club where 99.9% of the members never heard of each other." Conversely, a 30-year-old Caucasian man living in a medium-sized southern city mused over whether bisexuals might be "too mainstream to be visible," and a White Anglo-Saxon man living in San Antonio wondered whether the reason that bisexuals had made so little progress is because they are more threatening to society.

Although most men who lack a sense of bisexual community seem to wish that they could belong to one, a few do not see a need for such a community. A couple feel that the gay, lesbian, and straight communities are sufficient to fulfill the needs of bisexuals. For example, John, a 26-year-old White man living in a northeastern suburb who identifies himself as gay or homosexual because "being gay, to me, means not only being attracted to members of the same sex, but also identification with an oppressed minority with a distinct identity and subculture," feels that bisexuals are a subgroup of the lesbian and gay community and wrote that "I don't think [a bisexual community] will break off because although individuals may be bi, individual relationships are either same sex or opposite sex. 'Bi relationships' do not exist really. Also, bi issues are irretrievable from gay and lesbian ones." Perhaps John does not perceive the existence of a bi community or bi relationships because he is gay-identified; or, conversely, perhaps he is gay-identified because he does not perceive bisexual identity as a link to a distinct group and subculture.

Others object to the formation of a separate bisexual community on political grounds, for example because "separatism is so confining" or "because there is no need for one. It's ghettoizing." A 61-year-old White man living in a large midwestern city who does not identify as bisexual because he prefers not to label himself made a similar point with some apparent anger, "If there is a community, I could care less. Don't promote me on the job, hire me, fire me, talk to me or anything because I am a sexual person. Don't do nice things because I am a good person, worker, conversationalist, witty, sharp, loyal, etc. I'm sure there is a bisex community . . . Frankly, I would not associate with them. I am a live person *first* and a sexual person *secondly*." Paul, a 27-year-old Caucasian man living in a small midwestern city, expressed a similar sentiment with less anger; below his map, he wrote, "I'm standing in the corner because a separate community is not what I want when I try to imagine a better world. I realize I am in the community; this paradox leads to uncertainty." A man living in Denver, Colorado left the box provided for his map blank, writing that "Bisexuality is in the basement of society–we are unique, happy, free, kind, loving spirits–perhaps we should stay this way and let things be because not too many people can or could handle and/or understand their own feelings about bisexuality."

For some, the idea of a queer, or sexual freedom, movement is more attractive than the idea of a bisexual community or movement. For example, Joseph, a 31-year-old man of central European ancestry living in a southern state, approves of the fact that the bisexuals he knows put their energy toward building the queer movement rather than a bisexual community because "Pushing queer politics . . . expands the room for everyone." Dylan, a 25-year-old White European American, notes that the lack of bisexual identification and community-building could reflect either more sophisticated ideas about sexual liberation, or a pre-liberation lack of consciousness. Comparing two California cities in which he had lived, he reported that in one city, "[my friends and I] all identified/identify as bisexual to a certain extent but also tried/try not to label [our] sexuality. We all felt/feel . . . that it allow[s] us more freedom to experience different modalities (tapped and untapped) of the sexual." In contrast, in the other city, "People that I have met there seem to continue to buy into the monosexual consciousness that I see as pervasive in an overwhelmingly large part of the United States."

INSIDE THE BISEXUAL COMMUNITY–
KNOCK, KNOCK, WHO'S THERE?

Despite widespread feelings of isolation and lack of community among bisexual men, many–one in three in the current study–do feel that there is a bisexual community, and that they are or could be members of it. In their maps, several of these men represented their bisexual communities with circles, squares, or amoeba-shapes containing nothing but empty, undifferentiated space. Whatever exists inside the bisexual community for these men remains a mystery.

But other men's maps help peel away the layers of that mystery. More detailed maps of the bisexual community, including some maps drawn by men who would not use the term "community" to describe their drawings, distinguish bisexual men, bisexual women, and bisexual transgenderists; activist, open, and closeted bisexuals; asexuals, pansexuals, and sadomasochists; and friends and family. Some maps show organizations or other social structures, and several include the Internet.

Gender Differences

In some maps, bisexual men and women are shown as members of the same community or population, that is, popumunity. Jacob, a 34-year-old Jewish man living in a large midwestern city, for example, drew a single circle filled with numerous male and female symbols (Figure 5). Other men drew separate popumunities for bisexual men and women, or indicated that within a single bisexual popumunity are separate sub-popumunities for men and women. In some cases, the bisexual men's popumunity is shown as being much smaller than the bisexual women's popumunity. For example, Monty, a 31-year-old Caucasian man living in suburban California, drew a small circle

FIGURE 5

Pseudonym: Jacob
Would you say there is a "bisexual community"? Yes, there is an active
bi network in [my city]. For me it is a place where bisexuals affirm and strength-
en their bi identities. Some of us are also active in queer communities.

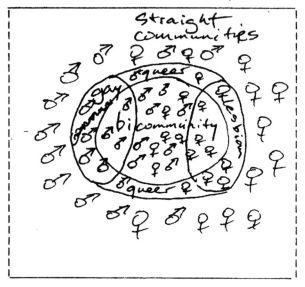

representing the "bi" community, and inside that placed a smaller circle,
about one tenth as large, labeled "Bi M." Other maps depict bi men's and bi
women's popumunities of approximately equal sizes. As shown in Figure 1,
Herman drew a single circle representing "bisexuals" and then drew a jagged
line through the middle, with one side designated male and the other female.
He labeled a smaller circle, straddling the line, "Bi Note" on the women's
side and "Bi Male" on the men's side, apparently representing twin organizations for bisexual women and men. Jordan, a rural 44-year-old Caucasian man,
similarly split a single circle through the center, labeling the sides "presenting
male" and "female presenting," indicating that the important gender distinction is social presentation, not biological sex or assigned gender.

Several map-makers specifically included transgendered people within
their bisexual popumunities, often not as marginal or minority members but
as a third gender alongside men and women. Larry, a 35-year-old White,
Anglo-Saxon man, divided the bisexual population into three unequal sized
segments: "bi women," "bi men," and "bi transgenderists" (Figure 6). The
"bi transgenderists" section is the smallest, but a marginal note indicates that

FIGURE 6

Pseudonym: Larry
Would you say there is a "bisexual community"? No. I have never had any experiences with such a group large enough to be defined as a community.

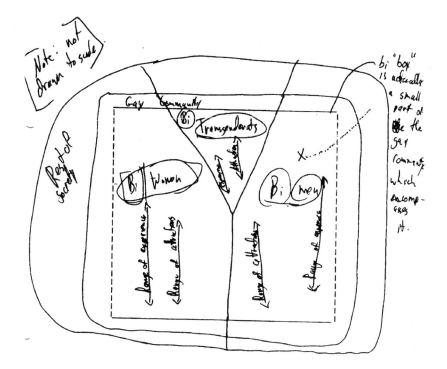

the map is not drawn to scale. Arnold, a 57-year-old Caucasian man, commented that including transgenderists in the map would require a third dimension, that is, "a plane above and/or below the [questionnaire] page." Inside his bisexual circle, Jim, a 27-year-old who describes himself as "half Asian-American and half Caucasian," wrote "phreaky" near the border with the lesbian/gay circle, "transgender" and "transsexual" near the center of the circle, and "kinky" near the border with the heterosexual circle. What does the placement of these words in the bisexual circle signify, if anything? Are all bisexuals phreaky, kinky, and transgendered? Or, are bisexuals who gravitate toward heterosexuality or heterosexuals "kinky," whereas those who gravitate toward lesbianism/gayness or lesbians/gays "phreaky"?

Political and Social Differences

Some map-makers distinguished between bisexuals who are open or politically active and those who are closeted or less vocal. For example, as shown
in Figure 7, Karl, a Philadelphia resident, differentiated "activists" from
"apolitical bisexuals" (see also Figure 8). In another map, Martin, a White,
33-year-old Los Angeles resident, represented "open bisexuals" with a
small, darkened area at the tip of a space called "bi." The rest of the bi space
presumably represents bisexuals who are closeted or at least less vocal and
visible. The only bisexual presence in Gene's map is a circle labeled "bisexual activism groups," suggesting that activist groups *are* the bisexual community. Floyd, a 40-year-old Caucasian suburban midwesterner, estimated that
only 10% of the population are "true gay/lesbians" and 10% are "true
hetero"; the rest are "society-dictated heterosexuals (50%)," "non-practic-
ing bisexuals (15%)," "closeted bisexuals (10%)," and "admitted, practic-

FIGURE 7

Pseudonym: Karl
Would you say there is a "bisexual community"? "Bisexual community,"
to me, is the growing number of bisexuals who have chosen to ally themselves
together for both social, support, and political purposes.

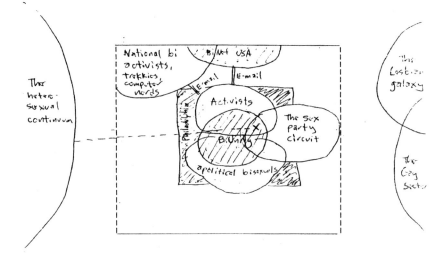

FIGURE 8

Pseudonym: Josh

Would you say there is a "bisexual community"? Yes. It is small and sketchy, not well-defined, because bisexuals are a very diverse group and many are very private or not interested in developing community. I like my "bi community" as a place to be among like-minded people; but the value is limited because sexuality is only one part of life and beyond it–an important basic attitude to life–the bisexuals in my bi community and I share little in common.

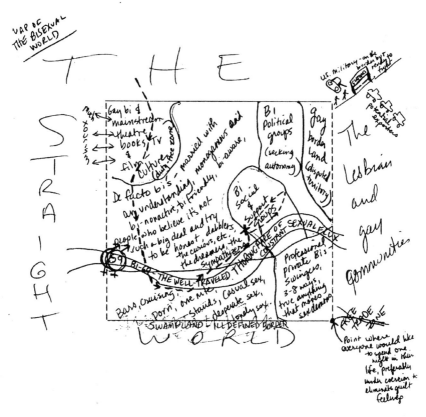

ing, bisexuals (5%)." Oswald, a 77-year-old White/Jewish man who identifies himself as heterosexual "most often" although he has had "several
bisexual experiences," drew individual bi females, bi males, gay females,
gay males, swingers, and nonmonogamists, and then enclosed some of these
individuals inside closet icons. Several individuals who are grouped in a
corner are enclosed together inside a larger closet icon labeled "military."

In several maps, closeted bi people are included as members of the gay/
lesbian or heterosexual communities. An example is Figure 9, drawn by Cole,
a 30-year-old Caucasian man who lives in Hawaii and identifies himself as
gay because he "primarily desire[s] emotional, sexual, and spiritual intimacy
with people of the same gender"; perhaps he considers himself one of the
closeted bi people he depicts. In another map, not pictured, the aforementioned resident of San Antonio drew "The Sexuality Classroom," with individual "Bisexuals" who "won't come out in this rigid society so they stick to
their strict labels that pose no threats to the next guy/girl" sitting silently
among "homosexual" and "straight" students. One "openly bisexual" student sits in the back corner, farthest from the teacher, who is also a closeted
bisexual. Ian, a 32-year-old of mixed European ancestry, used several colors
in his map and indicated that there are areas of "self-defined heterosexual
society" contiguous with the bisexual community which consist of individuals who "have suppressed feelings or desires toward same sex" or who "are
also sexual with [same] sex persons," and that similar areas exist in the
landscape of "self-defined gay and lesbian society." Likewise, Allan, a
25-year-old White man who lives in a large western town, placed "bis defin-

FIGURE 9

Pseudonym: Cole
Would you say there is a "bisexual community"? Yes. I feel comfortable
with its emergence.

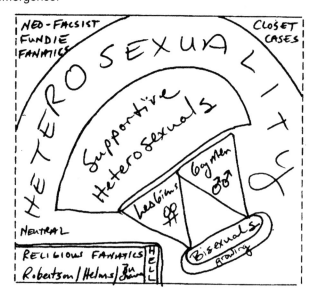

ing as gay/lesbian" inside the "gay/lesbian community," and "bis acting as straights" in "hetero-community/society."

In other maps, individuals who are not out as bisexual–especially those who self-identify as gay, lesbian, or heterosexual but who are or could be bisexual–are shown as members of the bisexual popumunity. A particularly elaborate map by Thomas, a 26-year-old White man living in a small mid-western city, shows a large circle representing the bisexual community (Figure 10). Inside this community, two smaller circles drawn with dashed lines represent "self-identified gay men" and "self-identified lesbians," symbolizing the permeability of these boundaries and the idea that many self-identified gay men and lesbians are bisexual or could identify as bisexual. A third circle, slightly larger and drawn with a solid line except for "a few tiny openings for those who bother to look or venture outside," represents "self-identified straights." Inside this circle, a drawing of a closed closet suggests that many self-identified straights are really closeted bisexuals. Francisco, a

FIGURE 10

Pseudonym: Thomas
Would you say there is a "bisexual community"? Yes. We're out there and we describe ourselves in the same ways. I guess the most important issue is that we realize we are not alone and have some common experiences with others.

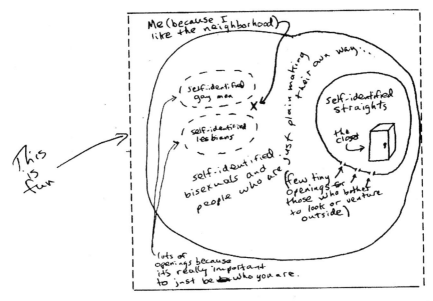

White/Hispanic man living in the Pacific northwest, noted in his map that an entire spectrum of sexual identities exists–gay/lesbian, gay/lesbian-identified bi man/woman, bi-identified gay man/lesbian, bi-identified straight man/woman, straight-identified bi man/woman, and straight man/woman–although he did not indicate which he would include within the bisexual community.

Rudy, a 28-year-old, gay-identified White man living in a medium-sized southern city, pointed out that sexual identities sometimes reflect an individual's politics rather than their sexual practices or even their sexual or affectional inclinations. He also noted that the identity/practice knife cuts both ways; in addition to people who identify as lesbian, gay, or "strayt" but who are bisexual in practice, there are also closeted gay people who call themselves bi. His map (Figure 11) includes amoeba-shaped blobs for several types of people defined by the combination of their sexual practices and identities,

FIGURE 11

Pseudonym: Rudy
Would you say there is a "bisexual community"? There is not a bisexual community here in [name of southern city]. I believe there could be one of more progressive strayts/gays/bisexuals who are not so inclined to be bounded by social categories. I often think of *Details* magazine as an example of a bisexual community magazine: all types of sexualities without assumptions as to what a person's sexuality is.

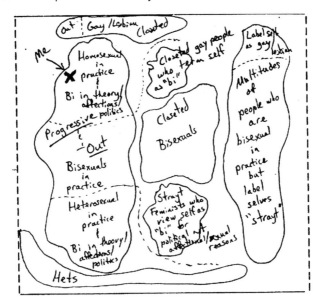

including a blob for those who are "bi in theory/affections/politics," among whom are "progressive and out bisexuals in practice" and individuals who are "homosexual in practice" or "heterosexual in practice." Separate blobs represent "closeted gay people who term self as 'bi,'" "closeted bisexuals," "strayt feminists who view self as 'bi' for political not affectionate/sexual reasons," and the "multitudes of people who are bisexual in practice but who label selves 'strayt,'" or, alternatively, who "label selves gay/lesbian."

Sexual Differences

In some maps, bisexuals are distinguished by their sexual practices or philosophies. Mitch, a 27-year-old White man living in Brooklyn, New York, for example, carved out a space inside the realm of "bisexuality" for "pan-sexuals." Frank, a 40-year-old Caucasian Italian man living in a small California town, distinguished "monogamous bisexuals" from "non-monogamous bisexuals"; the amoeba-shape representing the former is smaller than, and embedded within, the amoeba-shape representing the latter (Figure 12). Francisco drew distinctions between forms of bisexuality (transitional, serial, concurrent), and sexual philosophies or practices (monogamy, polyfidelity, sex radical). Lou distinguished "situational" bisexuality, such as occurs among "prisoners, sailors, [and] youth," from "trade" and "general" bisexuality, and further distinguished men who take both the active and passive sexual roles with other men from those who take only the passive role. Kaleb, whose ancestry is "mixed middle Eastern," included "hot tub queens" and "bi boy party babes," as well as "all purpose core activists" and "bi's discovering selves/coming out." Larry, in each of his three segments representing bi women, bi transgenderists, and bi men, drew double-headed arrows labeled "range of experience" and "range of attraction," suggesting Kinsey-like variations in the feelings of attraction and sexual experiences among bisexuals of all three genders (Figure 6). Larry's own sexual attractions to women and men have ranged from a 70:30 to a 40:60 ratio during his lifetime, yet he identifies as gay, explaining that "my sexual *orientation* is bisexual (clinical definition). My sexual *identity* is gay."

Three maps show particular detail regarding sexual variation within the bisexual popumunity. For Albert, a 25-year-old White Jewish man, relationship status is a key distinction. He used the box provided on the questionnaire to represent the bisexual population and drew irregular shapes inside it to represent bisexuals with different relationship statuses. The largest, most central shape is labeled "bis in no steady relationship." Occupying corner positions, represented by shapes of substantial size, are "bi men and women

FIGURE 12

Pseudonym: Frank
Would you say there is a "bisexual community"? There is one, but it is very fluid (people coming in and out often).

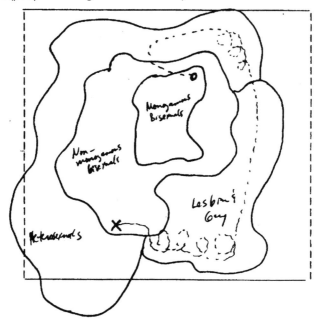

in straight relationships," "bi women in lesbian relationships," "bi men in gay relationships," and "?straights." A small shape, clinging to the side of the box, is labeled "bis in relationships with each other." These shapes do not overlap, suggesting that a "straight relationship" is not just a relationship with a person of another gender; it is a relationship with a heterosexual of another gender. Thus, bisexuals are shown as being differentiated from each other not only on the basis of the genders of their current partners, but on the basis of the sexual identities of those partners. For Albert, it appears to be the heterosexual identity of a bisexual's partner, not their different gender, that makes the bisexual's relationship with that person "straight." In this view, contrary to John's opinion, "bi relationships" do exist–they are relationships between two bisexuals.

The other two maps showing great sexual variation among bisexuals are reproduced in Figures 4 and 8. In Ricky's map, several amoeba-like shapes represent swingers, experimenters, "closeted bi women pretending to be lesbians cause they know they'd lose their friends if they came all the way out," "gay men who occasionally end up in bed with women friends," "trans folk for whom the label is meaningless," "children before monosexist indoctrination," "just bi-curious," "a couple with a girlfriend," and "married guys who suck dick in subway toilets." In Josh's map, two smallish areas labeled "bi social and support groups" and "bi political groups" are surrounded by much larger, more irregular shaped areas representing: "de facto bi's–married with an understanding, monogamous and bi-nonactive, bi friendly, bi-aware people who believe it's not such a big deal and try to be honest, dabblers, the curious, etc., the dreamers and the sympathizers," "Bars, cruising, porn, one nite stands, casual sex, desperate sex, lonely sex," and "Professional, private bis–swingers, 3-8 ways, true anything that moves, sex dreams."

Demographic Differences

Other distinctions made by some map-makers include race or ethnicity, political orientation, and religion. For example, inside a kite-shaped bisexual community, a 26-year-old Asian-Indian man drew a circle labeled "people of color, bisexual," within which he placed an "X" representing himself. A 38-year-old Black man noted the existence of "Persons of Color," as well as parents, leather groups, and recovery groups; crosscutting these categories are distinctions based on level of political activity and age, with individuals under 30 distinguished from those aged 30-50, or over 50. Noting that the bisexual community's "strengths and weaknesses [are] centered on its diversity," Francisco commented that it is "too diverse to map in two dimensions" and listed six dimensions, including religion (Pagan, Judeo-Christian, Unitarian) and political orientation (conservative, moderate, liberal radical).

Individual Members

Many men included individuals in their maps. Often, these individuals are real people whom the map-maker knows personally. For example, George, who feels that there is "not so much a bisexual community as a loose population which coalesces around institutions of the lesbian/gay community," drew individuals labeled "friends" and "family" inside part of his bisexual popumunity, which he hesitatingly labeled a community (Figure 13). Sean drew a spiral labeled "GLBU Bi-Group." Dots and stars are strewn along the length of the spiral; dots are labeled with the names of individuals, and stars

FIGURE 13

Pseudonym: George
Would you say there is a "bisexual community"? I am aware of some
bisexual groups that are organized through the Gay and Lesbian Resource
Center. I have not participated in them. My sense is that there is not so much
a bisexual community as a loose population which coalesces around institutions of the lesbian/gay community.

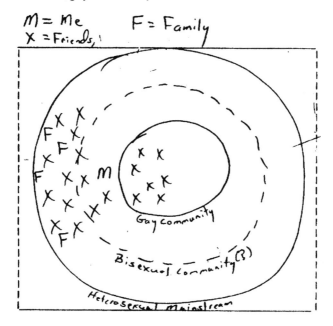

are designated as "open seats." Phillip, a 23-year-old living in a small southwestern city, drew stick figures representing his bi friends, asking that we
"notice that I know them as individuals–not as a community." He also drew
a cloud-shaped blob peopled with smiling faces but distant from himself and
his friends, writing, "This is the larger bi community–distant and cloudy. I'm
loosely connected only through reading." Indeed, a dotted line leads from
himself, through a picture of the book *Bi Any Other Name*, and then on to the
cloudy bi community. In the map drawn by Kilroy, a 39-year-old midwesterner of northern European and American Indian descent, amoeba-like blobs
twist around each other like exaggerated puzzle pieces. One blob is labeled
"self," and others are labeled "other bi," suggesting that each is a single
individual; additional blobs are labeled "hetero" and "G&L," suggesting
communities or populations.

Other maps include nationally prominent bisexual activists who are known to many by reputation. Among the activists named in maps are Lani Ka'ahumanu, Alan Hamilton, ben factory, Loraine Hutchins, Michael Beer, Deb Kolodny, Luigi Ferrer, Elias Farajajé-Jones, Regina (Reinhardt), Alexei Guren, and Peggy Walsh. In some cases, the map-maker himself is an activist who works directly with these bisexual activists. In other cases, he does not know them personally but draws a sense of community from the fact that visible bisexual activists exist. As one man wrote, "Lani Ka-ahumanu–the only real name I know in the bisexual movement." Ricky also mentioned "lani k" in his map (Figure 4).

Sometimes the individuals named in the maps are not real people. For example, Edward, a 43-year-old White suburban Californian, drew a number of stick figures. Bearing labels such as butcher, baker, candlestick maker, t-shirt seller, ex-lover, conference organizer, total jerk, parent, kid, doctor, lawyer, Indian chief, punk, teenager, and PWA, these figures apparently represent individual variety among bisexuals.

Internal Organizations and Social Structures

Some men drew structural features within the bisexual popumunity or indicated the lack of such structures. In one map, drawn by a German/Irish-American resident of Washington, D.C., a crosshatched box extends partially into the "homo" community on one side, and the "hetero" community on the other side. The box is labeled "bi institutions and culture" with a footnote reading "ideally. Currently it is not in hetero as much as homo," suggesting that bi institutions and culture should be visible within both the heterosexual and the gay/lesbian communities, and that this visibility is particularly lacking in heterosexual society. Paul drew an empty space inside the bisexual community, symmetric to a space outside the bisexual community labeled "gay club," and explained that the space is empty "because there are no bisexual clubs."

Other map-makers were more specific; a New York City man drew "Audrey's apartment," where "bi-culture salon meetings" take place; "Gramp's restaurant," where bi meetings take place on Sunday; and "our little corner" of the Gay and Lesbian Center, where there are bisexual meetings and monthly parties. A man in his 50s living in Florida drew a central circle representing sources of social support, including a regional bisexual network and a "political action support group." Intersecting this circle are circles labeled "spirituality support"–including Interweave and the Unitarian Universalist Church– and "Bi friends." Amid the wealth of different sexual lifestyles visible in

Ricky's map are also a number of bisexual organizations, including the Boston Bisexual Women's Network, BiPol in San Francisco, and the San Francisco Sex Information telephone line (Figure 4). Ricky's map also shows small groups of bisexuals who apparently are neither characterized by particular sexual lifestyles nor belong to the organizations named; additional amoeba-like blobs represent "2 bis," "3-4 bisexuals," "4 bis," and "30 bis in a city." A 34-year-old White man who completed the questionnaire while incarcerated drew a map of the dorms in his correctional institution.

BiNet USA, the primary national bisexual organization, and regional bisexual networks play a role in many men's bisexual popumunities, appearing in many maps as a central or overarching structure linking other bisexual groups and individuals to each other (e.g., Figure 7). This is particularly common in maps drawn by bisexual men living in Seattle; several maps show BiNet in relation to the Seattle Bisexual Men's Union (SBMU) and the Seattle Bisexual Women's Network (SBWN). For example, a 32-year-old Seattle resident drew two contiguous circles representing SBMU and SBWN, both overlapping a series of concentric circles representing, from the inner to the outer circle, BiNet Seattle, BiNet Northwest, and BiNet USA. In this map, the names of bisexual activists are as prominent as the organizations they are associated with. In another map, drawn by a 24-year-old Seattle resident, SBWN takes up about half the space inside the bisexual community, whereas SBMU takes up one fourth; the leftover quadrant appears to represent unaffiliated bisexual men, implying that bisexual men are less likely than bisexual women to be connected to local bisexual organizations. SBWN and SBMU overlap in an area labeled "BiNet," implying that the men and women belonging to these local gender-specific organizations come together under the umbrella of the national gender-inclusive bisexual network. A few men living in areas other than Seattle made similar maps; for example, a 33-year-old suburban man of Russian Jewish heritage living in New England drew a blob representing the "East Coast Bisexual Network" intersecting a blob labeled "BiNet USA," each blob sprinkled with the initials of well-known activists in that network.

A 44-year-old man of European descent living in a medium-sized midwestern city arranged the structural features of the bisexual community hierarchically, from micro to macro structures. At the lowest level are individual male and female symbols, arranged in various combinations, and captioned "individual-relationship-encounter-friend-group." Above these micro structures are social groups, followed in turn by support and political groups. At the top of the map is the "national community," consisting of BiNet, conferences, magazines, and books. Superimposed on this hierarchy are drawings of flowers, implying that each level supports, or grows into, the next. The national community would not be possible if not for local political groups, which would not be possible if not for social groups, which in turn depend on individual relationships. Ian also envisioned a hierarchical arrangement, but with a much more global perspective; he drew two concentric circles, labeling the inner circle "BiNet USA" and the outer circle "BiNet International: BiNets of other countries." Similarly, Peter, a 38-year-old Caucasian man living in a large California city, distinguished micro and macro levels of organization, with the macro level consisting of a network connecting bi groups in the large cities of the U.S. and Europe.

Internal Connections

In many of the maps already described, contiguous or overlapping borders indicate overlapping memberships or relationships between different segments of the bisexual popumunity. Such connections help foster solidarity, communication, and stability. In other maps, connections are represented by lines drawn between individuals and groups. For example, Andrew, a 22-year-old living in suburban New England, drew an international network of bi groups and individuals connected by lines labeled "fantasy links," "real links," and "identity links." A man living in rural New England outlined the continental United States and covered the map with dots (Figure 14). The dots are sparse in the south and much of the west and midwest, but densely grouped along the west coast and in the areas of Boston, Madison, and New York. Lines connect dots in the dense areas with each other, but no lines connect the isolated dots spread across the rest of the country. He wrote "I see clusters of bi's around the country . . . The lines represent communication links. My wife and I are outside any cluster as are many (maybe most) others. We feel very separated except through our mail box." In his map of the macro international network, Peter used lines to indicate direct connections, and dots to indicate bisexuals who are "plugged in via mail or computer."

Organizations and e-mail are often shown connecting various segments of the bisexual popumunity. Karl, who defines the bisexual community as "the growing number of bisexuals who have chosen to ally themselves together for both social, support, and political purposes," drew a particularly detailed map (Figure 7). Inside a shaded box labeled "Philadelphia," a circle representing the organization "BiUnity" intersects circles representing "activists," "apolitical bisexuals," and "the sex party circuit," indicating that BiUnity serves as a central structure bringing together individuals with these different political and sexual lifestyles, who would otherwise operate in different social networks. Conduits labeled "e-mail" lead from the "activist" circle, cross the border of "Philadelphia," and link up with "National bi activists, trekkies, computer nerds" and "BiNet USA." Thus, activists in different areas are linked not only to a variety of non-activists by local

FIGURE 14

Pseudonym: None
Would you say there is a "bisexual community"? I think one is developing, but certainly not out here in the backwoods. B.NET. *Anything That Moves, Bi Any Other Name*, and numerous local groups (not local to this area) are starting to make a cohesive movement.

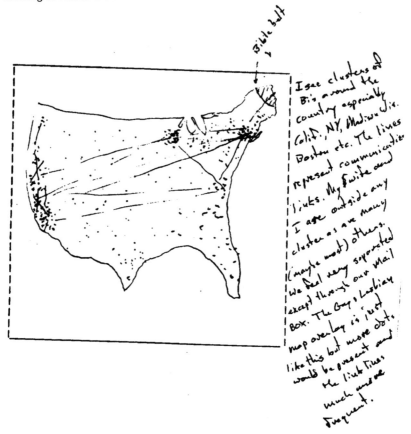

groups, but to activists across the country through the Internet and national organizations.

Several men gave the Internet a central position in their maps. Evan drew soc.bi, a bisexual Internet news group, as a central structure overlapping the University of Chicago Bisexual Union and the Champaign Urbana Bisexual Network. The CUBN, in turn, overlaps a bisexual support group and a bisexual discussion group, which also overlap each other. Groups of friends also appear in this map: "net friends" are found within soc.bi; "friends in Texas" overlap soc.bi; "supportive friends" exist in the straight community; and the "men's chorus," the map-maker's "best friend and his friends," and the "massage guy" are located in the gay community. Warren also prominently featured soc.bi, referring to it as an "internet *community*," yet noting that the majority of "self-identified bisexuals . . . don't know about soc. bi community." Paul drew two isolated stick figures at opposite sides of the box outline–a woman and a man each sitting at a computer with a long, thin line labeled "internet" connecting them; in answer to the verbal question, he indicated that computer networks *are* the bisexual community.

The theme of connection is especially dominant in the map drawn by David, a European-American living in a small town in New Jersey, who divided the space provided for his map into political, communication, professional, and personal quadrants. In the political quadrant, he listed the bisexual groups BNNJ and BiNet USA. Straddling the line between the political and communication quadrants are bisexual electronic-mail discussion groups such as BISEXU-L, BIACT-L, and soc.bi. In the personal and professional quadrants are "published bi essays and poems" and "bi scholarship," as well as "bi friends" and his bisexual same-sex lover. In contrast to most other map-makers, who emphasized individuals, organizations, and population segments in their maps, David apparently considers connections–including cultural products, which abstractly connect artist to audience–to be the defining features of the bisexual community. Sam, a 38-year-old White man living in a medium-sized northern city also views communities as consisting of connections, writing next to his map of a bisexual network spanning the breadth of the United States and Canada, "I don't 'see' the lesbian/gay/heterosexual communities as being geographically distinct from the bisexual community–the lines of connection would be stronger [in some communities than others]." Like David, Emmett and Gregory consider cultural products an aspect of community; in addition to soc.bi, Emmett, who lives in a small city in Georgia, included *Bi Any Other Name* as a feature of his bisexual community, and Gregory, who lives in San Francisco, captioned the "bi community" with "music/TV/make-up/disco."

Community as Philosophy

Instead of representing the bisexual popumunity in terms of the types of people and organizations in it, or as a network of connections, some men described community more abstractly as consisting of certain beliefs or goals. For example, inside a circle labeled "BiNet USA," Ian listed a number of sociopolitical philosophies and objectives that he apparently believes are integral to the bisexual popumunity: "multiculturalism, feminism, egalitarianism, sex positivism, differently abled, reaching out to one another, reaching out to other oppressed people/groups, improving relations between males/females, transgender empowerment and rights, pushing and helping the gay/lesbian community to be more inclusive, progressive." Peter, commenting that bisexuals are "composed of components," represented the "micro" level of the bisexual community with a network connecting feminists, new age people, anti-racists, and sex radicals. Raul, a White/Hispanic man living in a large midwestern city, drew five islands in a circle, connected to each other by bridges meeting in the center as clasped hands; the bridges are labeled, respectively, "peace, kindness, women, open mindedness, men." A 35-year-old Anglo man living in a medium-sized northeastern city drew a map representing political and social goals or ideals; in it, relationships are "based on love, straight or gay," "gay and lesbian couples can marry and adopt children," "youths are given rights, including sexual rights," and "straight people use birth control, only children who are wanted or adoptable are born." Similarly, the center of a map made by a man living in Philadelphia consists of "generous ideas about sex, sexuality, love, faithfulness, community," with arrows radiating outward toward–for the purpose of changing?–cultural institutions that often work to regulate sexual expression in the larger world, including "religious views and institutions," "government institutions," "educational and cultural institutions," "sports and entertainment," and "communities, family, neighborhood."

FENCES AND BRIDGES, OVERLAPS AND BORDERS: RELATIONS BETWEEN THE BISEXUAL COMMUNITY AND OTHER COMMUNITIES

How does the bisexual popumunity fit into the larger society? Which other communities and populations–both sexual identity-based and non-sexually based–are linked in bisexual men's minds to the bisexual popumunity? What connections exist between bisexuals and these other popumunities? Are the relationships supportive or antagonistic? For men who see themselves as part of a bisexual community, how does this membership situate them in the larger scheme of things?

By far, the most common vehicle map-makers used to illustrate the relationships between the bisexual community or population and other communities or populations is Venn diagramming. Two aspects of bisexual men's Venn diagram maps are especially important for understanding their perceptions of the relationship between the bisexual popumunity and other popumunities. The first aspect is their physical arrangement vis-à-vis each other in a map. Physical arrangement means, for example, whether any popumunities are pictured as central, which popumunities are pictured as proximal to which others, and which popumunities are larger or smaller than others. The second aspect is the character of the boundaries between physically proximate communities or populations. These boundaries can take at least three forms: the boundaries of neighboring popumunities can be distinct from each other and separated by intervening space, they can be contiguous, or they can overlap each other.

In mathematics, Venn diagrams accurately convey clear, specific meanings; an overlap, for example, represents members shared by two or more sets. However, when Venn diagrams are used by non-mathematicians to illustrate their social worlds, interpretation–especially in the case of overlapping boundaries–becomes a complex process. Distinct boundaries probably simply represent the borders of two separate popumunities, without any implications regarding the relationship between them aside from the distinction of identity. Contiguous boundaries might similarly represent a simple distinction, or they might imply that a close relationship exists between the popumunities. Overlapping boundaries, on the other hand, have a multitude of interpretations, depending on the identities of the communities or populations involved. How, for example, are we to interpret an overlap between lesbian and gay male communities? Following the mathematical use of Venn diagrams, we would interpret the overlap as representing shared members. But what kind of individual would belong to both lesbian and gay male communities? If membership is identity-based, then that individual might be a transgenderist with both lesbian and gay male identities. This is a possible interpretation, but the map-maker might have had something different in mind. Perhaps membership in an identity-based community need not be contingent on individual identity. Or, perhaps the overlaps in such maps represent something other than shared members. Although some map-makers labeled their overlaps or wrote marginal comments explaining them, most provided no verbal translation, leaving the problem of interpretation to the viewer. The possible interpretations of overlaps in bisexual men's maps of their bisexual popumunities will be explored after the various physical arrangements among the popumunities depicted in these maps are described.

Relationships with Lesbian, Gay, and Heterosexual Communities

The instructions for the map question specifically asked respondents to include the lesbian, gay, and heterosexual communities in their maps, and most did so using Venn diagrams. Most of these maps show the bisexual popumunity as centrally located, partially overlapped or bounded on one side by heterosexuals and on the other by lesbians and gays. In a few maps, gays and lesbians are shown at opposite ends of the bisexual popumunity, with heterosexuals falling somewhere else along the border of the bisexual popumunity. For example, in the map drawn by the 44-year-old resident of Wisconsin, "bi" and "hetero" are represented by long ovals lying side by side and overlapping, with "gay" and "lesbian" ovals at opposite ends, each overlapping both the bi and hetero ovals. Thus, there are points of intersection representing every possible combination except for a combination of the gay and lesbian communities, and including the triplicate combination of bisexual, heterosexual, and either gay or lesbian popumunities. In such maps, the axis appears to be gender distinctions rather than a Kinsey-like concept of sexual orientation–men and women, rather than straights and gays/lesbians, mark the poles. Whether the axis is sexual orientation or gender, however, these depictions of the bisexual popumunity as between and partially overlapping heterosexual, lesbian, and gay communities reflect, superficially at least, common conceptions of bisexuality as an "intermediate" form of sexuality, either residing "between" heterosexuality and homosexuality as on the Kinsey scale, or as composed of a hybrid combination of heterosexuality and homosexuality.

In other maps, the entire bisexual popumunity is formed by an overlap between heterosexual and lesbian/gay communities. In the map drawn by Martin, for example, areas labeled "gay" and "straight" extend from opposite sides of the page, merging in the center to form an area labeled "bi." Similarly, in Figure 15, "bisexual" is constituted by the intersection of "hetero," "lesbian," and "gay." In such maps, the bisexual popumunity is not only portrayed as intermediate or "in between" other communities, but as having no existence wholly independent of these other communities. Indeed, some of the men who drew these maps are among those who said, in the verbal part of the questionnaire, that there is no bisexual community.

In some maps, no communities or populations are central and the bisexual popumunity is no more intermediate than any other. For example, Gene drew circles representing the heterosexual community, bisexual activism groups, and social and political gay communities. The heterosexual, bisexual, and

FIGURE 15

Pseudonym: Jesse
Would you say there is a "bisexual community"? [No written comment]

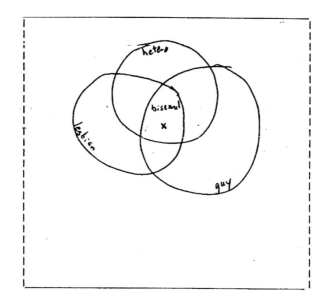

gay areas are arranged like the points of an equilateral triangle, overlapping in every possible two- and three-way combination near the center of the diagram.

Another variation on the Venn diagram theme is the complete encompassing or surrounding of one popumunity by another. In some maps, overlapping or separate bisexual and gay/lesbian communities and populations are surrounded by an all-encompassing, and much larger, heterosexual society. For example, Jacob's map depicts the "bi community" overlapping separate gay and lesbian communities at its poles and a slightly broader queer community encompassing all three communities, which in turn is surrounded by "straight communities" (Figure 5). Chris, a crossdresser of White European ancestry living in a California suburb drew a three-way overlap between "bi's," "lesbians and gay men," and "transgendered," all surrounded by the larger straight society. Gordon, a 32-year-old man who lives in a small northwestern city and prefers not to label his sexual orientation, believes that "there is a bisexual community in as much as there are people who call themselves 'bisexual' and feel a belonging to a certain community they call by that name." He drew overlapping heterosexual, bisexual, and homosexual communities surrounded by stick figures in a landscape of trees, stars, birds, and planets, representing "those of us creatures who choose to belong to the whole of creation." Sometimes the bisexual popumunity is shown wholly encompassed by lesbian and gay communities, which in turn might be wholly encompassed by straight community, heterosexual society, or the "rest of society," as in Figure 6, or the bi popumunity might be surrounded partially by heterosexual society and partially by the lesbian and gay community, as in Figure 12. In Kenneth's map, "lesbians" are shown surrounded by "gay men," both of whom overlap "bisexuals." Conversely, George's "gay community" circle is entirely contained within his "bisexual community(?)" circle (Figure 13), and in Ralph's map, the amoeba-shape representing the heterosexual community is completely contained within the amoeba-shape representing lesbian and gay communities (Figure 2).

Finally, in some maps, none of the popumunities overlap or encompass each other. For example, Herman drew distinct gay, lesbian, heterosexual, and transgender communities, linking them to "bisexuals" with paths (Figure 1). In another map, Manfred, a 26-year-old Caucasian man of English and German descent living in a small midwestern town, drew circles representing straight men, gay men, straight women, and lesbians. A diamond shape resting between the four circles is labeled "baby queers." The apparent implication is that a person either belongs to one and only one of the four populations pictured or is still in the process of coming out. "Bisexuals," Manfred wrote, "are poised for organization and an independent identity that includes political and social definition," but did not explicitly depict this emerging identity in his map.

Sometimes very similar relationships are represented without Venn diagrams. Kilroy's map uses amoeba-shapes rather than the usual Venn diagram circle, and the amoebas representing "G&L," "hetero," and several "bi's" wind around each other, usually separated by a buffer zone but occasionally overlapping. This design maximizes the opportunities available for contact or overlap between individuals and popumunities and minimizes the isolating effects of community boundaries. A marginal note suggests that this was Kilroy's intention: "all divisions slightly overlap in a common background." Several non-Venn diagram maps reflect the concept of bisexuality as intermediate to, or a combination of, heterosexuality and lesbianism/gayness. Jake, Evan, and Porter, for example, each drew two parallel lines either diagonally or horizontally through the box provided. In each map, the area between the lines is labeled "bi," with "gay" or "lesbian/gay community" on one side and "straight," "hetero," or "heterosexual community" on the other. Some map-makers used the box provided to represent the bisexual community or population, and then indicated that heterosexual society and lesbian and gay communities exist outside the box, on different sides from each other (e.g., Figure 8). Xu, an Asian man living in a medium-sized southwestern city, drew a bell curve, with "bi" surrounding the modal point and "gay/lesbian" and "hetero" at the tails. In this map, upward slanting lines shade the gay/lesbian area and downward slanting lines shade the hetero area; these lines combine to form crosshatching in the bi area, suggesting that bisexuality is the combination of heterosexuality and lesbianism/gayness. Indeed, in answer to the verbal question, Xu wrote that there is no bisexual community because there is "no common identity; less forced oppression than gays/lesbians," a perception that often results from the conceptualiza-tion of bisexuality as a hybrid combination of heterosexuality and homosexu-ality. In contrast to these representations of bisexuality as intermediate to or composed of heterosexuality and homosexuality, Edward drew a fence and wrote, "The Fence (notice no one is sitting on it)."

What do the various overlaps between bisexual and lesbian, gay, and heterosexual popumunities in these maps, whether Venn or not, represent? Each type of overlap–partial, entire, and encompassing–can be interpreted in terms of shared members or, alternatively, in terms of other shared character-istics or connections, but the meanings vary depending on the type of over-lap. Exploring the possible meanings for partial overlaps will prepare the way for an analysis of the meanings invoked when the bisexual popumunity is shown entirely composed of the overlap of two or more other popumunities, or as encompassed by or encompassing other popumunities.

If overlapping boundaries represent shared members as they would in Venn diagrams, then partial overlap between the bisexual popumunity and another popumunity suggests that some bisexuals are also members of other popumunities. There are, however, different ways of conceptualizing dual or multiple membership. In the case of overlap between the bisexual popumun-ity and lesbian, gay, and/or heterosexual communities, the overlap might indicate that some members of the bisexual popumunity are *simultaneously* members of lesbian, gay, and/or heterosexual communities. Or, it might mean that some members of the bisexual popumunity have the potential to *shift* their membership to these communities, perhaps alternating between com-munities, or that they *pass* as "monosexuals," thereby appearing to belong to another popumunity in certain circumstances. The fact that, in some maps, the dotted line representing the respondents' own path begins in one commu-nity and then moves into another by passing through the overlap between the communities suggests that overlap can also represent individuals who are in transition–another form of dual membership.

As noted above, map-makers did not necessarily follow mathematical conventions in drawing their Venn diagram maps, and overlaps need not represent shared members. Partial overlap might instead represent social connections between members of overlapping popumunities. In this case, an overlap between the bisexual popumunity and lesbian, gay, and/or heterosexual communities would indicate that some members of the bisexual popumunity have platonic, sexual, or political relationships with lesbians, gay men, and/or heterosexuals, although they are not members of those communities themselves. Overlaps between lesbian and gay male communities are particularly likely to represent social connections rather than shared membership, because dual membership in both lesbian and gay male communities is implausible except for transgendered people. For example, Gus, a Chicago resident of French and German descent, labeled a small overlap in his map between "lesbians I've known" and "gay men" as a "creative interactive space," suggesting that this overlap represents social connections between lesbians and gay men. Gus also labeled the overlap between the "hetero world" and "gay men" in his map "cutting edge contact," implying social relations between heterosexuals and gay men.

A third interpretation for partial overlap is suggested by a marginal comment made by Orin, a 43-year-old New York City resident of Eastern European descent (Figure 16). In his carefully drawn map, "most of the bisexual world is submerged by overlapping interests," indicating that overlaps represent shared concerns. The largest overlap in his map occurs between the "bi" and "heterosexual" worlds. If the sizes of the overlaps denote the degree to which the interests of particular worlds overlap each other, then Orin perceives bisexual interests as more aligned with heterosexual interests than with "lesbian" or "male homosexual" interests. His descriptions of the heterosexual world as "children world," the lesbian world as "no-men world," and the male homosexual world as "no-women world" provide a clue as to what the interests might be that bisexuals share with heterosexuals, lesbians, and male homosexuals, and why Orin perceives bisexuals' interests as most similar to heterosexuals'. Orin indicated that he himself inhabits the small section of the bisexual world that does not overlap with either the lesbian, male homosexual, or heterosexual worlds, a section that presumably represents the extent to which bisexuals have specific interests unique to themselves as bisexuals.

A fourth possible interpretation for partial overlap is suggested by Timo-

FIGURE 16

Pseudonym: Orin
Would you say there is a "bisexual community"? [No written comment]

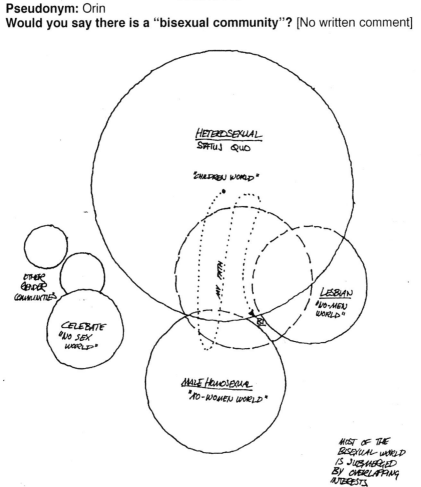

thy, a 20-year-old White crossdresser living in a rural area of the northeast who labeled the three-way overlap between the gay and lesbian, straight, and bi popumunities in his map "me and Ani Difranco." Perhaps, for Timothy, the overlap represents not membership in all three popumunities, but a rejection of membership in any particular community or identity-based group, and possibly a rejection of identity-based sexual distinctions in general. Indeed, when Timothy was asked for his sexual identity, he answered that he is not sure what it is and prefers not to label himself. However, when asked whether a bisexual community exists, he commented, "I hope to find one, but I haven't yet."

Still another interpretation is suggested by Henry, a 22-year-old White man living in a large northeastern town, whose map "is less about community than about a cross section through a few dimensions of sexual identification." Bisexual, lesbian, gay, and heterosexual communities or populations per se do not appear in Henry's map; rather, they are implied by the overlaps of the various characteristics that individuals in those popumunities might have. Thus, overlaps in Henry's map represent the multiple identities an individual might have, rather than communities or populations that an individual might belong to or which might be sociopolitically related to each other. Four circles, representing "male-attraction," "female-attraction," "male-identified," and "female-identified," overlap in all possible combinations. Some of these overlaps are labeled. For example, the overlap of female-identified and female-attracted is labeled "femme/dyke," the overlap of male-identified and male-attracted is labeled "gay/stud," and the overlaps of male-attracted and female-identified and of female-attracted and male-identified are labeled, respectively, "vanilla [female symbol]" and "vanilla [male symbol]," apparently indicating individuals who would be called "heterosexual" using the language of sexual orientation. The areas of female-identification and male-identification that do not overlap either of the circles representing female- or male-attraction are, respectively, "nuns" and "monks." The very center, representing male- and female-attraction and male- and female-identification, is called "Buddha"–followed by a question mark.

The plausibility of each of these possible interpretations changes if, instead of a partial overlap, the bisexual popumunity is shown as entirely composed of the overlap of two or more other communities or populations. Interpreted in terms of shared members, such overlap suggests that *all* bisexuals are necessarily members of these two or more other popumunities. In most such maps, these other popumunities are lesbian/gay and heterosexual communities. How might a map-maker conceive of bisexuals as necessary members of both lesbian/gay and heterosexual communities? A look at three maps suggests three different conceptions of this membership. Alex, a 28-year-old of German descent residing in New York City, drew two triangles labeled "straight community" and "gay community," whose overlap is labeled "bisexual community," with the marginal explanation "I see the bisexual community this way: Although I am bisexual I have to live on the edges of both the gay world and the straight world." This comment suggests that bisexuals are members of heterosexual and lesbian/gay communities because, as bisexuals, they necessarily participate in these communities rather than having the ability or choice to participate in multiple communities, as might be indicated by a partial overlap. The fact that the entire bisexual community is composed of the overlap indicates that *all* bisexuals, like Alex himself, "have to" participate in both lesbian/gay and heterosexual communities.

In contrast, in the map drawn by Aaron, a 37-year-old White Jewish man living in suburban California, the two circles whose overlap is labeled "bisexual people" are designated, respectively, "straight *people*" and "gay *people*" (emphasis mine). In this map, a small third circle labeled "transgendered people" overlaps both circles, including their overlap with each other–a recognition that straight, gay, and bisexual people can also be transgendered. Analogously, therefore, the map implies that bisexual people are members of heterosexual and gay populations because they *are* both "straight" and "gay" by virtue of their bisexuality. Here, in other words, bisexuality *is* heterosexuality and gayness, hence the necessary inclusion of all bisexuals in both heterosexual and gay populations.

Third, rather than seeing all bisexuals as participatory or essential members of lesbian/gay and heterosexual communities, Joseph considers bisexuals to be *partial* members of multiple popumunities because they don't fit neatly into any one single popumunity. He indicated that the overlaps between the "straight" area and the "lesbian" and "gay" areas in his map consist of "the women who don't really know or care why, but 'do' other women/men outside of their own label," and "the men who 'do' what is not in their label, and don't really think of it."

In some maps, a bisexual popumunity composed of the overlap of two or more other popumunities is more readily interpretable in terms of shared social connections rather than shared members. For example, Jesse, a 25-year-old Anglo man living in a small midwestern city, drew three circles that show lesbian, gay male, and heterosexual communities overlapping each other in all possible combinations (Figure 15). The three-way overlap in the center of the diagram is labeled "bisexual." In this case, the overlaps are probably meant to represent social connections rather than shared memberships, given that it is unlikely Jesse intended to suggest that *all* individual bisexuals are also heterosexual, lesbian, *and* gay male or that they are otherwise simultaneously members of lesbian, gay, and heterosexual communities. The overlap of the lesbian and gay male communities alone suggests, as discussed earlier, that something other than dual or multiple membership is intended. The implied meaning here is that the bisexual popumunity is a social network wholly embedded in both lesbian/gay and heterosexual social networks, even though individual bisexuals might not be members *per se* of lesbian/gay and heterosexual communities.

Whichever interpretation is given to maps in which the bisexual community is shown composed entirely of the overlap of two or more other communities, the inescapable conclusion is that these map-makers perceive no independently extant bisexual community or population. If the overlap represents shared members, then there is no distinct bisexual population. If the overlap represents social connections, then the bisexual community, like a telecommunications company renting line usage from a larger telecommunications company, has no core composed solely of intra-bisexual connections. For the men who drew these maps, whatever the bisexual popumunity is, it is not a distinct or autonomous community but a social entity dependent on the existence of the lesbian, gay, and/or heterosexual communities.

Like partially or entirely overlapping areas, the complete encompassing of one popumunity by another could have various meanings. At least three different interpretations appear possible; the plausibility of each depends on which popumunities are shown encompassing which other popumunities. For example, the encompassing of the bi popumunity by the gay community has a different set of plausible interpretations than does the encompassing of lesbian, gay, bi, and/or queer popumunities by heterosexual society.

One interpretation is that the encompassing popumunity is a larger, umbrella community or population that includes the encompassed popumunity. For example, when the bi popumunity is shown encompassed by a larger gay, or queer, community, this might reflect the perception that the bi popumunity is part of a larger gay community, that is, that bisexuals, like lesbians and gay men, are members of a "gay" community that includes bisexuals–by virtue of their bisexuality–under its umbrella. This appears to be Larry's intention; he allowed the box provided for his map to represent the bisexual population, and drew a slightly larger box surrounding it, writing "[the] bi 'box' is actually a small part of the gay community which encompasses it" (Figure 6). The role of the "gay" community in this map is similar to the role of the "queer" community in Jacob's map; here, the queer community is the umbrella community that encompasses bi, gay, and lesbian popumunities (Figure 5).

This interpretation is probably not what George intended, however (Figure 13). Here, the ring representing the "bisexual community(?)" completely surrounds the ring representing the gay community. Although it would be possible to conceive of the bisexual popumunity as encompassing a smaller, more exclusive gay community, the placement of the labels in this map–seemingly marking the perimeter rather than the area enclosed by each ring–and the fact that the ring representing the bi community is dotted and ambivalently referred to as a "community" suggest that this was not George's intention. In this case, it appears that the aim of the map-maker was to depict the bisexual popumunity as *between* the gay community and the heterosexual mainstream, rather than as a superset of the gay community and a subset of the heterosexual mainstream. In this view, the popumunities that appear encompassed by others are not part of the popumunities that encompass them; rather, they are distinct popumunities that are surrounded by, but separate from, other popumunities. This would indicate that the bi popumunity exists as an appendage to, or is embedded within, the gay community without actually being part of that community.

The distinction between these two different interpretations for the encompassing of one popumunity by another might be clarified by a concrete example. If a bisexual group meets in a lesbian and gay community center, it might be seen as evidence that bisexuals are part of the larger gay community served by the center, or it might be seen as the dependence of a resource-poor but distinct bisexual community on the resources of a separate gay community; in the latter case, bisexuals in the group are embedded within, but not part of, the gay community served by the center.

In maps in which both bisexual and gay popumunities are encompassed by heterosexual society–or by "straight communities," the "rest of society," or the "heterosexual mainstream," as in Figures 5, 6, and 13–the second interpretation initially appears more plausible than the first. It is possible that map-makers perceive gay men, lesbians, and bisexuals as separate from but dependent upon heterosexual society, whereas it is unlikely that these map-makers perceive gay men, lesbians, and bisexuals as included by virtue of their gayness, lesbianism, or bisexuality under a large umbrella called "heterosexuality"; bisexual, and particularly lesbian and gay, sexualities are constructed as distinct from, not as a variation of, hegemonic heterosexuality. But, on second thought, is a person's sexuality the only possible basis for membership in a sexuality-based community? Specifically, does a lack of heterosexuality mean that bisexuals, lesbians, and gay men cannot be members of heterosexual society on some basis other than their individual sexualities? Cannot one be a member of heterosexual society without being heterosexual? One can, if that society is defined not by the heterosexuality of all its members, but by the hegemony of heterosexuality within that society. If "heterosexual society" means "mainstream society," then bisexuals, lesbians, and gay men *are* members of that society, despite the fact that they themselves are not heterosexual. In Cole's map, the word "heterosexual*ity*" (emphasis mine) arches over not only "supportive heterosexuals," but also lesbians, gay men, and bisexuals (Figure 9). The map drawn by Kenneth, in which "gay men" encompass "lesbians," lends itself to a similar interpretation. By specifying "gay *men*," Kenneth clearly indicates that his intention is to depict the lesbian community not as part of the larger gay community, but instead as embedded in or surrounded by the gay *male* community. In summary, a third interpretation for the encompassing of one popumunity by another is that members of encompassed popumunities are members of the encompassing popumunities, not by virtue of their individual sexualities, but by virtue of their status as minority citizens whose sexualities should be, but are not, represented in the dominant conceptualization of the encompassing popumunity.

This third interpretation is also plausible in maps showing the bisexual popumunity encompassed by gay and/or lesbian communities. Interpreted in this way, these maps suggest that bisexuals are members of the lesbian and gay community not because the lesbian and gay community is an umbrella that encompasses bisexuality or because bisexuals are distinct from yet dependent on the lesbian and gay community, but because bisexuals often find themselves participating in a community that is dominated by lesbian and gay identities, despite the fact that not all of its members are lesbian/gay. In this view, bisexuals are minoritized, rather than included or appendaged, by lesbian and gay communities. Just as lesbians, gay men, and bisexuals are members of a larger society that is dominated by heterosexuality and heterosexuals, bisexuals are members of a larger community that is dominated by lesbianism and gayness, and by lesbians and gay men. See Figure 12, for example. Here, "bisexuals" are surrounded partially by "heterosexuals" and partially by "lesbian[s] and gay [men]," suggesting that lesbians/gays and heterosexuals have similar dominating positions vis-à-vis bisexuals; although heterosexuality might be hegemonic to bisexual, lesbian, and gay communities, from a bisexual point of view, lesbianism and gayness can be equally hegemonic.

Map-makers who drew the bisexual popumunity and other popumunities with distinct boundaries that do not overlap or encompass each other often used other vehicles to represent the relationships between the popumunities. In many of these maps, popumunities are connected to each other with lines, arrows, bridges, or other similar symbols. In some maps, these connections appear to represent the flow of people. For example, a 30-year-old Caucasian man living in Kentucky drew pathways of various widths between bisexual, gay/lesbian, and heterosexual popumunities; the dotted line marking his own path circles through these pathways. The path from the bi popumunity to the gay/lesbian community is very wide, whereas the path in the other direction is very narrow, suggesting that he believes that more people move from the bi to the gay/lesbian community than vice versa. Similarly, Herman drew a network of paths, representing the movements individuals might make, among bisexual, gay, lesbian, heterosexual, and cross-gender/transgender popumunities (Figure 1), and Josh created "Bi-69, the well-traveled thoroughfare of constant sexual flux" (Figure 8). Lou placed a wall between the lesbian and gay communities on his map, but he also drew male symbols with their shafts arching across the borders between the bisexual male popumunity and the gay and straight male popumunities, suggesting that gay and straight men might also have bisexual experiences.

In other maps, these connections appear to represent relationships between members of different popumunities. Recall, for example, the spiral made by Sean to represent the "GLBU Bi-Group." As the spiral crosses the border of the group, it splits into several arrows, each of which curves gracefully toward another group or community, including GLBU and gay, straight, and lesbian communities. The implication appears to be that Sean's friendship network includes individuals who connect him to various communities. Similarly, Edward depicted couples, some of whom are holding hands across the borders of bisexual and heterosexual, or bisexual and "non-bi queer," spaces. Phillip drew his wife and himself holding hands across a divide; the caption next to his wife reads "straight but not narrow." Emmett sketched lines radiating from soc.bi and "queer computer sources" toward heterosexuals and homosexuals, indicating that electronic networks connect individuals with different sexual orientations to each other. Likewise, Paul drew a long line from a person sitting at a computer outside the bisexual community to individuals sitting at computers inside the bisexual community. Recall, also, Sam's comment that lesbian, gay, and heterosexual communities are not geographically distinct from the bisexual community; instead, these communities consist of networks of connections that are more dense in some areas than in others.

Connections between popumunities are sometimes friendly, sometimes antagonistic, and sometimes characterized by ignorance or negligence. Different map-makers have different perceptions of the affective quality of the bisexual popumunity's relations with other sexual-identity based popumunities. Some focus on the lack of support or outright hostility they feel from heterosexual society. For example, Allan drew angry-looking arrows radiating from "anti-gay/lesbian forces" in "hetero-community/society," indicating that they represented "targeting homophobia and bigotry." Andrew placed double-headed arrows between the bisexual community and lesbian and gay communities and a broken, jagged double-headed arrow between "hetero" and the bisexual community, suggesting that the bisexual community's relationships with lesbian and gay communities are friendlier than relations with heterosexual society. Paul drew doors in the border of the bisexual community, with captions indicating greater understanding and recognition from gays than from heterosexuals. One door is labeled the "invisible door," and the stick figures outside it are "self-identified heterosexuals who don't see the door." Stick figures outside another door are "self-identified homosexuals who can at least consider the potential." Understanding is a two-way street, however, and a double door is captioned, respectively, "door a monosexual has to open to understand other side," and "door a bisexual has to open to understand other side."

In contrast, Ricky, who is "bummed out" by the lack of a bisexual community, emphasized the antagonism of other sexual minority communities toward bisexuals; as shown in Figure 4, he drew hate rays from lesbians to bisexuals, and a wall between gay men and bisexuals is labeled "screen of complete invisibility." In his map, even the division between the "het world" and the sexual minority popumunities is defined in terms of intra-minority tension by the caption "this is the arc of total non-understanding that there is any difference or tension between lesbian/gay and bi people." Kaleb perceives a more supportive world, but nevertheless depicts tension between bisexuals and some lesbians. He drew arching lines connecting various components of the bisexual community to various components of lesbian and gay communities, labeling them with comments regarding relations between these communities. For example, a line between the gender community and the local bisexual men's group is labeled "very positive/good alliance," and a line between the gay men's community and the bisexual men's group is labeled "good relations," whereas a line between the lesbian community and the bisexual men's group is labeled "most activists supportive, some old grand dykes suspicious of us."

Amid these connections, the bisexual popumunity is pictured by a number of map-makers as having a privileged position. For some, this privilege arises from its central position, which enables it to have connections to a wide variety of other communities and populations and to serve as a link between them. For example, Augustín, a Hispanic man living in New Jersey, drew "bisexuals" as a smiling octopus, with tentacles reaching out toward other populations, including gays, lesbians, heterosexual men, and heterosexual women at the four corners of the box provided, and transvestites, liberals, feminists, and right wingers occupying positions along the sides of the box (Figure 17). The positions of these groups are meaningful; for example, transvestites are placed between gays and heterosexual men, whereas feminists are placed between lesbians and heterosexual women. Island and bridge imagery is also frequently used to portray the intermediary role of the bisexual popumunity. For example, in Raul's map, gay and heterosexual communities are pictured as islands with bridges linking them to a central bisexual community consisting of several islands.

For other map-makers, the privilege of the bisexual popumunity lies in its lack of definition. For example, Michael drew the "lesbian community is-

FIGURE 17

Pseudonym: Augustín
Would you say there is a "bisexual community"? I think there are a lot of Bisexuals out there but they are not unified enough to form a "Bisexual Community." Each bisexual is so different from another that at times it is difficult to find a common unity. I think, however, that by exploring our differences and similarities, and becoming more visible we can achieve a "Bisexual Community."

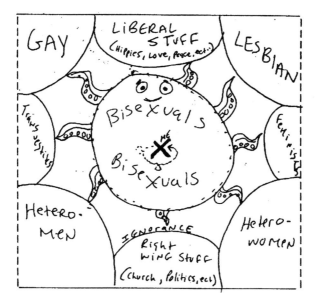

land," the "gay male community island," and the "mainland of heterosexual patriarchal, imperialistic, theocratic, hierarchic, oppressive society" (Figure 18). In the vast expanse separating these well-delineated land masses are the "bisexual community shoals and sandbars" and the "'T' [Transgender] community delta," with "inexact boundaries" indicated by broad shaded areas. Similarly, an Anglo-American living in Chicago drew a stream with "happy bisland" in the middle. One bank is "the fertile land of the straights" and the other bank is "the rocky gay world." The caption reads, "In this geography, the fertile land of the straights is where life is easy. Cattle graze but lack of struggle keeps people lazy. The rocky Gayland is mountainous and people will not

FIGURE 18

Pseudonym: Michael
Would you say there is a "bisexual community"? The "bi community" is amorphous, indistinct and probably will remain so. For me a community has to be more identifiable and members have to be somewhat self identified as belonging to the group. Also "bisexual" suggests only one's sexuality is the determinant of community identity, and this is insufficient, I think. Thus, I feel more at "home" as part of the "T" or "gender" community, encompassing more than just sexuality.

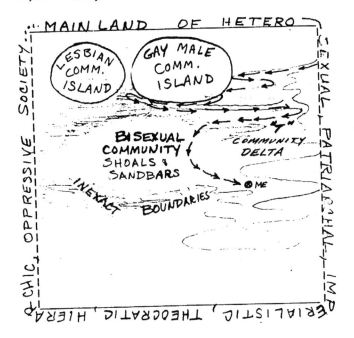

survive if they get lazy. In the Happy Bisland people live between. Occasionally Bisland floods and people choose which shore they will swim to."

Maps differ in the relative sizes of the bisexual, lesbian, gay, and heterosexual popumunities. In many maps, size might not be meaningful, but in some maps, size appears to be symbolic of either population size or different levels of importance to the map-maker. In many maps, the bisexual popumunity is shown as the smallest, followed by lesbian and gay communities, both of which are surpassed in magnitude by the heterosexual community or society. In these maps, size most likely represents the relative numbers of people belonging to each popumunity or the different degrees of sociopolitical influence of the different popumunities. Floyd explicitly noted the relative sizes of the bisexual, lesbian/gay, and heterosexual populations; he used most of the box provided to depict bisexuals, and indicated that two extreme corners of the box represented "true gays/lesbians-10%" and "true hetero-10%?," respectively. The magnitudes of the circles that Orin drew to represent the bisexual, male homosexual, lesbian, heterosexual, and celibate worlds might also be reflective of population size or, perhaps, sociopolitical power (Figure 16). In other maps, the bisexual popumunity is centrally located, more elaborately drawn, and larger than other sexual identity popumunities. In these maps, the relative size might reflect the map-makers' own greater knowledge of and involvement with the bisexual popumunity (e.g., Figure 1).

Relationships with Other Communities

In addition to lesbian, gay, and heterosexual communities, many map-makers included other communities and populations in their maps and illustrated the relationships of these popumunities to the bisexual popumunity. Some of these popumunities are ones that other map-makers included *within* their bisexual popumunities. Some are defined by sexuality, including polyfidelitous and polyamorous, S&M/B&D, asexual, celibate, transgender, pansexual, sex radical, swinging, sex party, and sex work communities or populations. Others are not primarily identified by sexuality, including recovery groups, the disabled, HIV communities or populations, and the U.S. military. In some maps, these latter groups were included to illustrate diversity within the bisexual popumunity; in other maps, they were included because of the sexual implications of these populations. For example, those who included the military generally characterized its members as closeted non-heterosexuals; as Josh put it, the U.S. military is "on the border but ready to fight" (Figure 8). Some map-makers, like Cole, whose map is shown in Figure 9, also included social and political constituencies, such as "homophobic big-ots," "anti-gay and lesbian forces," "neo-fascist fundie fanatics," liberal heterosexuals, feminists, anti-racists, new agers, and separatists.

Communities and populations defined by their sexuality, when drawn distinct from, rather than included within, the bisexual popumunity, are often depicted as crosscutting sexual orientation distinctions. For example, pan-sexual, polyfidelitous, S&M, and transgender popumunities are usually shown overlapping the bisexual popumunity and often also overlapping or intersecting lesbian, gay, and/or heterosexual communities, as in Figure 6. By crosscutting or transcending sexual orientation distinctions, such groups pro-vide venues for contact between bisexuals, lesbians, gay men, and heterosex-uals. The notion of transcendence is especially apparent in the map drawn by Monty. In this map, adjacent circles representing "bi," "gay," and "het" communities are all intersected by a fourth circle. The interior of the fourth circle is unnamed, but the perimeter has several labels: BBS/Internet, SCA, Renaissance Faire, Polyamorous, and Group/swing. The implication is that these are spaces and events in which the three sexual orientation communi-ties–bi, gay, and het–come into contact with each other or intermix. A map drawn by Harlan, an Anglo-Celtic man living in California, depicts the S&M popumunity in a similar way, suggesting that interest in S&M transcends sexual orientation or that the S&M popumunity includes bisexuals, lesbians, gay men, and heterosexuals. The transgender popumunity is likewise de-picted by Aaron, who drew three intersecting circles: a large circle represent-ing "straight people," a much smaller circle representing "gay" (with the overlap between them labeled "bi"), and a very small circle overlapping all three areas that is identified as "transgendered people." In some maps, the transgender popumunity is shown having a closer relationship to the bisexual popumunity or to bisexual, lesbian, and gay popumunities than to either the lesbian/gay community alone or to heterosexual society. For example, al-though the map in Figure 1 does not show overlap between the transgender community and bisexuals, the transgender community is closer and con-nected to bisexuals by a shorter path than the other sexual communities. Also, whereas the paths between bisexuals and heterosexual society and between bisexuals and the gay community are marked, respectively, by homophobia and biphobia and by heterophobia and biphobia, the path between bisexuals and the cross-gender/transgender community is without phobia. Such repre-sentations suggest that although transgenderism transcends sexual orientation distinctions and constitutes its own distinct communities and identities, there is a particular resonance between bisexuality and transgenderism in a social world dominated by binary notions of sexuality and gender that similarly oppress transgenderists and bisexuals.

THE IMPACT OF RACE, AGE, AND GEOGRAPHIC LOCATION

One might expect Men of Color to be more likely than White men to have greater difficulty finding a community and more likely to mention race in their maps, and younger men living in large cities to report stronger bisexual communities than older men or men living in small towns or rural areas. Only some of these expectations are borne out.

Racial patterns are surprisingly absent among the bisexual men in this study; there is no greater tendency for Men of Color to report a lack of community, to be more likely to mention race in their maps, or to discuss the impact of race on the development of the bisexual community. Several Men of Color in this study report belonging to strong, vibrant, bisexual communities, and some feel completely isolated. Only one Man of Color–a self-described "yellow Japanese" man–mentioned race or ethnicity in his verbal answer, and his comment dismissed the importance of race by analogy. He said that there is no need for a bisexual community because "It's ghettoizing, an ethnic group, people sticking together at a certain location." Another man made an apparent implicit reference to racial/ethnic differences, commenting that "what must be kept in mind is that there are competing communities that overwhelm the subtle needs of other communities. This gives the simplistic outward illusion that certain communities do not really exist."

But these findings do not imply that there are no racial and ethnic differences in men's experiences of bisexual community. In answer to a more specific question, "Do you think that bisexual people of color have concerns, needs, or problems that bisexuals of White ancestry do not share? If so, what are they?," many Men of Color–as well as many White men–answered yes. The issues raised include the problem of being a minority within a minority, the double oppression of belonging to two minorities, the predominant Whiteness of the individuals and the culture in bisexual and gay organizations, the need to negotiate at least two cultures (that is, one's own ethnic culture as well as mainstream White-dominated culture), differences between the meanings given (bi)sexuality in these two cultures, and sexual repression in one's own ethnic culture. Some bisexual Men of Color commented that they experience the same racism within the bisexual community as they do anywhere else; a few commented that they have found greater understanding of racial dynamics within the bisexual community than anywhere else. Most agree, however, that regardless of how much progress has already been made, the bisexual community–like the rest of society–still has considerable work to do in the effort to eradicate racism.

Age-related patterns are also strikingly absent from respondents' verbal comments and maps. The verbal comments of respondents aged 15-25, 30-39, and 55-83 were compared to identify any differences in whether they felt part of a bisexual community or in what they were looking for in a community, and no such differences were apparent. In all age groups, some men find themselves actively involved in a thriving bisexual community, some men feel completely isolated, some don't believe a bisexual community would be possible or even desirable, and some hope and expect that a bisexual community will emerge and develop. The Internet was mentioned as a resource by old and young, and the possibility of a queer, rather than a bisexual, community was mentioned by at least a few men in each age group except the very oldest.

Geographic location does, however, influence bisexual men's access to bisexual community. Men living in areas known as centers of bisexual activism–most notably, Seattle–are more likely to feel that they are part of a thriving bisexual community. But, outside these areas, many bisexual men feel isolated or rely on the Internet or books and newsletters for knowledge of a bisexual community that exists elsewhere. Even in other large and medium-sized cities, such as New York City; Denver, Colorado; Chicago, Illinois; and Phoenix, Arizona, or in cities with reputations for tolerance of sexual diversity, such as Berkeley and San Francisco, many men feel there is no bisexual community to which they can belong. The problem of isolation is even more intense for residents of small towns (ironically, the prototype for the concept of "community"), suburbs, and rural areas. Although isolation is a problem for men in all areas of the country, the lack of community is particularly apparent in the comments of men living in southern and midwestern states. Perhaps the most telling evidence of a lack of community, however, comes from the non-coastal western states; very few questionnaires were completed by men living in this region, suggesting that bisexual men in the western interior of the United States are even more isolated than men in other areas of the country who, despite their dissatisfaction, are at least well enough connected to bisexual information sources to have received copies of the questionnaire.

Although the Internet has revolutionized the process of community building by making it possible for people to make connections with each other almost without regard for geographic distance, the types of connections permitted by the Internet are limited and access is not available to everyone. Bisexual men who are either connected to an academic institution or who can afford private Internet access are glad to have at least some connection to other bisexuals, and some enjoy the unique qualities provided by the electronic community–for example, freedom from the burdens of physical appearance and social characteristics–but most see this as a weak substitute for the more substantial connections that can be made in person. Even this substitute, however, with its freedom from the constraints of the real world, is only possible if one can get on-line. Internet access itself is still limited by the same social characteristics that limit access to any other social resource, and bisexual men who are socially and economically disadvantaged in the real world find that these disadvantages also bar them from full participation in the virtual world.

INDIVIDUAL COMMUNITIES AND SOCIAL REALITIES

The traditional community, epitomized by the small town in which residents live and work together lifelong, no longer exists for most people. Held up to the standard of this traditional community, communities that exist today might seem lacking because they do not involve all aspects of ourselves and because our sense of belonging to them is not a secure one based on the essential accident of birth, but a tenuous one based on actively seeking, creating, and maintaining social connections. However, the social changes that eroded the traditional close-knit, ascribed communities that afforded such security are the same social changes that made voluntarily-formed communities based on individual preferences possible. Were it not for the individualism and the social and geographic mobility that destabilized the traditional community, alternative community forms based on sexual identities, preferences, or expressions would be inconceivable.

The traditional community, admittedly an ideal type that has rarely existed in pure form, is easy to recognize because all defining aspects of community–identifiability, visibility, clear boundaries, meeting places, geographical proximity, public accessibility, scope and inclusivity, variety of social and cultural resources, economic and social self-containment and independence, strong internal connections and cohesiveness, and holistic involvement of the individual–coincide, each identifying the same social space as a community. A small town, for example, is identifiable; it has a name and is known by that name to its inhabitants and to outsiders. Its borders are clear and visible; they are legally defined and marked by roadside signs welcoming visitors and announcing local regulations. Meeting places include the town hall and buildings for religious worship; all residents live in geographic proximity to each other; the town itself is not only publicly accessible but is a public institution officially recognized by other legal entities, such as neighboring towns and state and federal governments; and the scope of the community by definition includes all members of the town population. Social and cultural resources, although probably not adequate to satisfy the desires of all inhabitants, are sufficient to constitute a moderately self-contained system. Residents relate to each other as whole persons; social, economic, and political relationships overlap and involve the same population of individuals. The population that lives within the legal borders is identical to the population that meets or is represented in the town hall, and each member of that population conceptualizes him or herself as a member of the town–the same town conceptualized by other residents. There is a resonance between individual members' perceptions of the community and the social reality of the community. No questions need arise about which criteria are more important than others in defining a community, about whose network of social relations defines membership in the community, or about whose perception of whether there is a community and of what it consists is most accurate, because all criteria, all networks, and all perceptions define the self-same community.

The transformation of the traditional community into contemporary community forms has involved divergence among the defining aspects of community, the compartmentalization of social relationships, and, consequently, widening gaps between individuals' perceptions of their communities. The various definitional aspects of community no longer coincide; a social entity might have clearly defined boundaries and meeting places, but it might not be visible and it might involve only certain aspects of its members. Must a social entity meet all the traditional criteria to be considered a community, or are some aspects more crucial to the definition of community than others? If so, which aspects are critical? Social networks no longer correspond to each other, and might not even be reciprocal. Even if I consider you a member of my social network, my social network and your social network are not necessarily identical to each other. In fact, you might not consider me a member of your network, and neither of our networks necessarily coincides with any independently extant social reality. Populations in which all members' social networks reciprocally coincide, such that all members' networks identify the same population as a community, are rare in contemporary society. These changes–divergence in the defining aspects of community and divergence among individual social networks–lead to differences of opinion among individuals regarding what constitutes a community and whether a community exists.

The difficulties involved in defining contemporary communities are multiplied when the community in question is newly forming. Established communities, in which members have already attained a sense of community, can perceive themselves as "changing" with the times without losing their underlying sense that a community exists. But people who are engaged in developing a community during this historical period when the very definition of community is in flux have a different problem: how to know when they have "become" a community. Bisexuals are at this historical juncture, and the difficulties involved in defining bisexual community are evident in the differences of opinion among the bisexual men in this study. Some bisexual men feel that the bisexual groups and networks they belong to do not constitute a bisexual community because they fail to meet one or more definitional criteria. Others feel that there is a bisexual community, even though it might not meet all of these standards. Two bisexual men who belong to the same bisexual group or network might disagree as to whether this group or network is a community because they differ in their assessment of the importance of different aspects of community. Two other bisexual men might disagree as to whether there is a bisexual community because they belong to different groups or networks; one man's network meets his definition of community, whereas the other man's network does not.

Can all four of these hypothetical men's opinions be right? In each case, is one man a member of a bisexual community while the other is not? If only one is a member, then is there a bisexual community? The question of *whether* there is a bisexual community assumes the singular existence of a social reality; answering the question either way leaves this assumption unchallenged. But this assumption is undercut when different individuals who belong to the same social network have different opinions about whether the network is a community, or when different individuals' networks are either entirely distinct from each other or overlap, rather than coincide. To maintain the concept of a singular social reality, we would have to declare one man wrong in each case; either there is, or there is not, a community. Making such an assessment invokes the assumption that there is a true definition of community by which individual opinions on the subject can be judged. If all four men are right, then the question of whether there is a bisexual community is unanswerable because the underlying assumption of a singular social reality is violated.

This leads to a paradox. If we hesitate to assign ourselves the superior position necessary to declare any of these men's perceptions incorrect, choosing instead to declare all four men correct, it is probably because we desire to respect individuals' perceptions of their own experiences and possibly also because we reject the concept of a true essence by which perceptions could be declared correct or incorrect. Bisexuals, in fact, might be particularly aware of the need to avoid invalidating others' perceptions of their experiences because, as bisexuals in a binary world, we have so often found our own perceptions invalidated by others who appeal to a belief in the exclusive existence of monosexual essences. However, the individual perceptions in question here are perceptions regarding the existence of a *social reality*. If we respect individual perceptions that a bisexual community exists, how can we simultaneously eschew the existence of a singular social reality, thereby undermining the very question these individuals are answering?

The resolution to the paradox lies in reconceptualizing the social reality of community. A community is not a social entity composed of individual members or institutions, but a social construction composed of the individuals' perceptions of such a social entity. The social reality is not singular; it is a mega-map composed of myriad individuals' maps of that very social reality. This social reality is self-constructing (and self-destructing?). It is multidimensional, and it looks different from every angle; almost no two people see it the same way. These different views of that social reality are, in fact, the reality itself.

NOTE

1. Post-operative MTF transsexuals and other full-time women were excluded because they would belong in an essay on bisexual women, not one on bisexual men; other born-male transgenderists were included so as not to eliminate this aspect of gender diversity from the sample. There were no female-born post-operative transsexuals in the "first catch" portion of the United States sample; if there were, they would have been included in this analysis.

2. All maps reprinted with permission of Paula C. Rust on behalf of anonymous artists.

Male
Bisexuality
and
HIV Risk

Meaghan Kennedy
Lynda S. Doll

[Haworth co-indexing entry note]: "Male Bisexuality and HIV Risk." Kennedy, Meaghan, and Lynda S. Doll. Co-published simultaneously in *Journal of Bisexuality* (Harrington Park Press, an imprint of The Haworth Press, Inc.) Vol. 1, No. 2/3, 2001, pp. 109-135; and: *Bisexuality in the Lives of Men: Facts and Fictions* (ed: Brett Beemyn and Erich Steinman) Harrington Park Press, an imprint of The Haworth Press, Inc., 2001, pp. 109-135. Single or multiple copies of this article are available for a fee from The Haworth Document Delivery Service [1-800-342-9678, 9:00 a.m. - 5:00 p.m. (EST). E-mail address: getinfo@ haworthpressinc.com].

SUMMARY. The HIV epidemic has led to extensive research on sexual behaviors, and our knowledge of the range of sexual behaviors in which people engage has grown considerably. In this review, we examine the theoretical and empirical literature to consider the relationship between male bisexual behavior and HIV risk. We cover theories of bisexual behavior and critique methods used to study populations of bisexual men. We then provide a brief overview of data on the prevalence of bisexual behavior, HIV infection, and AIDS cases, the prevalence and determinants of HIV-risk behaviors, and the emerging findings on prevention approaches. A range of research methods, including ethnography and other qualitative methods, population-based studies, and surveys of targeted samples, will be necessary to fully address the HIV-prevention needs of bisexual men. Although the continued study of individual-level factors is important, a focus on social structural-level factors that may encourage the expression of bisexual behavior or HIV-related risk is also necessary. Basic research on bisexuality, conducted outside the context of HIV research, as well as additional HIV-related research on populations of behaviorally bisexual men, is needed to continue to add to the knowledge base in this area. *[Article copies available for a fee from The Haworth Document Delivery Service: 1-800-342-9678. E-mail address: <getinfo@haworthpressinc.com> Website: <http://www.HaworthPress.com>]*

KEYWORDS. Bisexual men, bisexuality, HIV, risk behaviors, prevention

Bisexual behavior and identity have long been of interest to sex researchers. More recently, however, the HIV epidemic has prompted extensive research on sexual behaviors by the public health community, and our knowledge of the range of sexual behaviors in which people engage has grown considerably. Therefore, much of what we have learned about bisexuality is colored by how bisexual behavior relates to HIV risk. Concerns about bisexuals constituting the HIV bridge from homosexual to heterosexual populations have led in some cases to an AIDS-era construction of bisexuality as a "problem." While it is clear that behaviorally bisexual men have indeed infected heterosexual women with HIV (Centers for Disease Control and Prevention [CDC], 1998), the problem probably has not reached the proportions many feared (Kahn et al., 1997). In this review, we examine the theoretical and empirical literature to consider the relationship between male bisexual behavior and HIV risk, a topic of interest to both sex researchers and HIV-prevention programs.

We begin our review with a brief discussion of theories of bisexual behavior and a critique of methods used to study populations of bisexual men. These sections provide a foundation for interpreting the empirical literature and for understanding the limitations of research related to HIV risk. We then provide a brief overview of data on the prevalence of bisexual behavior, HIV infection, and AIDS cases, and the prevalence and determinants of HIV-risk behaviors. We also review the emerging findings on prevention approaches. Our review ends with a synthesis of the data and a proposed research agenda to increase our understanding of bisexual behavior and HIV risk among men who engage in sexual behavior with both genders. In this essay, our focus is on bisexual behavior rather than on bisexual self-identification, because it is behavior that must be the focus of HIV-prevention messages. Therefore, when we refer to bisexual men, we are referring to behaviorally bisexual men. However, at several points in the article, we refer to and label self-identification because it is relevant to what is being discussed.

SOCIAL CONTEXT, IDENTITY, AND PATTERNS OF BISEXUAL BEHAVIOR

A discussion of bisexual behavior and HIV risk is best understood with some background on the societal context in which the behavior occurs, theories of sexual identity, and patterns of bisexual behavior. Self-identified bisexuals are often not well integrated socially into a community. Consequently, they may face ostracism by both heterosexuals and homosexuals. The sociological concept of marginalization is important in understanding the position of those who identify as bisexual in relation to heterosexual and homosexual communities (Guidry, 1999; Paul, 1984, 1996; Stonequist, 1937). Because they are not fully integrated into either group, self-identified bisexuals may be considered deviant in both (Paul, 1984). Biphobia, or negative attitudes toward bisexual identity and behavior, is found among members of both gay and straight communities (Eliason, 1997; Istvan, 1983; Morrow, 1989). In addition to the biphobia among members of the heterosexual and homosexual communities, internalized biphobia has begun to be discussed (Hutchins, 1996; Ochs, 1996).

The marginalization of self-identified bisexuals is not surprising when viewed in light of the traditional dichotomous view of sexual identity–that is, one is either heterosexual or homosexual. However, many researchers have proposed a much more fluid view of sexuality (Blumstein & Schwartz, 1977; Herdt, 1984; Kinsey, Pomeroy, & Martin, 1948; Nichols, 1988). Kinsey and colleagues (1948) first postulated sexuality as a continuum with exclusively heterosexual and exclusively homosexual on opposite poles. Since that time, multidimensional views of sexual orientation have taken into account factors such as sexual behavior, physical and emotional relationship preferences, erotic fantasies, self-identification, lifestyle, and temporal identity changes (Coleman, 1987; Klein, Sepekoff, & Wolf, 1985; Storms, 1980).

Coupled with this more complex view of sexuality has been an interest in the acquisition of sexual identity. There are several different theories of lesbian and gay identity acquisition (Cass, 1979; Coleman, 1982; Troiden, 1979). Typically, these theories presume that the experience or the expression of homosexual attraction leads in a linear fashion to the formation of identity (Paul, 1996). However, little has been written about the acquisition of bisexual identity. Paula Rust (1993) found that many bisexually identified women move from a heterosexual to a homosexual identity and back several times before adopting a bisexual identity. Thus linear identity formation theories may not adequately describe bisexual identity acquisition for some persons (Fox, 1995; Paul, 1996; Rust, 1992, 1993).

In addition to the variety of ways people may arrive at a bisexual identity, recent research has focused on the various patterns of bisexual behavior. Several patterns or taxonomies of bisexual behavior have been proposed (Ross, 1991; Stokes & Damon, 1995; Zinik, 1985). In order to describe the diversity of behavior in samples of men recruited for HIV research, Joseph Stokes and Will Damon (1995) developed four categories of men who have sexual contact with both male and female partners. *Transitional* bisexual behavior is part of the coming out process for many homosexual men. For them, bisexual behavior is a temporary stage on the way to exclusive homosexual behavior. The future sexual behavior of *Occasional Experimenters* will likely remain consistent with their baseline heterosexuality or homosexuality, with only limited incidents of experimentation with bisexual behavior. A third category of bisexual behavior is seen among men who seek sex with other men based on the availability of or their access to male partners. *Opportunists* often self-identify as heterosexual and engage in sex with men because of easy access in anonymous sex venues, their ability to find male partners who will pay them for sex (i.e., because of an economic motivation), or a lack of available female partners, such as in prison. Finally, some men experience emotional and sexual attraction to both men and women. Men in this category, those with *Dual Involvement*, will likely have relationships with both men and women, either serially or concurrently, and often self-identify as bisexual. More recently, Taywaditep and Stokes (1998) have developed a model of bisexual behavior that takes into account self-identified sexual orientation (gay, straight, bisexual), orientation of erotic fantasies, and sexual experience and relationship history. Data from a sample of men with both male and female sex partners in the past three years were cluster analyzed to identify eight subgroups of behaviorally bisexual men.

METHODOLOGIC ISSUES IN STUDYING BISEXUALITY

Understanding the relationship between bisexual behavior and HIV risk is made particularly difficult by the paucity of empirical literature. It is also made difficult by conceptual and methodological issues that continue to affect research on this topic. A recent examination of the peer-reviewed literature on male bisexuality published in the United States from 1986 through 1996 showed that most of the 166 articles that mentioned bisexual men aggregated gay and bisexual men into a single category. Of the total, eight articles included information exclusively on bisexual men, and only 21 assessed differences between gay and bisexual men. Forty-eight percent of these 29 articles with specific mention of bisexual men were HIV-focused (Doll, 1997).

The scarcity of research literature on these populations is puzzling, but may be related, in part, to three phenomena: (a) the tentativeness of social science to accept sexuality research, generally; (b) the continued ambiguity in the field over what constitutes bisexuality; and (c) the relatively slow development of theory related to bisexuality (Rust, 1993). Many social scientists have ignored or rejected sexuality research as an important area for investigation, seemingly because of its applied focus and apparent lack of a theory base. Societal norms, phobias, and stigma (biphobia and homophobia) may also work to divert research from this area to other, less marginalized issues.

In the various theories and taxonomies of bisexuality, there remains ambiguity about what constitutes bisexuality. This ambiguity has been complicated by the tendency for studies to aggregate diverse groups of persons who are behaviorally similar (e.g., they engage in sex with men and women) into a single group, bisexuals. In many studies, the construct of bisexuality is defined by a single, very narrow feature, namely the gender of one's partners, without consideration of the differences in the psychological and social contexts of their lives. This tendency may be a consequence of the fact that most of the recent literature on these populations has been HIV-focused and dominated by epidemiologic models, methods, and selection criteria. But, regardless of the genesis, both the definitional ambiguity and the very narrow behavioral definition hamper our ability to gain a fuller understanding of the range of bisexualities, as well as the cultural meanings associated with bisexual sexual behavior and identity. In turn, they also hamper theory and intervention development.

Our understanding of the sexual behaviors of bisexual men and women is also hindered by the methodologic limitations of published research. The lack of a generally agreed-upon definition of bisexuality is evident in the methods used to recruit study participants. For example, Ted Myers and Dan Allman (1996) conducted an inventory of major Canadian studies on male bisexuality and found that most of them used behavioral definitions. Six studies measured bisexuality on the basis of behavior in the past year, two on behavior in the past five years, and two on lifetime experience. Not surprisingly, the proportion of bisexual men in such studies varies tremendously. As an alternative to behavioral measures, self-identification as bisexual was used in five studies. Measures of sexual attraction, fantasy, desire, and satisfaction were not commonly included. Furthermore, even though several studies have used more than one measure of bisexuality, little attention has been given to the relationship between different measures, including how behavioral definitions are affected by different time frames or how they relate to other measures of sexual orientation, such as self-identification, sexual attraction, and sexual satisfaction.

Finally, to add still further difficulty, neither sampling methods nor the definitions of sexual contact have been standardized across studies. These concerns are not unique to the study of bisexuality, but they complicate an already confusing area of research. Some surveys have defined sexual contact as intercourse to the point of orgasm, others have required orgasm, and still others have failed to clarify how they define sexual contact. Most have also used convenience samples (samples that are necessarily representative of all bisexual men), making interpretation and generalization of study results difficult at best (Binson et al., 1995).

DISTRIBUTION AND CHARACTERISTICS
OF MALE BISEXUALS

Estimates of the prevalence of bisexual behavior among men in the U.S. range from approximately 1% to 7%, depending upon the questions on the survey and whether bisexual contact is measured since puberty, age 18, or the past five or ten years (Billy, Tanfer, Grady, & Klepinger, 1993; Binson et al., 1995; Laumann, Gagnon, Michael, & Michaels, 1994; Rogers & Turner, 1991; Smith, 1991). Greater consensus has been reached in estimates of recent bisexual behavior; according to most surveys, fewer than 1% of men report sexual contact with both women and men in the past year (Laumann et al., 1994; Rogers & Turner, 1991). In their review of studies of bisexual behavior in gay-identified men, Reinisch, Ziemba-Davis, and Sanders (1990) found that 62% to 79% of these men relate a history of heterosexual contact and 15% to 26% have been married. Little data on demographic characteristics of bisexual men have been published, and findings should be viewed with caution, given the small size of most studies. However, a synthesis of results from six national surveys showed that, compared with exclusively homosexual men, bisexual men were more likely to be younger, African American, married, and less formally educated (Binson et al., 1995).

HIV INFECTION AND AIDS

The prevalence of HIV infection among bisexual men in the United States is unknown. Through December 1998, 79,227 men with a history of bisexual behavior since 1977 had been reported with AIDS to the Centers for Disease Control and Prevention. This figure represents 21% of the cumulative total of AIDS cases among men who indicated having sex with men. AIDS case reports and more in-depth studies of persons with AIDS suggest that bisexual contact is more likely to be reported by African American and Hispanic men than by white men (Diaz et al., 1993). These same data show that bisexual men with AIDS are twice as likely as exclusively homosexual men with AIDS to report injection drug use.

Convenience samples of groups of men provide additional information on HIV seroprevalence among bisexual men. Of 5,480 men recruited for an intervention study in Seattle, HIV seroprevalence was highest for self-identified gay men (27%), followed by bisexually identified (12%) and heterosexually identified (8%) men who have sex with men (Wood, Krueger, Pearlman, & Goldbaum, 1993). This ordering of seroprevalence by sexual orientation seems to be a consistent pattern. In their review of the literature, Joseph Stokes and colleagues (Stokes, Taywaditep, Vanable, & McKirnan, 1996) repeatedly found higher HIV seroprevalence in homosexually identified, compared to bisexually identified, men. In studies that included heterosexually identified men, these men had the lowest HIV seroprevalence. The difference in seroprevalence between homosexually and bisexually identified men may reflect higher rates of HIV-risk behaviors among homosexually identified men or a lack of overlap in networks where partners are drawn from.

HIV TRANSMISSION TO FEMALE PARTNERS

The role of male bisexual behavior in the transmission of HIV to female partners is uncertain. AIDS cases reported to the CDC through 1998 show that, overall, 3,132 women with AIDS, or fewer than 8% of women infected through heterosexual contact, were known to be potentially infected through sexual contact with a bisexual man (CDC, 1998). Based on a telephone survey of AIDS-related risk behaviors, James Kahn and colleagues (1997) estimated an annual transmission of 408 HIV infections from bisexual men to their female partners in the 22 cities with the highest prevalence of AIDS in the U.S.

Prior to 1990, 61% of the AIDS cases in the United States occurred in these 22 cities. If HIV infections linked to male bisexual behavior have a similar geographic pattern to AIDS cases, these authors estimate that 669 infections would be expected to be transmitted from bisexual males to their female partners in the United States annually (408 is 61% of 669). Hence, at this point in the epidemic in the United States, widespread transmission of HIV from bisexual men to heterosexual women has probably not occurred or has not been detected.

HIV-RELATED RISK BEHAVIORS

Few quantitative studies of male bisexual behavior have been published in the United States and, of these, few examine risk behaviors, determinants of risk behaviors, or the extent of behavioral change by bisexual men over the course of their lives. Of the published studies, most are cross-sectional, which compare groups of men at a single point in time. This research suggests three overall trends. First, behaviorally bisexual men may be less likely than men with exclusively male partners to engage in receptive anal sex (Stokes, Vanable, & McKirnan, 1997). However, bisexual men do engage in relatively high rates of unprotected anal sex with male partners (approximately one-third in recent studies using community samples [McKirnan, Stokes, Doll, & Burzette, 1994], bar samples [Heckman et al., 1995], and samples recruited through media campaigns [Kalichman et al., 1998]). Later in this section, we will discuss four contexts in which we believe behaviorally bisexual men may be more likely to engage in risky sexual practices with male partners. Finally, bisexual men probably have less sex with male partners than do exclusively homosexual men; thus the risk of sexual transmission from a male partner may be lower for bisexual men (CDC, 1993; Doll et al., 1992; Lever, Kanouse, Rogers, Carson, & Hertz, 1992; Roffman et al., 1990; Stokes, Taywaditep, Vanable, & McKirnan, 1996).

A second group of studies found lower levels of risky sexual practices with male than with female partners (Ekstrand et al., 1994; Kalichman et al., 1998; McKirnan et al., 1994; Stokes, McKirnan, & Burzette, 1993; Wold et al., 1998; Wolitski, 1993). For example, in a survey of more than 500 African American and white behaviorally bisexual men (McKirnan et al., 1994), 42% reported unprotected vaginal sex and 31% reported unprotected anal sex with another man in the past six months. No racial differences were found in the rates of unprotected anal sex with male partners, though more African American men reported unprotected penetrative sex with both male and female partners. In another study, involving men recruited from public cruising areas in southern Los Angeles County, 56% of nongay-identified men (most of whom were bisexual) reported using condoms every time during anal sex with their main (primary) male partners, and 71% said they did so with their casual male partners. In contrast, only 33% reported consistent condom use during vaginal sex with their main female partners, and 25% with their casual female partners (Wolitski, 1993).

Research conducted with convenience samples of men suggests that bisexual men may engage in high rates of risk behaviors with female partners (Beeker et al., 1993; Padian et al., 1987). For example, in a sample of over 2,000 men recruited from inner-city streets in three U.S. cities, Beeker and colleagues (1993) found that 60% of the bisexual men with a main female partner acknowledged having anal sex with her in the past month, compared to 12% of the exclusively heterosexual men with a main female partner. Bisexual men with female primary partners were also more likely to report unprotected anal intercourse with these partners than were bisexual men without female primary partners (Kalichman et al., 1998). As many as 50-75% of bisexual men may not inform their female partners of male sexual contacts (Freeman et al., 1992; Kalichman et al., 1998; Roffman et al., 1990; Stokes, McKirnan, Burzette, Vanable, & Doll, 1996; Wolitski, 1996).

In addition to these studies assessing the prevalence of risk behaviors, Lynda Doll and Carolyn Beeker (1996) identified four contexts in which male bisexual behavior is more likely to occur and more likely to be associated with greater HIV risk: (a) male sex work (Elifson, Boles, & Sweat, 1993; Morse et al., 1992; Morse et al., 1991; Simon et al., 1993); (b) injection drug use (Lewis & Watters, 1994; CDC, 1995); (c) sexual identity exploration (Hays, Kegeles, & Coates, 1990; Lemp et al., 1994; Reinisch et al., 1990);

and (d) culturally specific gender roles and norms that may characterize some African American and Hispanic communities in the United States (Peterson, 1992; Stokes, Vanable, & McKirnan, 1996a, 1996b; Wright, 1993). In many situations, the same-sex behavior is economically motivated, engaged in secretly, or part of sexual experimentation. These conditions make delivery of HIV-prevention messages particularly challenging.

Some men engage in bisexual behavior in the context of survival sex (sexual activity in exchange for basic living necessities) or sex work (Doll & Beeker, 1996; Ross, 1991). Research has consistently shown that a substantial portion of male sex workers who have same-gender partners do not identify as gay and continue to have female sex partners (Boles & Elifson, 1994; Morse et al., 1991; Pleak & Meyer-Bahlburg, 1990). Therefore these men may engage in HIV-risk behaviors in the context of sex work yet not be reached by prevention messages specifically targeting gay men.

The relationship between injecting drug use and bisexual behavior and identity is not well understood. However, some studies indicate that behaviorally bisexual injecting drug users may be at a higher HIV risk than behaviorally heterosexual and homosexual injectors (Wolitski et al., 1992). In a comparison of behaviorally bisexual, heterosexual, and homosexual male injection drug users recruited from 42 sites in the United States and Puerto Rico, behaviorally bisexual injectors were more likely than behaviorally heterosexual or homosexual injection drug users to have traded sex for drugs or money and to have shared needles. Additionally, bisexual self-identification has been shown to be related to ever having injected drugs. In a study involving men who had sex with men, recruited from public sex environments in four U.S. cities, those who self-identified as bisexual were more likely than those who self-identified as either gay or straight to report ever injecting drugs or having sex within the previous month with a partner who had injected drugs within the last five years (Goldbaum et al., 1998).

Bisexuality in other contexts also has implications for HIV risk. Sexual-identity exploration often occurs in late childhood or adolescence (Coleman & Remafedi, 1989) and frequently includes sexual contact with both male and female partners (Doll & Beeker, 1996; Rosario, Hunter, & Gwadz, 1995). Studies of gay and bisexual male youth suggest that they may seek anonymous sex (Roesler & Deisher, 1992) and have survival sex (Pennbridge, Freese, & MacKenzie, 1992), and thus be at a particularly high risk for HIV. Among a random sample of high school students, those with same-sex experience were shown to be more likely than students with only heterosexual experience to be exposed to violence, seriously contemplate suicide, and use alcohol and drugs, including injection drugs (Faulkner & Cranston, 1998). In addition, as Mary Jane Rotheram-Borus, William D. Marelich, and Shobha Srinivasan (1999) have suggested, gay and bisexual youth may seek sex partners outside their neighborhoods, and often in marginalized settings, which may place them at risk for HIV. These researchers also found that self-identified bisexual youth have more sex partners than their self-identified heterosexual and homosexual peers. Therefore, sexual-identity exploration during adolescence or early adulthood, when many youth are particularly vulnerable (Remafedi, 1987), may involve engaging in behaviors that put them at risk for HIV infection (Doll & Beeker, 1996).

Several studies have found that male bisexual behavior is more prevalent among African American and Latino men than among white men in the United States (Carrier, 1985; Chu et al., 1992; Wright, 1993). Researchers have proposed that the higher rates of male bisexual behavior in communities of color may be attributed to community norms which narrowly define gender roles and pressure men to have female partners (Binson et al., 1995; Doll & Beeker, 1996). In many communities of color, men who have sex with men may do so secretly and also have wives and children (Peterson, 1992; Wright, 1993). Moreover, in Latino and African American cultures, male same-sex contact may be more acceptable for the man who is the insertive partner during anal sex (Carrier, 1985; Ross, 1991) and for men who also have female partners (Wright, 1993). The high rates of bisexual behavior for men of color may also reflect their differential participation in situations associated with same-sex contact, such as prolonged isolation from women because of incarceration (Doll & Beeker, 1996). Many of the situations where same-sex behavior is secretive may make HIV-prevention messages harder to deliver, thus contributing to HIV infection in bisexual men of color and their female sex partners. Though still an area that needs further study, these higher rates of both bisexuality and HIV risk may result from cultural factors, such as homophobia, strong ties to family and ethnic identity, gender role expectations, and attitudes about masculinity.

In summary, the relationship between male bisexuality and HIV risk is complicated. There is very little societal support for the development of bisexual identity and the expression of bisexual behavior. Additionally, men who identify themselves as bisexual or who engage in bisexual behavior are a heterogeneous group. At the same time, many patterns of bisexual behavior, and the factors influencing the expression of that behavior, may have implications for HIV transmission. For example, the eight subgroups of behaviorally bisexual men identified by Kittiwut Taywaditep and Joseph Stokes

(1998) demonstrated different rates of HIV-risk behaviors, both with male and female partners. These differential rates of HIV-risk behaviors were not related to self-identified sexual identity. This research underscores the need for continued study of the contexts of bisexual behaviors and their intersection with HIV-risk behaviors.

DETERMINANTS OF RISK BEHAVIORS

A limited number of studies have addressed the correlates of HIV-risk behaviors of bisexual men. As has been true in research involving exclusively homosexual men, these studies have largely emphasized social psychological factors. We know little about the relationship between HIV risk and social structural factors, such as survival needs, gender imbalances, and social network composition, that may be particularly relevant for bisexual men. Given the very limited number of studies examining determinants, these findings should be considered tentative until further research is conducted.

Several studies have examined factors that have been correlated with HIV risk among men who have sex with men. For example, Seth Kalichman et al. (1998) studied self-efficacy for safer sex, social skills, and perceived social norms in samples of gay and bisexual men. Low self-efficacy and perceived norms were significantly related to unsafe sexual behaviors; however, the groups differed only in perceived norms. Bisexual men were less likely to view safer sex as normative among their peers than were gay men (Kalichman et al., 1998; Stokes et al., 1996a). Additionally, Jeffrey Kelly and Seth Kalichman (1998) found that the reinforcement value (i.e., pleasure) of high-risk sex may be an important factor in determining frequency of risky sexual behavior among men who have sex with men (heterosexual behavior was not considered, so it is unknown to what extent bisexual men are represented in the sample). Finally, consistent with others who have studied men who have sex with men, David McKirnan, Peter Vanable, and Joseph Stokes (1995) reported that sexual risk is higher for bisexual men with primary male partners and when alcohol and drugs are used in the context of sex.

Several studies have suggested that, contrary to expectation, bisexual men with stronger ties to gay communities may engage in higher rates of unsafe sexual behaviors (Kalichman et al., 1998; McKirnan et al., 1995). Affiliation with gay communities is variously defined in these studies as being active in gay organizations, having a number of gay friends, participating in gay marches, and reading gay literature. Although the strength of the relationship between specific community involvement variables and HIV risk differs by study, research has generally supported the hypothesis that greater gay community involvement is not necessarily protective for bisexual men. Explanations for this lack of a protective effect are unclear but may be related to increased opportunities for male sexual contacts among men with stronger ties to gay communities.

A less clear relationship has been identified between HIV risk and sexual identity. David McKirnan and colleagues (1995) found that behaviorally bisexual men who were more strongly gay-identified (as measured on a Kinsey-type scale) were more likely to engage in unsafe sexual practices. In the same study, men who were lower on the scale of gay identity reported fewer male partners and more female partners and were more likely to seek out male partners in anonymous settings. The authors proposed that men who experience a conflict between their behavior and identity may be more tentative about their male sexual contacts and therefore may be safer overall. In contrast, Lynda Doll and colleagues (1992) found that of HIV-seropositive bisexual men who engaged in unprotected anal sex, those who were heterosexually identified were the least likely to use condoms with male partners. Differences in samples may largely account for these results, demonstrating once again the tentativeness of the findings of the few studies of bisexual men.

Finally, David McKirnan et al. (1995) and Joseph Stokes, Peter Vanable, and David McKirnan (1996b) have examined differences between African American and white bisexual men on several dimensions. African American and white bisexual men did not differ in internalized homophobia, but African American men were less likely to perceive their friends (though not their families) as accepting of their homosexual contacts. Interestingly, however, African American men also believed that more African American men than white men engaged in bisexual behavior.

PREVENTION APPROACHES: SCIENTIFIC DATA AND PROGRAMS

No data are available from efficacy trials of interventions specifically for bisexual men. However, in this section, we discuss an intervention trial targeting nongay-identified men who have sex with men (NGI-MSM) and a second intervention for which separate analyses have been conducted for gay and bisexual men. We also describe programs that may be relevant for bisexually active men, especially those in the four high-risk contexts identified by Lynda Doll and Carolyn Beeker (1996).

Intervention Trials

The AIDS Community Demonstration Project is an example of research testing a community-level intervention for nongay-identified men who have sex with men (Goldbaum et al., unpublished manuscript). Target populations for this study, conducted in Seattle, Denver, and Long Beach, California between 1991 and 1995, were NGI-MSM, that is, men who had ever had sex with another man and self-identified as either straight or bisexual. An intervention and a control community of NGI-MSM were used to study the impact of peer outreach and small-media publications, such as pamphlets and newsletters, on condom use with casual male partners and main female partners. Extensive research was conducted to identify population subgroups, settings in which to conduct outreach efforts, and relevant information to include in the small-media messages (Goldbaum, Perdue, & Higgins, 1996). Media consisted of theory-based role model stories that described behavioral change efforts by peers of the target population in the community. In the intervention communities, consistent (always or nearly always) condom use increased from 41% to 60% for casual male partners versus 48% to 54% in the control communities.[1] Consistent condom use during vaginal intercourse with primary female partners increased over the study period in both intervention and control communities, with no differences seen between the two types of communities. The authors conclude that community-level interventions show promise with difficult to reach populations and represent one of several complementary elements in an HIV-prevention strategy that includes HIV testing and risk-reduction counseling, social marketing of condoms, treatment of other sexually transmitted diseases, and early medical treatment of HIV to reduce infectiousness (Goldbaum et al., unpublished manuscript).

A second intervention, consisting of a 17-week, small-group counseling session, targeted gay and bisexual men who reported having difficulty engaging in safer-sex behaviors. Participants were randomly assigned to either a treatment or a waiting-list control condition, with treatment focused on coping with situations in which high-risk behaviors were likely to occur. Relative to the control condition, the intervention decreased rates of unprotected anal and oral sex among exclusively gay men for the three-month period studied.[2] The rates for bisexual men also declined, though the change was not statistically significant, given the small sample size (N = 32) (Roffman, Picciano, Wickizer et al., in press).

Programs with Relevance to Behaviorally Bisexual Men

In addition to reports of intervention trials, Lynda Doll and Carolyn Beeker (1996) reviewed information on programs that have been, or may be, useful for reaching bisexual men. In some locations in the United States, health and social service agencies and community outreach workers try to educate men who engage in covert homosexual behavior about HIV-risk reduction. They approach men where they live, work, socialize, and/or have sex to stress the need for them to use condoms during sex with both men and women (Beckstein, 1990; Beeker, 1993). Mobile vans, person-to-person outreach on street corners, and storefront drop-in centers have all been used with some apparent success. In one program, called Wake Up My Brother, heterosexually identified men conducted outreach in parks and bars where nongay-identified MSM meet one another (U.S. Conference of Mayors, 1994).

To sustain risk-reduction behaviors among bisexual men, organizational support may be particularly useful. For example, a growing number of bisexuality-oriented groups now provide opportunities for men to meet, learn to talk about sex, and consider different sexual options (Rubenstein & Slater, 1985). Gay organizations have also been encouraged to diversify their programs for a range of MSM, including married men, sex workers, youth, and gay men of color. However, Roffman and his colleagues (in press) have cautioned that perceived negative attitudes toward bisexual behavior may limit the effectiveness of such programs. These authors emphasized that programs targeting bisexual men need to be aware of the unique status of bisexual men within the larger population of MSM (Roffman, Picciano, Ryan et al., in press). In their research, bisexual men were less likely to enroll in, and more likely to drop out of, telephone and face-to-face counseling interventions. They hypothesized that bisexual men may fear reduced social support from exclusively gay counselors or group participants or may be concerned that issues raised during interventions will not address the specific challenges faced by bisexual men (Roffman, Picciano, Bolan, & Kalichman, in press; Roffman, Picciano, Ryan et al., in press). Thus focusing on both the contexts and the determinants of HIV risk and the unique experience of bisexual men is probably critical to successfully reaching and retaining bisexual men in HIV-prevention efforts.

A limited number of intervention models have been developed for each of the four high-risk subgroups described by Lynda Doll and Carolyn Beeker (1996). Interventions for male sex workers have typically used peer educators to distribute condoms and materials, provide social support, and refer men to services (Miller, 1993). Other intervention components that may be critical for this population are vocational training, drug and alcohol treatment, and training in negotiation skills to increase control for male sex workers over commercial sex transactions (Simon et al., 1993).

Syringe-exchange programs (as well as other programs that provide sterile syringes), methadone maintenance, and drug and alcohol treatment facilities are important access points for bisexual men who inject drugs. Interventions at these sites must effectively address both drug and sexual risk with male and female partners. Other important venues for community outreach and the distribution of condoms may include liquor stores and bars, barber shops, video arcades, and commercial or public cruising areas. Again, these programs should target all men; not requiring men to admit to bisexual behavior may be critical to reaching them with HIV-prevention messages.

Expanded services, including counseling, outreach, and shelter programs, are needed for youth and other men exploring their sexual identity. Such programs must promote self-acceptance and encourage individuals to access relevant social networks. Programs are also needed for homeless and runaway youth, many of whom engage in survival sex with male partners (Elie, 1993). Youth support groups offered through gay-identified community organizations may provide a sense of shared community; positive, gay-identified role models; and emotional support during the coming-out process (Herdt & Boxer, 1993; Martin & Hetrick, 1988). However, for youth who are bisexually identified or from cultures in which homosexual behavior is particularly stigmatized, an emphasis on gay-identified groups may be inappropriate (Martin & Hetrick, 1988). In fact, data from focus groups of 15-23-year-old British men who had recently become homosexually active suggest that safer-sex information should be delivered with other sexual and mental health information, using images and experiences taken from youth rather than gay culture (Scholey, 1998). In this same study, the respondents stressed the need for HIV-prevention information to be presented discreetly so as not to draw attention to the fact that it was intended for men who have sex with men. Because they may be covert about their same-sex activity, anonymous venues may be critical for reaching such youth. Additionally, youth who are most distressed may require an even more extensive intervention that combines HIV prevention with comprehensive health and mental health care (Rotheram-Borus et al., 1995).

Finally, intervention strategies for bisexual men of color must be developed within these communities to insure that such programs are compatible with community language, values, and norms. Issues of masculinity, family, reconciliation of sexual and racial identities, and homophobia may be particularly important for bisexual men of color (Stokes & Peterson, 1998). Also needed are training programs for health and social service providers and the staff of religious and other community-based organizations to help them better serve persons with diverse sexual preferences. Because male bisexual behavior is often linked to poverty, substance use, and commercial sex work, especially in communities of color, any effort to change sexual behavior must take into account the social and economic contexts in which such behavior is embedded (Schilling et al., 1989).

CONCLUSIONS AND NEXT STEPS

Early in the epidemic, bisexual males were a concern to public health policy makers responsible for establishing HIV-prevention programs in the United States. Though little was known about these men or their risk behaviors, discussions were concentrated on the potential threat to their sex partners and how sex educators and public health officials might notify unsuspecting female partners of their risk. This led to a construction of bisexuality as a "problem," but did little to focus HIV-prevention education on issues specific to bisexual subgroups. These early public health responses to bisexual behavior reflected the state of the research describing these populations at the time, in which data on gay and bisexual men were typically aggregated into a single category and the emphasis was on identifying the risk posed to female partners. However, as is true of other aspects of sexual behavior, the body of research on bisexual men has grown in tandem with the changing face of the AIDS epidemic. In this final section, we summarize themes in this scientific literature and point out continuing gaps in our understanding of bisexual behavior and its relationship to HIV risk.

In our review of current research, a number of themes emerged. First, studies with a range of samples and sampling methods suggest that, in general, bisexual men engage in less unsafe sexual behavior than do exclusively homosexual men. Still, some bisexual men may be at a particularly high risk for HIV; estimates generally show that from 20 to 35% of bisexual male study participants may engage in unprotected anal sex with male partners, and research involving bisexual subgroups suggests that bisexual men may have high rates of injection drug use.

Other findings relate to the specific risks for the female partners of behaviorally bisexual men. Bisexual men may use condoms less frequently with female than male partners and report higher rates of anal sex with female partners than do exclusively heterosexual men. Additionally, many bisexual men do not disclose their same-gender contacts to their female partners. Bisexual men in the U.S. who are younger, more involved in gay communities, and engage in commercial sex work are likely at an increased risk. Finally, rates of bisexual behavior, HIV seroprevalence, and possibly HIV-risk behaviors are greater in African American and Hispanic communities, suggesting that bisexual men of color represent a subgroup at a particularly high risk.

Not surprisingly, little intervention research involving bisexual men has been published. However, important themes that could be applied to interventions for bisexual men have begun to be used in prevention programs. These themes stress outreach in locations where men work, live, and interact with medical and other social service providers, as well as the use of anonymous venues, such as personal ads, hotlines, and HIV-testing centers. The focus of the outreach should be on HIV prevention with all partners, regardless of gender. Additionally, because HIV may be just one of many areas of concern for behaviorally bisexual men, some programs treat HIV prevention as part of a larger response to basic survival needs (Myrick, 1999). These programs try to provide men with skills to address a variety of dangerous situations, from unprotected sex with either men or women, to substance use and violence. Finally, some programs that target behaviorally bisexual men of color have had a hard time reaching these men because they may not be open about their same-sex behavior. These programs have responded by producing messages about a range of services and health information for the entire community. Within these messages, HIV prevention is addressed as it relates to sexual behavior with both men and women.

Because of the relative lack of research on bisexuality, our suggestions for additional research remain broad. It is critical to assess basic questions about male bisexuality, including theories of bisexual behavior and identity, and how persons integrate their bisexual behavior into their self-identity. We need to continue to explore the relationship between measures of bisexuality, including those based on sexual behavior, identification, fantasy, and attraction. We also need to know more about how bisexuals are organized and about their social and sexual networks. In particular, we need to understand the extent of their associations with gay, bisexual, and heterosexual communities and how factors such as ethnicity and culture may influence membership and association.

In relation to HIV, it is important to understand the risky and the protective sexual behaviors of bisexuals, the extent to which and under what conditions their behavior remains undisclosed, and how stigma, along with many other determinants of behavior, relate to risk taking. We must understand the sub-groups of bisexual men and the extent and context of risk for each group. Additionally, among subgroups of behaviorally bisexual men, the interaction between drug use and male bisexual behavior should be examined. We do not know whether the increased reports of HIV-risk behaviors, including commercial sex work, are being driven by drug use or some other factor(s). Finally, this information must be applied to interventions for bisexual men. We must determine how bisexual men can be reached and retained in HIV interventions and what messages should be delivered by whom. Also, we must understand under what conditions and with what success these men might be reached through prevention efforts targeting homosexual or heterosexual men, instead of bisexuals specifically.

More broadly addressing societal issues that impact bisexual men and their partners may also be a piece in the HIV-prevention puzzle. For example, Joseph Stokes and John Peterson (1998) argue that pervasive, virulent negative attitudes toward homosexuality in our society might contribute to the spread of HIV. They stress the need for open discussions of sexuality and contend that changing negative attitudes toward homosexuality or reducing the impact of negative attitudes on young people (i.e., combating homophobia) is an important part of a plan to stop the spread of HIV. Such changes will have to occur on a community level. One vehicle for reaching large portions of society is through the media. In a study that assessed sources of AIDS information among men recruited from public sex environments, Gary Goldbaum and colleagues (1998) found that television was the only medium to reach over half of the gay, bisexual, and straight-identified men who have sex with men in their study population. Similarly, in order to educate women about the diversity of men's sexual behavior (thus educating the female partners of bisexual men), a program in Australia produces educational campaigns, places articles in women's magazines, and collaborates with television drama writers (Lubowitz, 1998). However, the impact of such a program on HIV transmission may not be measurable.

In summary, a range of research methods, including ethnography and other qualitative methods, population-based studies, and surveys of targeted samples, will be necessary to answer these questions fully and to address the prevention needs of bisexual men. Although a continued focus on individual-level factors is important, a focus on social structural-level factors that may encourage the expression of bisexual behavior or HIV-related risk is equally important. If at all possible, the basic research on bisexuality should be conducted outside the context of HIV research. In this way, biases attributed to high HIV-seroprevalence locations, or to specific populations, such as persons living with HIV, injection drug users, or commercial sex workers, may be avoided. However, this need for more basic research on bisexuals does not diminish the critical importance of additional HIV-related research on these populations.

NOTES

1. Consistent condom use was almost twice as likely (adjusted odds ratio = 1.9) to occur in intervention versus control communities. However, this finding is not statistically significant (confidence interval = .07 to 4.9); it could have occurred by chance alone.

2. The intervention community was more likely than the control community to report increased abstinence from unprotected anal and oral sex in the previous three months ($p = .01$). These results could not have occurred by chance.

REFERENCES

Beckstein, D. 1990. *AIDS Prevention in Public Sex Environments: Outreach and Training Manual.* Santa Cruz, CA: Santa Cruz AIDS Project.

Beeker, C. 1993. *Final Report on Hispanic Nongay-Identified Men Who Have Sex with Other Men: A Formative Research Study.* Atlanta: Centers for Disease Control and Prevention.

Beeker, C., D. Schnell, D. Higgins, J. Sheridan, and K. O'Reilly. 1993. *AIDS Community Demonstration Projects: Bisexuality, Drug Use and Prostitution Among Men Intercepted in Urban Neighborhoods with High IDU Prevalence.* Paper presented at the IXth International Conference on AIDS, Berlin.

Billy, J. O. G., K. Tanfer, W. R. Grady, and D. H. Klepinger. 1993. The Sexual Behavior of Men in the United States. *Family Planning Perspective* 25: 52-60.

Binson, D., S. Michaels, R. Stall, T. Coates, J. Gagnon, and J. A. Catania. 1995. Prevalence and Social Distribution of Men Who Have Sex with Men: United States and Its Urban Centers. *Journal of Sex Research* 32: 245-54.

Blumstein, P. W., and P. Schwartz. 1977. Bisexuality: Some Social Psychological Issues. *Journal of Social Issues* 33: 30-44.

Boles, J., and K. Elifson. 1994. Sexual Identity and HIV: The Male Prostitute. *Journal of Sex Research* 31: 39-46.

Carrier, J. 1985. Mexican Male Bisexuality. *Journal of Homosexuality* 11: 75-85.

Cass, V. 1979. Homosexual Identity Formation: A Theoretical Model. *Journal of Homosexuality* 4: 219-35.

Centers for Disease Control and Prevention. 1993. Condom Use Among Men Who Have Sex with Men and the Relationship to Sexual Identity–Dallas 1991. *Morbidity and Mortality Weekly Report* 42: 13-14.

_____ . 1995. HIV Risk Factors of Male Injecting-Drug Users Who Have Sex with

Men–Dallas, Denver, and Long Beach, 1991-1994. *Morbidity and Mortality Weekly Report* 44: 767-69.

_____ . 1998. *HIV/AIDS Surveillance Report* 10: 1-43.

Chu, S. Y., T. A. Peterman, L. S. Doll, J. W. Buehler, and J. W. Curran. 1992. AIDS in Bisexual Men in the United States: Epidemiology and Transmission to Women. *American Journal of Public Health* 82: 220-24.

Coleman, E. 1982. Developmental Stages of the Coming-Out Process. *American Behavioral Scientist* 25: 469-82.

_____ . 1987. Assessment of Sexual Orientation. *Journal of Homosexuality* 14: 9-24.

Coleman, E., and G. Remafedi. 1989. Gay, Lesbian, and Bisexual Adolescents: A Critical Challenge to Counselors. *Journal of Counseling and Development* 68: 36-40.

Diaz, T., S. Y. Chu, M. Frederick, P. Hermann, A. Levy, and E. Mokotoff. 1993. Sociodemographics and HIV Risk Behaviors of Bisexual Men with AIDS: Results from a Multistate Interview Project. *AIDS* 7: 1227-32.

Doll, L. S. 1997. Studying Bisexual Men and Women and Lesbians. In *Researching Sexual Behavior: Methodological Issues*, ed. J. Bancroft. Bloomington: Indiana University Press.

Doll, L. S., and C. Beeker. 1996. Male Bisexual Behavior and HIV Risk in the United States: Synthesis of Research with Implications for Behavioral Interventions. *AIDS Education and Prevention* 8: 205-25.

Doll, L. S., L. R. Petersen, C. R. White, E. Johnson, J. W. Ward, and Blood Donor Study Group. 1992. Homosexually and Nonhomosexually Identified Men Who Have Sex with Men: A Behavioral Comparison. *Journal of Sexual Research* 29: 1-14.

Ekstrand, M. L., T. J. Coates, J. R. Guydish, W. W. Hauck, L. Collette, and S. B. Hulley. 1994. Bisexual Men in San Francisco Are Not a Common Vector for Spreading HIV Infection to Women: The San Francisco Men's Health Study. *American Journal of Public Health* 84: 915-19.

Eliason, M. J. 1997. The Prevalence and Nature of Biphobia in Heterosexual Undergraduate Students. *Archives of Sexual Behavior* 26: 317-26.

Elie, R. 1993. *Hetrick-Martin Institute's Project First Step.* Paper presented at the Hustler Network Peer Education Conference, San Francisco, CA.

Elifson, K. W., J. Boles, and M. Sweat. 1993. Risk Factors Associated with HIV Infection Among Male Prostitutes. *American Journal of Public Health* 83: 79-83.

Faulkner, A. H., and K. Cranston. 1998. Correlates of Same-Sex Behavior in a Random Sample of Massachusetts High School Students. *American Journal of Public Health* 88: 262-66.

Fox, R. C. 1995. Bisexual Identities. In *Lesbian, Gay, and Bisexual Identities Over the Lifespan: Psychological Perspectives*, eds. A. R. D'Augelli and C. J. Patterson, 48-86. New York: Oxford University Press.

Freeman, A. C., M. Krepcho, A. Hedrick, C. Schenk, B. Elwood, and A. Seibt. 1992. *Gay, Bisexual, and Straight Men Who Have Sex with Men: HIV Risk and Disclosure.* Paper presented at the VIII International Conference on AIDS, Amsterdam, Netherlands.

Goldbaum, G., W. Johnson, R. Wolitski, C. Rietmeijer, R. Wood, D. Kasprzyk, D. Montano, and the AIDS Community Demonstration Projects. *Sexual Behavior Change Among Non-Gay-Identified Men Who Have Sex with Men: Response to a Community-Level Intervention.* Unpublished manuscript.

Goldbaum, G., T. Perdue, and D. Higgins. 1996. Non-Gay Identifying Men Who Have Sex with Men: Formative Research Results from Seattle, Washington. *Public Health Reports* 33: 36-40.

Goldbaum, G., T. Perdue, R. Wolitski, C. Reitmeijer, A. Hedrich, R. Wood, M. Fishbein, and the AIDS Community Demonstration Projects. 1998. Differences in Risk Behavior and Sources of AIDS Information Among Gay, Bisexual, and Straight-Identified Men Who Have Sex with Men. *AIDS and Behavior* 2: 13-21.

Guidry, L. L. 1999. Clinical Interventions with Bisexual Clients: A Contextualized Understanding. *Professional Psychology–Research and Practice* 30: 22-26.

Hays, R. B., S. M. Kegeles, and T. J. Coates. 1990. High HIV Risk-Taking Among Young Gay Men. *AIDS* 4: 901-07.

Heckman, T. G., J. A. Kelly, K. J. Sikkema, R. Roffman, L. J. Solomon, R. A. Winett, L. Y. Stevenson, M. J. Perry, A. D. Norman, and L. J. Desiderato. 1995. Differences in HIV Risk Characteristics Between Bisexual and Exclusively Gay Men. *AIDS Education and Prevention* 7: 504.

Herdt, G. H. 1984. A Comment on Cultural Attributes and Fluidity of Bisexuality. *Journal of Homosexuality* 10: 53-62.

Herdt, G., and A. Boxer. 1993. *Children of Horizons: How Gay and Lesbian Teens Are Leading a New Way Out of the Closet.* Boston: Beacon Press.

Hutchins, L. 1996. Bisexuality: Politics and Community. In *Bisexuality: The Psychology and Politics of an Invisible Minority,* ed. B. A. Firestein, 240-59. Thousand Oaks, CA: Sage Publications.

Istvan, J. 1983. Effects of Sexual Orientation on Interpersonal Judgement. *Journal of Sex Research* 19: 173-91.

Kahn, J., J. Gurvey, L. Pollack, D. Binson, and J. Catania. 1997. How Many HIV Infections Cross the Bisexual Bridge? An Estimate from the United States. *AIDS* 11: 1031-37.

Kalichman, S. C., and D. Rompa. 1995. Sexual Sensation Seeking and Sexual Compulsivity Scales: Reliability, Validity, and Predicting HIV Risk Behavior. *Journal of Personality Assessment* 65: 586-601.

Kalichman, S., R. A. Roffman, J. F. Picciano, and M. Bolan. 1998. Risk for HIV Infection Among Bisexual Men Seeking HIV-Prevention Services and Risks Posed to Their Female Partners. *Health Psychology* 17: 320-27.

Kelly, J. A., and S. C. Kalichman. 1998. Reinforcement Value of Unsafe Sex as a Predictor of Condom Use and Continued HIV/AIDS Risk Behavior Among Gay and Bisexual Men. *Health Psychology* 17: 328-35.

Kinsey, A., W. Pomeroy, and C. Martin. 1948. *Sexual Behavior in the Human Male.* Philadelphia: W. B. Saunders.

Klein, F., B. Sepekoff, and T. J. Wolf. 1985. Sexual Orientation: A Multivariable Dynamic Process. *Journal of Homosexuality* 11: 35-49.

Laumann, E. O., J. H. Gagnon, R. T. Michael, and S. Michaels. 1994. *The Social Organization of Sexuality.* Chicago: University of Chicago Press.

Lemp, G. F., A. M. Hirozawa, D. Givertz, G. N. Nieri, L. Anderson, M. L. Lindegren, R. S. Janssen, and M. Katz. 1994. HIV Seroprevalence and Risk Behaviors Among Young Gay and Bisexual Men: The San Francisco/Berkeley Young Men's Survey. *Journal of the American Medical Association* 272: 449-54.

Lever, J., D. E. Kanouse, W. H. Rogers, S. Carson, and R. Hertz. 1992. *Behavioral Patterns and Sexual Identity of Bisexual Males*. Santa Monica, CA: Rand Corporation.

Lewis, D. K., and J. K. Watters. 1994. Sexual Behavior and Sexual Identity in Male Injection Drug Users. *Journal of Acquired Immune Deficiency Syndromes* 7: 190-98.

Lubowitz, S. 1998. *Working with Women Whose Male Partners Are Homosexually Active*. Paper presented at the XIIth International Conference on AIDS, Geneva, Switzerland.

Martin, A. D., and E. S. Hetrick. 1988. The Stigmatization of the Gay and Lesbian Adolescent. *Journal of Homosexuality* 17: 163-83.

McKirnan, D., J. Stokes, L. Doll, and R. Burzette. 1994. Bisexually Active Men: Social Characteristics and Sexual Behavior. *Journal of Sexual Research* 32: 64-75.

McKirnan, D., P. Vanable, and J. Stokes. 1995. *HIV-Risk Sexual Behavior Among Bisexually Active Men: The Role of Gay Identification and Social Norms*. Unpublished manuscript.

Michael, R. T., J. H. Gagnon, E. Laumann, and G. Kolata. 1994. *Sex in America: A Definitive Survey*. Boston: Little, Brown and Company.

Miller, R. 1993. *GMHC Hustler Peer Education Project*. Presented at the Hustler Network Peer Education Conference, San Francisco, CA.

Morrow, G. D. 1989. Bisexuality: An Exploratory Review. *Annals of Sex Research* 2: 283-306.

Morse, E. V., P. M. Simon, P. M. Balson, and H. J. Osofsky. 1992. Sexual Behavior Patterns of Customers of Male Street Prostitutes. *Archives of Sexual Behavior* 21: 347-57.

Morse, E. V., P. M. Simon, H. J. Osofsky, P. M. Balson, and H. R. Gaumier. 1991. The Male Street Prostitute: A Vector for Transmission of HIV Infection into the Heterosexual World. *Social Science and Medicine* 32: 535-39.

Myers, T., and D. Allman. 1996. Bisexuality and HIV/AIDS in Canada. In *Bisexualities and AIDS: International Perspectives*, ed. P. Aggleton, 23-43. Bristol, PA: Taylor and Francis Inc.

Myrick, R. 1999. In the Life: Culture-Specific HIV Communication Programs Designed for African American Men Who Have Sex with Men. *Journal of Sex Research* 36: 159-70.

Nichols, M. 1988. Bisexuality in Women: Myths, Realities, and Implications for Therapy. *Women and Therapy* 7: 235-52.

Ochs, R. 1996. Biphobia: It Goes More than Two Ways. In *Bisexuality: The Psychology and Politics of an Invisible Minority*, ed. B. A. Firestein, 217-39. Thousand Oaks, CA: Sage Publications.

Padian, N., L. Marquis, D. Francis, R. E. Anderson, G. W. Rutherford, P. M. O'Malley, and W. Winkelstein. 1987. Male-to-Female Transmission of Human Immuno-deficiency Virus. *Journal of the American Medical Association* 258: 788-90.

Paul, J. P. 1984. The Bisexual Identity: An Idea without Social Recognition. *Journal of Homosexuality* 9: 45-63.

_____. 1996. Bisexuality: Exploring/Exploding the Boundaries. In *The Lives of Lesbians, Gays, and Bisexuals*: *Children to Adults*, eds. R. C. Savin-Williams and K. M. Cohen. Fort Worth, TX: Harcourt Brace and Company. .

Pennbridge, J. N., T. E. Freese, and R. G. MacKenzie. 1992. High-Risk Behaviors Among Male Street Youth in Hollywood, California. *AIDS Education and Prevention* (Suppl): 24-33.

Peterson, J. L. 1992. Black Men and Their Same-Sex Desires and Behaviors. In *Gay Culture in America*: *Essays from the Field*, ed. G. Herdt, 147-64. Boston: Beacon Press.

Pleak, R. R., and H. Meyer-Bahlburg. 1990. Sexual Behavior and AIDS Knowledge in Young Male Prostitutes in Manhattan. *Journal of Sex Research* 27: 557-87.

Reinisch, J. M., M. Z. Ziemba-Davis, and S. A. Sanders. 1990. Sexual Behavior and AIDS: Lessons from Art and Sex Research. In *AIDS and Sex*, eds. B. Valor, J. M. Reinisch, and M. Gottlieb, 37-80. New York: Oxford University Press.

Remafedi, G. 1987. Adolescent Homosexuality: Psychosocial and Medical Implications. *Pediatrics* 79: 331-37.

Roesler, T., and R. W. Deisher. 1992. Youthful Male Homosexuality. *Journal of the American Medical Association* 219: 1018-23.

Roffman, R. A., M. R. Gillmore, L. D. Gilchrist, S. A. Mathias, S. Krueger, and S. Leigha. 1990. Continuing Unsafe Sex: Assessing the Need for AIDS Prevention Counseling. *Public Health Reports* 105: 202-08.

Roffman, R. A., J. F. Picciano, M. Bolan, and S. C. Kalichman. In press. Factors Associated with Attrition from an HIV-Prevention Program for Gay and Bisexual Males. *AIDS and Behavior.*

Roffman, R. A., J. F. Picciano, R. Ryan, B. Beadnell, D. Fisher, L. Downey, and S. C. Kalichman. In press. HIV Prevention Group Counseling Delivered by Telephone: An Efficacy Trial with Gay and Bisexual Men. *AIDS and Behavior.*

Roffman, R. A., J. Picciano, L. Wickizer, M. Bolan, and R. Ryan. In press. Anonymous Enrollment in AIDS Prevention Telephone Group Counseling: Facilitating the Participation of Gay and Bisexual Men in Intervention and Research. *Journal of Social Science Research.*

Rogers, S. M., and C. F. Turner. 1991. Male-Male Sexual Contact in the U.S.A.: Findings from Five Samples, 1970-1990. *Journal of Sexual Research* 28: 491-519.

Rosario, M., J. Hunter, and M. Gwadz. 1995. *Sexual, Alcohol, and Drug Risk Acts of Lesbian/Bisexual Female Youths*. Paper presented at the HIV Infection in Women Conference, Washington, DC.

Ross, M. W. 1991. A Taxonomy of Global Behavior. In *Bisexuality and HIV/AIDS*: *A Global Perspective*, eds. R. A. P. Tielman, M. Carballo, and A. C. Hendriks, 21-26. Buffalo, NY: Prometheus Books.

Rotheram-Borus, M. J., W. D. Marelich, and S. Srinivasan. 1999. HIV Risk Among

Homosexual, Bisexual, and Heterosexual Male and Female Youths. *Archives of Sexual Behavior* 28: 159-76.

Rotheram-Borus, M. J., M. Rosario, H. Reid, and C. Koopman. 1995. Predicting Patterns of Sexual Acts Among Homosexual and Bisexual Youths. *American Journal of Psychiatry* 152: 588-95.

Rubenstein, M., and C. A. Slater. 1985. A Profile of the San Francisco Bisexual Center. *Journal of Homosexuality* 11: 227-30.

Rust, P. C. 1992. The Politics of Sexual Identity: Sexual Attraction and Behavior Among Lesbian and Bisexual Women. *Social Problems* 39: 366-86.

_____. 1993. "Coming Out" in the Age of Social Constructionism: Sexual Identity Formation Among Lesbian and Bisexual Women. *Gender and Society* 7: 50-77.

Schilling, R. F., S. P. Schinke, S. E. Nichols, L. H. Zayas, S. O. Miller, and M. Orlandi. 1989. Developing Strategies for AIDS Prevention Research with Black and Hispanic Drug Users. *Public Health Reports* 104: 2-11.

Scholey, R. 1998. *Delivering HIV Prevention Information to Young Gay and Bisexual Men.* Paper presented at the XIIth International Conference on AIDS, Geneva, Switzerland.

Simon, P. M., E. V. Morse, P. M. Balgon, H. J. Osofsky, and H. R. Gaumier. 1993. Barriers to Human Immunodeficiency Virus Related Risk Reduction Among Male Street Prostitutes. *Health Education Quarterly* 20: 261-73.

Smith, T. W. 1991. Adult Sexual Behavior in 1989: Number of Partners, Frequency of Intercourse and Risk of AIDS. *Family Planning Perspective* 23: 102-07.

Stokes, J., and W. Damon. 1995. Counseling and Psychotherapy with Bisexual Men. *Directions in Clinical Psychology* 5: 1-14.

Stokes, J. P., D. J. McKirnan, and R. G. Burzette. 1993. Sexual Behavior, Condom Use, Disclosure of Sexuality, and Stability of Sexual Orientation in Bisexual Men. *Journal of Sex Research* 30: 1-10.

Stokes, J., D. McKirnan, B. Burzette, P. Vanable, and L. Doll. 1996. Female Sexual Partners of Bisexual Men: What They Don't Know Might Hurt Them. *Psychology of Women Quarterly* 20: 267-84.

Stokes, J., and J. Peterson. 1998. Homophobia, Self-Esteem, and Risk for HIV Among African American Men Who Have Sex with Men. *AIDS Education and Prevention* 10: 278-92.

Stokes, J. P., K. Taywaditep, P. Vanable, and D. J. McKirnan. 1996. Bisexual Men, Sexual Behavior, and HIV/AIDS. In *Bisexuality: The Psychology and Politics of an Invisible Minority*, ed. B. A. Firestein, 149-68. Thousand Oaks, CA: Sage Publications.

Stokes, J. P., P. A. Vanable, and D. J. McKirnan. 1996a. *Differences in Sexual Behavior Between Black and White Bisexual Men.* Paper presented at the annual meeting of the American Psychological Association, Toronto, Canada.

_____. 1996b. Ethnic Differences in Sexual Behavior, Condom Use, and Psychosocial Variables Among Black and White Men Who Have Sex with Men. *Journal of Sex Research* 33: 373-81.

_____. 1997. Comparing Gay and Bisexual Men on Sexual Behavior, Condom Use, and Psychosocial Variables Related to HIV/AIDS. *Archives of Sexual Behavior* 26: 383-97.

Stonequist, E. B. 1937. *The Marginal Man.* New York: Scribner.

Storms, M. D. 1980. Theories of Sexual Orientation. *Journal of Personality and Social Psychology* 38: 783-92.

Taywaditep, K., and J. Stokes. 1998. Male Bisexualities: A Cluster Analysis of Men with Bisexual Experience. *Journal of Psychology and Human Sexuality* 10: 15-41.

Troiden, R. 1979. Becoming Homosexual: A Model for Gay Identity Acquisition. *Psychiatry* 42: 362-73.

U.S. Conference of Mayors. 1994. *Assessing the HIV-Prevention Needs of Gay and Bisexual Men of Color.* Washington, DC: U.S. Conference of Mayors.

Wold, C., G. R. Seage III, W. R. Lenderking, K. H. Mayer, B. Cai, T. Heeren, and R. Goldstein. 1998. Unsafe Sex in Men Who Have Sex with Both Men and Women. *Acquired Immune Deficiency Syndromes and Human Retrovirology* 17: 361-67.

Wolitski, R. J. 1993. *HIV Risk Practices of Nongay-Identified and Gay-Identified Men Who Have Sex with Men.* Paper presented at the meeting of the American Public Health Association, San Francisco, CA.

Wolitski, R. J., G. Humfleet, J. Lee, and N. Corby. 1992. *HIV Risk-Related Practices of Male Homosexual, Bisexual, and Heterosexual Injection Drug Users.* Paper presented at the VIIth International Conference on AIDS, Amsterdam, Netherlands.

Wolitski, R. J., C. Rietmeijer, and G. Goldbaum. 1996. *Men's Disclosure of HIV Risk to Their Female Sex Partners.* Paper presented at the XIth International Conference on AIDS, Vancouver, Canada.

Wood, R. W., L. E. Krueger, T. C. Pearlman, and G. Goldbaum. 1993. HIV Transmission: Women's Risk from Bisexual Men. *American Journal of Public Health* 3: 1757-59.

Wright, J. W. 1993. African-American Male Sexual Behavior and the Risk for HIV Infection. *Human Organizations* 52: 421-31.

Zinik, G. 1985. Identity Conflict or Adaptive Flexibility? Bisexuality Reconsidered. *Journal of Homosexuality* 11: 7-19.

Bi-Negativity

The
Stigma
Facing
Bisexual Men

Mickey Eliason

[Haworth co-indexing entry note]: "Bi-Negativity: The Stigma Facing Bisexual Men." Eliason, Mickey. Co-published simultaneously in *Journal of Bisexuality* (Harrington Park Press, an imprint of The Haworth Press, Inc.) Vol. 1, No. 2/3, 2001, pp. 137-154; and: *Bisexuality in the Lives of Men: Facts and Fictions* (ed: Brett Beemyn and Erich Steinman) Harrington Park Press, an imprint of The Haworth Press, Inc., 2001, pp. 137-154. Single or multiple copies of this article are available for a fee from The Haworth Document Delivery Service [1-800-342-9678, 9:00 a.m. - 5:00 p.m. (EST). E-mail address: getinfo@ haworthpressinc.com].

SUMMARY. The purpose of this study was to examine the attitudes of heterosexual college students about bisexuality. Although there is considerable information about attitudes toward lesbians and gay men, much less is known about the structure and degree of attitudes about bisexual men and women. This article focuses on the results regarding bisexual men, who were rated more negatively than bisexual women, gay men, or lesbians. Some of the potential reasons for and implications of this finding are discussed. *[Article copies available for a fee from The Haworth Document Delivery Service: 1-800-342-9678. E-mail address: <getinfo@haworthpressinc.com> Website: <http://www.HaworthPress.com>]*

KEYWORDS. Attitudes, biphobia, bisexual men, bisexuality

This essay is an expanded and revised version of an article I published in 1997 which received an inordinate amount of attention. I have been writing articles on sexual identity development and lesbian and gay issues in health care for the past several years with little fuss. However, when this article was published in the *Archives of Sexual Behavior* (Eliason, 1997), I was inundated with phone calls from reporters and even talk show hosts who wanted to discuss bisexuality. Apparently, the "bisexual moment of fame" has arrived. This essay emphasizes the portion of my research study that focused on bisexual men.

Until recently, bisexual people have been a largely invisible segment of both the general population and lesbian and gay communities. In spite of work by Sigmund Freud, Alfred Kinsey, and many other researchers that conceptualizes sexuality as a continuum, and even proposes that bisexuality is the "natural state" of most human beings, many people still view sexual identity as a dichotomous variable–that is, people are either homosexual or heterosexual (Ochs, 1996). This dichotomization effectively erases all other points on the continuum, implying that heterosexuality and homosexuality are polar opposites, clearly distinguishable from one another (Kaplan, 1995; Paul, 1985; Udis-Kessler, 1990). Although the reduction of sexual identity to an either/or, "us versus them" framework helped lesbians and gay men to organize politically and socially, based on the belief that they were a cohesive minority group, the assumption of sexual sameness ignored important differences of race, class, age, religion, and other aspects of identity. It also contributed to a number of bi-negative attitudes, including the notion that bisexuality doesn't really exist.

As lesbian and gay people became more visible on college campuses, in the media, and in society at large in the 1970s, studies of "homophobia" (a term coined by psychologist George Weinberg in 1972 to describe negative attitudes about homosexuality and/or homosexual people) began to appear in the social scientific literature. The naming of homophobia was empowering, as it put the onus for negative attitudes about lesbians and gay men on the individuals holding such beliefs and removed the blame from those with the negatively perceived characteristic. This was an important first step toward ending societal prejudice and discrimination based on sexual identity, and in the past twenty years, studies of homophobia have become increasingly common. However, the concept of homophobia is not without its limitations. It can lead to too much attention being focused on individual prejudices and not enough on the societal institutions that create the climate for negative attitudes to flourish (Kitzinger, 1987). Additionally, homophobia is not a true phobia in the psychological sense of the word. A phobia is an irrational, uncontrollable fear that leads to physiological distress, whereas homophobia is often rational and intentional and fueled by anger, hostility, or hatred, rather than fear. And unlike many people with phobias, homophobes usually do not want to change (Haaga, 1991). For these reasons, I have recently decided not to use the term "homophobia" in my own writing, opting instead for "homo-negativity" or the more cumbersome, but descriptive, "negative attitudes about lesbians and gay men." In this same vein, I will use "bi-negativity" to refer to negative attitudes about bisexuals.

People who identify as bisexual have historically not been very visible in society. If they are in an other-sex relationship(s), they are perceived as heterosexual and if in a same-sex relationship(s), they are seen as lesbian or gay. Many writers have also refused to recognize bisexuality, maintaining that everyone really belongs to one of the two "legitimate" categories. Consequently, studies of homo-negativity have rarely addressed bisexuality or bi-negativity. Some researchers assume that bi-negativity, if it exists at all, is simply a variant of homo-negativity–that is, bisexuals only encounter hostility when in a same-sex relationship, just as a lesbian or gay man experiences homophobia. However, the fact that many lesbians and gay men have negative attitudes about bisexuals demonstrates that homo-negativity and bi-negativity are not identical (Rust, 1995).

There are very few published empirical studies of bisexuality or bi-negativity. Anecdotal information and personal accounts of bisexual experiences are provided in anthologies such as Thomas Geller's *Bisexuality: A Reader and Sourcebook* (1990), Loraine Hutchins and Lani Kaahumanu's *Bi Any Other Name: Bisexual People Speak Out* (1991), Elizabeth Reba Weise's *Closer to Home: Bisexuality and Feminism* (1992), Naomi Tucker's *Bisexual*

Politics: Theories, Queries, and Visions (1995), The Bisexual Anthology Collective's *Plural Desires: Writing Bisexual Women's Realities* (1995), and The Off Pink Collective's *Bisexual Horizons: Politics, Histories, Lives* (1996). These books suggest that stereotypes of bisexuals are widespread, such as the myths that bisexuals are confused about their sexuality, that they are gay or lesbian people who lack the courage to come out, that they are promiscuous and unable to commit to any one person, that they have more than one partner at a time, that they spread AIDS to heterosexuals and lesbians, and that they are obsessed with sex (anything that moves!). As important as these anthologies are, though, there is also a need for empirical research on issues related to bisexuality. Paula Rust (1993a, 1993b, 1996) is one of the few empirical researchers who takes bisexual identities seriously. However, her focus until recently has been on the attitudes of lesbians toward bisexual women and how bisexual women achieve a sense of identity. Although her studies add critical information to the literature on sexual identity formation and change, they do not consider the attitudes of gay men or heterosexuals toward bisexuals, nor do they provide information about specific attitudes about bisexual men.

Although bisexuality was not the original focus, some of my earlier work suggested that bi-negativity might be a serious problem among non-bisexuals. For example, in one study (Eliason, 1996), I found that 1,130 heterosexual respondents to a campus climate survey felt that bisexuals were less socially acceptable than lesbians or gay men. Thirty percent of the heterosexual sample rated bisexuals as "somewhat" or "very unacceptable," compared to 22% who rated lesbians as "unacceptable" and 23% who rated gay men as "unacceptable." Of the 58 lesbian and gay respondents to the survey, 5% considered bisexuals to be "unacceptable."

In another study, Salome Raheim and I found that heterosexual nursing students, 94% of whom were female, reported that they often felt uncomfortable around people who had different sexual identities than themselves (Eliason & Raheim, 1998). They were equally uncomfortable around bisexuals (43%) and lesbians (44%), but somewhat less uncomfortable around gay men (35%). One could speculate that gay men were the only group that were not perceived as a potential sexual threat. However, the reasons that the students gave for their discomfort were similar for gay men, lesbians, and bisexuals: lack of exposure to people in these categories, lack of knowledge about sexual orientation and identities, disapproval of same-sex relationships, and feeling personally endangered. One student made a comment specific to bisexuality: "I feel they are the people who spread AIDS. I think they should be either heterosexual or homosexual."

Neither of the above studies considered male and female bisexuals separately. Therefore, I decided to design a study that would collect more detailed information about heterosexual students' attitudes toward bisexuality. Empirical research certainly has its limitations, but it can also greatly increase our understanding of the concept of bi-negativity. Most of the previous writing on bi-negativity consists of bisexuals' personal accounts of discrimination. As useful as these narratives are, they are necessarily one-sided perceptions and can only describe the experiences of that individual. These narratives also focus primarily on bisexual women's experiences, especially with lesbians, and provide little information about bisexual men. I decided to survey the attitudes of heterosexual college students to begin to explore how pervasive bi-negativity might be. Paper and pencil surveys are easier and more convenient than face-to-face interviews and also allow the respondent to be anonymous, which increases the possibility of honest responding on sensitive topics. College students may not be representative of the population as a whole, because white middle- and upper-class individuals have more opportunities to attend college. However, they do represent a group of people who may sway public opinion in the future.

In this essay, I will compare the results of my findings about bi-negativity to studies of homo-negativity to determine whether the same demographic variables are related to both, and to determine the degree of overlap between bi-negativity and homo-negativity. There have been several empirical research studies of the predictors or correlates of homo-negativity. I summarized these in a recent article (Eliason, 1995), and found that the most frequently identified correlates include:

- gender (men are usually more negative than women)
- gender role ideology (people with traditional views of gender, who believe that women and men have very separate roles in society, are more negative about homosexuality than people with more open views)
- personality traits (a few studies have found that people with rigid, authoritarian, or dogmatic views are more negative about homosexuality)
- religion (members of fundamentalist and conservative religions are more likely to be homo-negative than members of progressive religions or people with no religious affiliation)
- geographic region (people from the south and midwest tend to have more negative attitudes than people from either coast, and rural residents tend to be more negative than urban residents)

- age (adolescent and young adult males are the most likely to be homo-negative, and elders tend to be more negative than middle-aged adults)
- education (people with lower levels of formal education tend to be more homo-negative than people with a higher education)
- familiarity with a gay or lesbian person (although one recent Harris poll found no relationship between knowing a person who is gay/lesbian and negative attitudes, several other studies have found such a relationship)

All of these studies are somewhat suspect, because the measurement of homo-negativity is nearly as varied and unscientific as the meaning of the term homophobia. Survey instruments often mix affective statements (such as expressions of disgust, revulsion, and fear) with cognitive statements (such as attitudes about workplace discrimination and civil rights), thereby measuring two very different things. Most of the attitude scales also rely on a single score to determine whether or not someone is homophobic, thus erasing differences between individual respondents and making meaningful comparisons between studies extremely difficult. Some surveys even use stereotypical language that might perpetuate homo-negativity.

At the time of my study, there were no published questionnaires about attitudes toward bisexual people. If bi-negativity is the same as homo-negativity, one would expect that the same variables would predict bi-negativity. That is, a young male with a low level of education from the rural midwest who belongs to a fundamentalist religion and does not know any gay, lesbian, or bisexual people would likely express comparable levels of bi-negativity and homo-negativity. There should not be a significant difference in ratings of bisexual and gay men. The next two sections will describe how I went about studying this question.

SAMPLE

Students enrolled in two undergraduate courses in psychology at a large midwestern university served as the participant pool. These courses are general education requirement electives, thus students from a wide variety of majors were enrolled. Participation in the study was voluntary and the surveys were anonymous and completed outside of class. Out of a potential pool of 320 students, 255 completed surveys. Twenty-six of these were not included in the data analysis because the respondents indicated that they were lesbian, gay, bisexual, or uncertain of their sexuality. Thus the final sample consisted of 229 self-identified heterosexual students, 170 of whom were female and 59 male (none indicated that they were transgendered). Women students predominate because the courses surveyed–classes on growth and development–attract substantially more women than men.

INSTRUMENT

The author-designed survey contained questions about demographic variables, such as age, gender, race, sexual identity, and religion; attitudes about and experiences with people who identify as bisexual; attitudes about and experiences with people who identify as gay or lesbian; the Beliefs about Sexual Minorities Scale (BSM; Eliason & Raheim, 1996); and a set of 23 statements describing common stereotypes about bisexuality that the students were asked to agree or disagree with. These statements were worded both positively and negatively to discourage respondents from answering in a particular way and not really reading the items. The statements were based on a review of the literature on bisexual stereotypes and subsequent feedback from a person who is a bisexual political activist and academic. The final revised instrument took about 15 minutes to complete.

The Beliefs about Sexual Minorities Scale provided respondents with six statements depicting a range of attitudes about sexual minorities, and asked them to check the one that most closely resembled their own current beliefs. For this study, four different versions of the BSM were used in order to collect information about beliefs toward lesbians, gay men, bisexual women, and bisexual men. The statements were as follows for each sexual identity group:

- celebration: I believe that lesbians, gay men, bisexual women, or bisexual men (L/G/BW/BM) contribute in a positive and unique way to society.
- acceptance: L/G/BW/BM people deserve equal protection and the same rights as heterosexual people.
- tolerance: L/G/BW/BM people have a right to exist, but should keep their sexuality private and hidden.
- disapproval: L/G/BW/BM lifestyles go against my religious or moral beliefs.
- disgust: L/G/BW/BM people are disgusting and should not be given any rights.
- hatred: I despise L/G/BW/BM people and believe their lifestyles should be punished.

Raheim and I have used this scale in several studies and found it to be a useful and reliable measure of the range of people's attitudes. Although the scale is ordered from the most positive to the most negative, it is not strictly linear because the items represent qualitatively different types of attitudes that may have vastly different underlying reasons. For example, the person who disapproves of bisexuality on the grounds of religious beliefs may have quite different motivations from the person who feels disgust about homosexual sexual practices or who hates bisexuals because of unacknowledged sexual issues of his/her own.

THE RESULTS OF THE STUDY

The respondents ranged in age from 18 to 34, with a mean age of 20.6. Not surprisingly, 60% of the sample fell into the 18- to 20-year-old age bracket, which is typical for lower-level undergraduate courses at this university. Over 95% were European American, and only a few already had an undergraduate degree (2%). Eighty-five students (37%) indicated that they belonged to a fundamentalist religion, which was much higher than I expected, given that the school does not have a strong religious character.

Few of the respondents knew anyone who had come out to them as bisexual: 76% of the sample said that they did not have any bisexual friends and 64% had no bisexual acquaintances. Most indicated that they had little (59%) or no (14%) knowledge about bisexuality. When asked how acceptable bisexuality was to them personally, they rated bisexual men as much less acceptable than bisexual women. The list below shows the percent of students who rated each group as "very unacceptable":

- Bisexual men: 26%
- Gay men: 21%
- Lesbians: 14%
- Bisexual women: 12%

Conversely, more students rated lesbians and gay men as "very acceptable" (22% for both groups), than bisexual women (14%) or bisexual men (12%). The responses to the BSM revealed a very similar picture: while very few respondents checked "celebration" for any of the sexual identity groups (only 6-7%), a larger segment of the sample marked "acceptance" for lesbians and gay men (53%) than for bisexual women and men (46% for both).

Likewise, "disapproval" on the basis of moral or religious grounds was greatest for bisexual men (21%), followed by bisexual women (18%), gay men (15%), and lesbians (14%). This is rather puzzling, since, to my knowledge, neither fundamentalist biblical interpretations, nor the rhetoric of the Religious Right, makes much of a distinction between lesbians, gay men, bisexual women, and bisexual men. The categories of disgust and hatred were rarely endorsed, thankfully, but here again, the most hostility was directed against bisexual men (2.5% versus less than 1% for the other groups).

When asked how likely it was that they would have a sexual relationship with a bisexual partner, 3.5% (five men and three women) indicated that they had already done so. Other students considered the possibility of such a relationship to be "very unlikely" (52%) or "somewhat unlikely" (25%). Only 9% thought it was "very likely" that they would choose a relationship with a bisexual partner.

Table 1 lists the stereotypical statements about bisexuality provided on the questionnaire and shows the students' responses. The lack of knowledge about bisexuality was evident in the high rates of "don't know" answers, ranging from 9-57%, depending on the item. For many of the stereotypes, the students were equally divided. For example, 27% agreed and 27% disagreed that bisexuals have more sexual partners than heterosexuals, and 31% agreed and 33% disagreed that bisexuals spread AIDS to heterosexuals (the rest didn't know). Some of the stereotypes garnered more support. For example, a majority of respondents believed that "bisexuals have more flexible attitudes about sex than heterosexuals," and didn't feel that "bisexuals are just gay and lesbian people who are afraid to admit they are gay." At the same time, a majority didn't think that "bisexuals are more psychologically well-adjusted" than heterosexuals or gays/lesbians, and felt that "bisexual rights are the same as gay and lesbian rights." The bottom line seems to be that heterosexual students do not have clear-cut beliefs about bisexuals.

GENDER DIFFERENCES IN RESPONDING

In many studies, heterosexual men have been found to be more homo-negative than heterosexual women, so I divided the sample by gender to determine if the men and women would have different levels of bi-negativity. Even though the men in the survey were slightly older than the women (means of 21.4 and 20.3 years, respectively), this factor did not seem to lead

TABLE 1. Percent of the sample who agreed, disagreed, or did not know about stereotypical statements about bisexual people.

Statement	Agree	Disagree	D.K.
Bisexuals tend to have more sexual partners than heterosexuals	27%	27%	46%
Bisexuals tend to have more sexual partners than gays or lesbians	20%	23%	57%
Bisexuals have more flexible attitudes about sex than heterosexuals	76%	7%	17%
People are probably born bisexual	26%	38%	36%
Bisexuals are more likely to have more than one sexual partner at a time than heterosexuals	39%	33%	28%
Bisexuals are more likely to have more than one sexual partner at a time than gays/lesbians	27%	33%	41%
Bisexuals are more psychologically well-adjusted than heterosexuals	3%	63%	34%
Bisexuals are more psychologically well-adjusted than gays/lesbians	4%	52%	44%
Bisexuals are more confused about their sexuality than heterosexuals	39%	35%	25%
Bisexuals are more confused about their sexuality than gays/lesbians	30%	38%	32%
Bisexuals are just gay and lesbian people who are afraid to admit they are gay	7%	69%	23%
Gender of sexual partners should not be an issue–we should all select partners based on personality or other human qualities	36%	54%	9%

TABLE 1 (continued)

Statement	Agree	Disagree	D.K.
A bisexual person is likely to leave you for someone of the other sex	15%	29%	56%
Bisexual rights are the same as gay and lesbian rights	55%	8%	36%
Bisexuals need to have political organizations separate from gay and lesbian groups	24%	24%	52%
Bisexuals are more accepted in society than gays/lesbians	32%	45%	23%
Bisexuals are less accepted in society than gays/lesbians	21%	48%	31%
Bisexuals have more privilege in society than gays/lesbians	19%	44%	38%
Bisexuals spread AIDS to the lesbian community	24%	34%	42%
Bisexuals spread AIDS to heterosexuals	31%	33%	36%
Bisexuals are just going through a phase or experimenting with sex	12%	45%	43%
Bisexuals have the best of both worlds	12%	50%	38%

them to have more positive attitudes, as might normally be expected. The heterosexual men showed a greater tendency to believe in a number of stereotypes about bisexuality: that bisexuals have more sexual partners than heterosexuals and gays/lesbians, are more likely to have more than one sexual partner at a time than heterosexuals, are really gays/lesbians who are afraid to admit that they are gay, spread AIDS to lesbians and heterosexuals, and are more accepted in society than gays/lesbians.

There was no difference between heterosexual women and men on the mean number of bisexual, gay, or lesbian friends and acquaintances, but men were more likely to report that they would have a sexual relationship with a bisexual woman. While seemingly a positive attitude, for a number of the men, this willingness to be sexually involved with a bisexual woman probably stems from the stereotype that bisexual women need or want to be involved with a man and a woman at the same time, thereby enabling the man to have sex with two female partners. The questionnaire did not specifically ask for explanations, but three men wrote comments to the effect that a female bisexual partner would allow them to experience a threesome.[1] The different attitudes toward bisexual men and women were also apparent on the BSM. Heterosexual men gave more negative ratings to gay men, lesbians, and bisexual men than did heterosexual women, but there was no statistical difference between the men's and women's ratings of the acceptability of bisexual women. Thus the heterosexual men's bi-negativity appears to be directed largely at bisexual men, just as their homo-negativity is directed more at gay men.

Several factors help to explain why heterosexual men may be more hostile toward gay and bisexual men than heterosexual women are toward lesbians and bisexual women. Men may have less experience with, and thus a greater concern about, being "hit on" by another man, whereas women are often relatively experienced at turning down unwanted advances from men, and as a result, have developed effective strategies that give them confidence in their ability to deal with an unwanted advance from a woman. Men also may perceive sexual advances by other men as a threat to their masculinity, where-as women may consider sexual advances by other women as "flattering." That men are often intimidated by sexual advances from other men was recently highlighted by the widely publicized murders of Matthew Shepard and Billy Jo Gaither, both of whom were killed by heterosexual men who subsequently argued that they felt threatened by the murder victims' homo-sexuality. This "homosexual panic" defense has been used by many lawyers to obtain lesser sentences for gay bashers, whose crimes are minimized because the gay or bisexual man supposedly "asked for it."

Some heterosexual men also stigmatize gay and bisexual men because of their perceived relationship to HIV/AIDS. That is, they assume that all gay and bisexual men are HIV-positive because they believe that same-sex sexual activity (anal sex, specifically) causes AIDS. Bisexual men may actually be even more threatening than gay men to many heterosexual men because bisexuals are not readily marked as non-heterosexual. Stereotypes about gay men include a number of physical indicators: "effeminate" gestures, limp wrists, a lisp, lack of athletic ability, and so on. But there are no similar bi male stereotypes, and thus, in the general perception of heterosexual men, bisexual men represent a hidden danger and a direct challenge to the creation of a clear, "us-them" sexual division.

FACTORS ASSOCIATED WITH NEGATIVE ATTITUDES ABOUT BISEXUAL MEN AND WOMEN

I used a type of statistical analysis called a multiple regression analysis that identifies the potential contributing factors to a particular attitude or behavior. Contributors to negative attitudes about bisexual women included a lack of bisexual friends and acquaintances, younger age, and belonging to a conservative religion. The factors that correlated with negative attitudes about bisexual men were the same, but also included male gender. Homo-negativity was strongly related to bi-negativity, and in fact, was the strongest relationship–a respondent who was homo-negative was almost always bi-negative as well. This was true for all the women in the sample, but there was a small subset of men who expressed little animosity toward lesbians, gay men, and bisexual women, but who were very hostile toward bisexual men. Some authors have argued that many homo-negative people are prone to "generalized prejudice," suggesting that they have a personality style or particularly rigid belief system that leads them to reject or fear people who differ from them in any way, such as by race, gender, class, or sexuality (Bierly, 1985; Eliason, 1998; Ficarrotto, 1990). This hypothesis was not tested in this survey, but if homo-negativity and bi-negativity typically go hand-in-hand (as my study suggests), it offers support for the theory.

CONCLUSIONS

As a group, heterosexual students were quite divided on their attitudes about the acceptability of bisexual women. Overall, 50% rated bisexual women as "acceptable" and 50% rated them as "unacceptable." Attitudes about bisexual men were more negative, with 61% considering them "unacceptable." This finding was more pronounced when the sample was divided by gender–many heterosexual men rated bisexual men as "very unacceptable," but were more tolerant or even accepting of bisexual women. Heterosexual men also tended to disapprove more of gay men than of lesbians.

Why are negative attitudes about another person's private, consensual sexual behavior so prevalent? One reason is that these stereotypical beliefs generally have benefits for the holder, such as a sense of moral superiority, the ability to fit into a peer group, a defense against one's own unacknowledged sexual desires and/or anxieties, and the reduction of uncertainty by reinforcing an "us-them" paradigm. In addition, homo-negativity and bi-negativity serve to maintain the patriarchal status quo, keeping heterosexual men in positions of perceived power. This heterosexual privilege makes such negative attitudes very resistant to change. Visibility itself is not sufficient, as the history of different civil rights movements has taught us. Nor is mere education and increased awareness adequate to eliminate negative attitudes. The very structures of society, especially the ways in which men are socialized and taught gender roles, must be changed to eliminate bi-negativity.

Predictors of homo-negativity vary widely, depending on the sampling and statistical methods used, but several consistent findings appear in research on the subject (Eliason, 1995). Factors such as being male (D'Augelli & Rose, 1990), being an adolescent or young adult (Marsiglio, 1993), holding traditional gender role beliefs (Herek, 1988), regularly attending a Christian church (Seltzer, 1992), and having little or no contact with lesbians and gay men (Herek & Glunt, 1993) often predict the degree of homo-negativity. The results of my study suggest that many of the same variables may help to explain bi-negativity, supporting the link between masculine gender socialization and negative attitudes about sexual minorities.

Since my study was published, there has been another quantitative study of attitudes about bisexuality. Jonathan Mohr and Aaron Rochlen (1999) gave an 18-item scale about bisexuality to nearly 600 heterosexual college students and found, as in my study, that heterosexual men rated bisexual men much more negatively than they rated bisexual women. They also found that race, religious attendance, and political ideology were associated with attitudes about bisexuality. Specifically, African Americans (especially men), those who attended church more often, and those with conservative political views had more negative attitudes about bisexuality. On the other hand, Leah Spalding and Letitia Anne Peplau (1997) asked heterosexual students to rate stories about dating couples on a variety of dimensions and found no differences in attitudes toward bisexual men and bisexual women–both were seen as less likely to be monogamous, more likely to give a sexually transmitted disease to a partner, and less able to satisfy a partner sexually than gays or lesbians (but more able to satisfy a partner sexually than heterosexuals).

The fact that the same variables are related to bi-negativity to nearly the same degree as to homo-negativity shows that the two stem from the same root oppression of heterosexism. However, there are some differences in the underlying stereotypes that drive bi-negativity and homo-negativity. Bisexuals are considered to have more flexible attitudes about sex, and they are not thought to be "born that way," as many respondents claim about lesbians and gay men. Some of the stereotypical statements used in this study were derived from the experiences of bisexual women in lesbian communities or in gay/lesbian political organizations and are particular to those settings. Heterosexual people may not make such clear distinctions between lesbians, gay men, bisexual men, and bisexual women as gays and lesbians do. As the writing of many bisexual women indicates, they typically face more significant prejudice from lesbians than from heterosexuals (see, for example, The Bisexual Anthology Collective, 1995; Hutchins & Kaahumanu, 1991; Weise, 1992). This prejudice may not be greater in degree, but it has greater personal consequences for bisexual women who attempt to have sexual and social relationships within lesbian communities. Bisexual men may find greater acceptance in lesbian and gay social and political organizations, which are not driven by the separatism of some lesbian feminist groups, where "male energy" and "heterosexual privilege" are frequently issues.

This study has a number of significant limitations that are evident from the results. First, I assumed that students would be familiar with and have a similar definition of bisexuality. However, the widespread lack of knowledge about bisexuality that was demonstrated by the high number of "don't know" responses seems to suggest otherwise. This fact should not be surprising, though, because even people who self-identify as bisexual do not agree on a common definition. It is also not clear if respondents were considering sexual behavior, sexual fantasy, or only self-identification when they read the stereotypical statements related to bisexuality (for a discussion of the different meanings of bisexual, see Fox, 1996). Secondly, I gave the students a list of preconceived stereotypes based on a reading of the literature and my experiences in lesbian, gay, and bisexual communities. I did not ask them to generate their own stereotypes, and as a result, I may be overlooking other important stereotypes that might be prevalent among heterosexual students. Finally, as I noted earlier, college undergraduates may not be typical of the general population, and therefore the findings of the study cannot be generalized beyond this particular group, which was predominantly white and midwestern.

In conclusion, the heterosexual students in this sample showed a relatively high degree of bi-negativity, especially directed at bisexual men. These negative attitudes may stem from many factors, such as a lack of accurate information about sexuality and sexual identities, especially bisexuality; the sexual taboos that permeate U.S. society; a misguided fear of AIDS; and a process of masculine gender role socialization that does not permit sexual (or even emotional) expression between men. Gender role socialization is difficult to change, and will involve a long process; nevertheless, the lack of knowledge demonstrates the necessity of providing accurate information about bisexuality (and all other forms of sexuality), whether in an educational setting or simply in our daily encounters.

NOTE

1. Another factor here is that heterosexual men often do not take female-female eroticism seriously, believing that two women cannot have "real" sex without a penis present. For example, pornography marketed to heterosexual men regularly depicts two or more women in sexual activities as a prelude to heterosexual sex or for male erotic pleasure, whereas male-male eroticism is almost never shown.

REFERENCES

Bierly, Margaret M. 1985. Prejudice Toward Contemporary Outgroups as a Generalized Attitude. *Journal of Applied Social Psychology* 15: 189-99.

Bisexual Anthology Collective (Nancy Acharya et al.), eds. 1995. *Plural Desires*: *Writing Bisexual Women's Realities*. Toronto: Sister Vision: Black Women and Women of Colour Press.

D'Augelli, Anthony R., and Melissa L. Rose. 1990. Homophobia in a University Community: Attitudes and Experiences of Heterosexual Freshmen. *Journal of College Student Development* 31: 484-91.

Eliason, Michele J. 1995. Attitudes about Lesbians and Gay Men: A Review and Implications for Social Service Training. *Journal of Gay and Lesbian Social Services* 2: 73-90.

_____. 1996. The Campus Climate for Lesbian, Gay, and Bisexual University Members. *Journal of Psychology and Human Sexuality* 8: 39-58.

_____. 1997. Prevalence and Nature of Biphobia in Heterosexual Undergraduate Students. *Archives of Sexual Behavior* 26: 317-26.

Eliason, Michele J., and Salome Raheim. 1996. Categorical Measurement of Attitudes about Lesbian, Gay, and Bisexual People. *Journal of Gay and Lesbian Social Services* 4: 51-65.

_____. 2000. Experiences and Comfort with Culturally Diverse Groups in Undergraduate Nursing Students. *Journal of Nursing Education*.

Ficarrotto, Thomas J. 1990. Racism, Sexism, and Erotophobia: Attitudes of Heterosexuals Toward Homosexuals. *Journal of Homosexuality* 19: 111-16.

Fox, Ronald C. 1996. Bisexuality in Perspective: A Review of Theory and Research. In *Bisexuality*: *The Psychology and Politics of an Invisible Minority*, ed. Beth A. Firestein, 3-50. Thousand Oaks, CA: Sage Publications.

Geller, Thomas, ed. 1990. *Bisexuality*: *A Reader and Sourcebook*. Ojai, CA: Times Change Press.

Haaga, David A. 1991. Homophobia? *Journal of Social Behavior and Personality* 6: 171-74.

Herek, Gregory M. 1988. Heterosexuals' Attitudes about Lesbians and Gay Men: Correlates and Gender Differences. *Journal of Sex Research* 25: 451-77.

Herek, Gregory M., and Eric K. Glunt. 1993. Interpersonal Contact and Heterosexuals' Attitudes Toward Gay Men: Results from a National Survey. *Journal of Sex Research* 30: 239-344.

Hutchins, Loraine, and Lani Kaahumanu, eds. 1991. *Bi Any Other Name*: *Bisexual People Speak Out*. Boston: Alyson.

Kaplan, Rebecca. 1995. Your Fence Is Sitting on Me: The Hazards of Binary Think-ing. In *Bisexual Politics: Theories, Queries, and Visions*, ed. Naomi Tucker, 267-79. Binghamton, NY: Harrington Park Press.

Kitzinger, Celia. 1987. *The Social Construction of Lesbianism*. London: Sage Publi-cations.

Marsiglio, William. 1993. Attitudes Toward Homosexual Activity and Gays as Friends: A National Survey of Heterosexual 15-to 19-Year-Old Males. *Journal of Sex Research* 30: 12-17.

Mohr, Jonathan J., and Aaron B. Rochlen. 1999. Measuring Attitudes Regarding Bisexuality in Lesbian, Gay Male, and Heterosexual Populations. *Journal of Counseling Psychology* 46: 353-69.

Ochs, Robyn. 1996. Biphobia: It Goes More than Two Ways. In *Bisexuality: The Psychology and Politics of an Invisible Minority*, ed. Beth A. Firestein, 217-39. Thousand Oaks, CA: Sage Publications.

Off Pink Collective (Sharon Rose, Cris Stevens et al.), eds. 1996. *Bisexual Horizons: Politics, Histories, Lives*. London: Lawrence and Wishart.

Paul, Jay P. 1985. Bisexuality: Reassessing Our Paradigms of Sexuality. *Journal of Homosexuality* 11: 21-34.

Rust, Paula. 1993a. Neutralizing the Political Threat of the Marginal Woman: Les-bians' Beliefs about Bisexual Women. *Journal of Sex Research* 30: 214-28.

_____. 1993b. "Coming Out" in the Age of Social Constructionism: Sexual Identi-ty Formation Among Lesbian and Bisexual Women. *Gender and Society* 7: 50-77.

_____. 1995. *Bisexuality and the Challenge to Lesbian Politics: Sex, Loyalty, and Revolution*. New York: New York University Press.

_____. 1996. Sexual Identity and Bisexual Identities: The Struggle for Self-De-scription in a Changing Sexual Landscape. In *Queer Studies: A Lesbian, Gay, Bisexual, and Transgender Anthology*, eds. Brett Beemyn and Mickey Eliason, 64-86. New York: New York University Press.

Seltzer, Richard. 1992. The Social Location of Those Holding Antihomosexual Atti-tudes. *Sex Roles* 26: 391-98.

Spalding, Leah R., and Letitia Anne Peplau. 1997. The Unfaithful Lover: Heterosex-uals' Perceptions of Bisexuals and Their Relationships. *Psychology of Women Quarterly* 21: 611-25.

Tucker, Naomi, ed. 1995. *Bisexual Politics: Theories, Queries, and Visions*. Bing-hamton, NY: Harrington Park Press.

Udis-Kessler, Amanda. 1990. Bisexuality in an Essentialist World: Toward an Under-standing of Biphobia. In *Bisexuality: A Reader and Sourcebook*, ed. Thomas Geller, 51-63. Ojai, CA: Times Change Press.

Weise, Elizabeth Reba, ed. 1992. *Closer to Home: Bisexuality and Feminism*. Seattle: Seal.

Writing Our Own Script

How Bisexual Men and Their Heterosexual Wives Maintain Their Marriages After Disclosure

Amity Pierce Buxton

[Haworth co-indexing entry note]: "Writing Our Own Script: How Bisexual Men and Their Heterosexual Wives Maintain Their Marriages After Disclosure." Buxton, Amity Pierce. Co-published simultaneously in *Journal of Bisexuality* (Harrington Park Press, an imprint of The Haworth Press, Inc.) Vol. 1, No. 2/3, 2001, pp. 155-189; and: *Bisexuality in the Lives of Men: Facts and Fictions* (ed: Brett Beemyn and Erich Steinman) Harrington Park Press, an imprint of The Haworth Press, Inc., 2001, pp. 155-189. Single or multiple copies of this article are available for a fee from The Haworth Document Delivery Service [1-800-342-9678, 9:00 a.m. - 5:00 p.m. (EST). E-mail address: getinfo@haworthpressinc.com].

SUMMARY. By conservative estimates, at least two million men and women who are or were married come out as gay, lesbian, or bisexual. Once they disclose to their heterosexual spouses, divorce results in the majority of cases. Little is known about the number of marriages that endure or how many of the disclosing spouses are bisexual, given the invisibility of such marriages, the mislabeling of bisexuals as gay or lesbian, and the reluctance of spouses to identify themselves as gay, lesbian, or bisexual. This article reports on the experiences of 56 self-identified bisexual husbands and 51 heterosexual wives of bisexual men who maintained their marriage after disclosure. Their responses to a survey questionnaire are compared with those of 32 self-identified gay married men and 28 heterosexual wives of gay men. The convenience samples, largely from the United States, came from Internet mailing lists, support groups, and members of the Straight Spouse Network. Strategies that they found most helpful in maintaining their marriages are analyzed alongside circumstances in their lives that supported their staying married and those that worked against them. Helpful for the largest numbers of all spouse samples were honesty, communication, peer support, therapy, and taking time. The bisexual men and heterosexual wives of bisexual men also relied on the husbands' empathy and the wives' flexibility.

The findings demonstrate the importance of the couple's working together to maintain a satisfying post-disclosure marriage. The relationship of the bisexual husbands and heterosexual wives of bisexual men with their respective spouses was marked by a multileveled interaction that included mutual sexual pleasure, as well as cognitive, verbal, behavioral, and emotional engagement. Their joint effort over time enabled them to deconstruct not only traditional concepts of marriage, but also dichotomous views of sexual orientation. *[Article copies available for a fee from The Haworth Document Delivery Service: 1-800-342-9678. E-mail address: <getinfo@haworthpressinc.com> Website: <http://www.HaworthPress. com>]*

KEYWORDS. Bisexual husbands, bisexuality, heterosexual wives of bisexual/gay men, mixed-orientation marriages

When the opposites are realized to be one, discord melts into concord, battles become dances, and old enemies become lovers. We are then in a position to make friends with all of our universe, and not just one half of it.

–Ken Wilber, *No Boundary*

What happens to a marriage when a spouse discloses his or her bisexuality? What are the odds that the couple stays married? Are bisexual-heterosexual couples a special case, compared with gay-heterosexual couples? Given an apparent increase in the number of spouses who are coming out nationwide, these questions can no longer be ignored by therapists, social scientists, or other researchers. Because the literature to date suggests that the majority of known mixed-orientation couples divorce after one of the spouses comes out,[1] marriages that endure command particular attention. Among them, bisexual-heterosexual marriages seem to outnumber those of gay- or lesbian-heterosexual couples. This essay provides a glimpse of how 56 bisexual husbands and 51 heterosexual wives in 89 marriages rewrote their marital scripts so that their marriages could last. Their experiences are compared with those of gay-heterosexual couples and are also considered in relation to all types of mixed-orientation couples, as described in the research literature and found in my own research over the past fourteen years.

The number of all mixed-orientation marriages, closeted or disclosed, is not known with any degree of certainty. Based on the most conservative estimates of the incidence of homosexuality and bisexuality, at least one to two million gay men, lesbians, and bisexual men and women living in the United States are or once were married.[2] In view of the stigmatizing nature of disclosure, especially for married persons, and the difficulty of measuring all relevant factors in sexual orientation, a dependable figure may never be generated.

How many of these spouses or former spouses are bisexual is unknown. While higher figures have been posited for bisexual spouses than for gay or lesbian spouses,[3] we cannot make any reasonable estimate because of the relative invisibility of bisexuality and the inaccurate labeling of bisexual individuals as gay or lesbian in most studies.[4]

More important than numbers is the apparent increase over the past twenty years of spouses who have come out, as indicated by research reports, media accounts, and my own study and observation. While this trend may partially result from a growing awareness of the phenomenon, the increase is quite likely real. Given the social and political changes and technological developments over the past four decades, it has become easier and more acceptable for married gay, lesbian, and bisexual individuals to self-identify, express, and disclose their sexual orientation.

MIXED ORIENTATION MARRIAGES: AN OVERVIEW

> Our therapist told us the odds were against us staying together. That
> made us so angry, we never went back to him. We were going to beat
> the odds!
>
> –the heterosexual wife of a gay man

According to research studies, as well as data I have gathered since 1986
and my experience facilitating support groups and directing the international
Straight Spouse Network (roles I continue to perform), mixed-orientation
marriages are found among all adult age groups, occupations, and educational and socio-economic levels in the United States, regardless of race, ethnicity, religion, or geographic region. In most cases, the bisexual, gay, or lesbian
spouses did not know, acknowledge, or disclose their sexual orientation before marrying. Many have come out to their spouses, some have not, and
others never will. Typically, when they come out, their heterosexual spouses
are devastated and their children confused. Some couples separate quickly,
while others stay together to figure out implications of the new information
or to try to resolve issues raised by the disclosure in order to stay married.
After several years, a majority divorce.[5]

The coming out of married persons and its impact on families are unfore-
seen consequences of the post-World War II movements for civil rights,
sexual freedom, women's liberation, and most centrally, gay liberation, following the 1969 Stonewall uprising. Through the 1970s and 1980s, these
socio-cultural forces gradually weakened traditional roles, rules, and expectations.[6] During the 1990s, advances in telecommunications accelerated the
pace of community building by gay men, lesbians, and bisexual men and
women and extended their visibility and political strength.[7] The expansion of
the Internet and the launching of the World Wide Web provided venues
through which they could find support for their coming out and form virtual
communities and cyber friendships, regardless of location, that sometimes
led to real-life relationships (see Peterson, this volume).

Concomitantly, public acknowledgment if not acceptance of homosexuality has grown, as noted in public opinion polls and signaled by the 1998
declaration by the American Psychiatric Association that reparative therapy
to change a person's sexual orientation is ineffective and potentially dangerous.[8] Nevertheless, as the new millennium dawns, bisexuality remains relatively unacknowledged and more circumspect than homosexuality.

These societal and technological developments affected married as well as single bisexual, lesbian, and gay persons, as alternatives to heterosexual marriage became more viable options. Research on married gay, lesbian, and bisexual spouses mirrors these changes. For example, studies conducted prior to the Stonewall uprising addressed the closeted "tearoom trade" and the clinical problems of gay husbands, and researchers continued to study clinical samples until the American Psychiatric Association declassified homosexuality as a disorder in 1973.[9] Thereafter, studies involved non-clinical samples and addressed such issues as the child custody and parenting concerns of divorced lesbian mothers, the process by which gay husbands integrate their homosexuality within marriage and/or fatherhood, and the experiences of gay-heterosexual couples.[10] Once bisexuality was acknowledged as a distinct sexual orientation in the late 1970s, researchers began to examine the lives of bisexual husbands and wives.[11] Similarly, as more married men and women came out during the 1980s, studies increasingly focused on the effects of disclosure on one or both spouses,[12] and popular books on the subject were published.[13] Few of these works, however, looked at bisexual or heterosexual spouses, and even fewer examined couples who stayed married.

The lack of attention to enduring marriages is not surprising, because the preponderance of data suggests that only a minority last more than a few years after disclosure. The convenience (i.e., non-representative) samples that I have used in my research, totaling more than 3,500 spouses,[14] show a fairly constant ratio of couples who separate and those who stay married. Roughly a third divorce within a year; another third stay together for two or three years to sort out pragmatic implications of the disclosure; and another third work jointly toward maintaining the marriage. Of the latter group, about half keep their marriages intact for three years or more. Most of these seem to be bisexual-heterosexual couples.

Reasons for separation and divorce abound. The bisexual, lesbian, or gay spouse may be drawn to the gay or lesbian world, fall in love with another person, or find that "leading two lives" is unbearable. The heterosexual spouse may not tolerate the idea of homosexuality or fear AIDS, may not want to give up sex, may not wish to share the partner with a lover or have the relationship cease being primary, or cannot rebuild the trust broken by the disclosure. Some couples end their relationship because of problems unrelated to sexual orientation.

The task of staying married is daunting. Having a spouse who is sexually attracted to and may have sex with someone else of the same gender poses extraordinary cognitive and relational challenges: dealing with misconceptions about sexual orientation and the resolution of conflicting personal, social, and religious attitudes about homosexuality, same-sex behavior, and the institution of marriage. To stay married requires finding ways to satisfy the moral values and sexual, emotional, and social needs of each spouse.

Besides the relatively small number of couples who stay married, the lack of information about enduring marriages is further explained by their invisibility. Mixed-orientation couples are generally indistinguishable from heterosexual couples, especially when they remain closeted because of privacy concerns or a fear of being stigmatized and rejected by their family, friends, employer, or community.

Along with invisibility, the misconceptions that sexual orientation is solely a matter of sexual behavior and exists only in two forms, homosexuality and heterosexuality, make it difficult to identify mixed-orientation couples. Viewing sexual orientation as sexual behavior alone excludes other significant dimensions, such as self-identity, attraction, fantasies, social preferences, and emotional-spiritual bonding.[15] It also fosters false assumptions about a person's sexual orientation, based only on observed or reported sexual behavior and the gender of one's sexual partner(s). Rather than acknowledging the complexities of sexual orientations, society dismisses the possibility of mixed-orientation couples. Similarly, the misconception that one's sexual orientation is either heterosexual or homosexual excludes bisexuality and the possibility of attraction to and sexual pleasure with partners of more than one gender.[16] Seen within an either/or paradigm, a person who is married has to be heterosexual.

Research studies of spouses in mixed-orientation marriages often reflect such binary thinking. Few distinguish between gay/lesbian and bisexual spouses, despite the availability of analytic tools that measure the multiple dimensions of sexual orientation, such as the Klein Sexual Orientation Grid or adaptations of the Kinsey scale.[17] Many investigators categorize respondents as gay or lesbian solely on the basis of reported same-sex behavior. Even researchers who make such distinctions frequently treat gay and/or lesbian and bisexual respondents as one group when discussing the total sample. Collapsing the data in this way presents a distorted picture of married bisexuals, gay men, and lesbians, as well as their heterosexual spouses.

Mislabeling, along with invisibility and a dichotomous view of sexual orientation, has led to an underreporting of mixed-orientation marriages and the misrepresentation of those who stay married. The present study was undertaken to provide a fuller, more accurate view. Since married bisexual men and their heterosexual spouses more often report enduring marriages than do married gay men and lesbians and their heterosexual spouses, bisexu-al-heterosexual marriages became the primary focus.

The goal was to present a vibrant picture of bisexual husbands and hetero-sexual wives of bisexual men that might expand our understanding of the "redefining" process undertaken by such spouses. The findings might pro-vide data-based examples for other mixed-orientation couples as they chart their way through this territory for themselves. Locating "invisible" re-spondents would not be easy, but I felt compelled to try.

FRAMING THE STUDY: THE FAMILY CIRCLE AND SOCIAL CONTEXT

Two themes emerged from my prior research to frame the current study and my analysis of the data: coming out in a marriage is not an individual event but a family matter, and coping with the disclosure is embedded in a social context. A family's experience in dealing with a hitherto unknown or closeted orientation of a spouse occurs in waves. The first wave comprises the struggle of the bisexual, gay, or lesbian spouse to address his or her sexual orientation. The second wave involves disclosure to the heterosexual spouse, who then begins her or his own struggle to deal with the revealed sexual orientation. If the couple has children, the third wave commences once they are told or find out that their parent is bisexual, gay, or lesbian. Although family members may learn about the new orientation at different times and cope in different ways, they often have similar areas of concern: sexuality, marriage, parent-child relationship, identity, integrity, and belief system.

In coping with the disclosure, family members are also affected by norms of heterosexuality and traditional concepts of marriage that prevail in their community, workplace or school, house of worship, or social network. How-ever liberal their social milieu, spouses and their children often feel stigma-tized by anti-gay attitudes outside the home. Most fear negative reactions should they share the information with friends, co-workers, kin, neighbors, playmates, social groups, or faith communities. If they tell others, or if others learn of the disclosure, some encounter criticism or rejection. While less often a personal attack than an expression of shock or discomfort to unex-pected news, such negativity hurts everyone in the family. .

Couples who decide to stay married, even those who commit to being monogamous, are viewed as non-traditional at best and immoral at worst. Heterosexual spouses find little understanding of their struggle and a lack of support for remaining in the marriage from the dominant society. While many bisexual, lesbian, and gay spouses receive support for their coming out from members of their respective communities, their desire to stay married is likewise not affirmed.

THE STUDY

It saddens me. We *still* don't have a book . . . that provides a model or the message that these matters can be (and *are*) successfully woven into the tapestry of an integrated marriage/relationship.

–a bisexual husband

Besides a desire to address a significant gap in the literature, this study was driven by two realities drawn from research and observation: about half of the couples who worked jointly to maintain their marriage were able to do so, and the increasing number of such couples across the country who seek role models for staying married. Existing research involving spouses who have succeeded in maintaining their marriage after disclosure reveals that these relationships often share a number of characteristics: open communication, primary commitment to the marriage, commitment to making the marriage work, rewriting marriage "rules," love, honesty, the wife's autonomy and acceptance, the husband's compromise, and personal capacities of empathy and flexibility.[18] Such elements contribute to the longevity of any marriage, but their viability is tested in the case of mixed-orientation couples by the impact of disclosure.

RESEARCH DESIGN

This study is the most recent of three projects undertaken within an ongoing investigation, begun in 1986, of spouses in all types of mixed-orientation marriages after the husband or wife comes out. The project reported here involves a sample of bisexual husbands and heterosexual wives of bisexual men and a comparison group of gay married men and heterosexual wives of gay men, who are examined against a background of self reports collected over the last fourteen years from over 3,500 heterosexual, bisexual, lesbian, and gay spouses in the United States and fifteen other countries.[19]

This cumulative data base–augmented by continued review of the literature, nine years of leading support groups in the San Francisco Bay Area, and experience as director of the international Straight Spouse Network since 1991–informed my understanding of issues typically faced by spouses after one partner comes out.

In the current project, "bisexual husbands" refers expressly to married men who self-identify as "bisexual" and are sexually attracted to both women and men, whether or not they act upon their same-gender desire. "Gay married men" specifies husbands who describe themselves as gay or "one woman short of being gay." Many feel emotionally and socially wedded to their wives and some continue sexual relations with or feel attracted to them, even though they are predominantly or exclusively attracted to men.

METHODOLOGY

The objective of the study was to reveal the process by which bisexual husbands and heterosexual wives of bisexual men redefined their marriages after disclosure, as distinct from the structure of the relationship that they devised. The focus was on coping strategies that they deemed helpful and factors that supported or hindered this process. Of particular interest were the individual perceptions of each spouse, couple interactions, and the interplay between their efforts and family and social contexts. The research design was qualitative, using a phenomenological approach to tap the spouses' experience as reported from their perspective.[20] No "a priori" hypothesis was formulated; self reports would identify the key behaviors, dynamics, and factors.

To elicit perceptions of the post-disclosure experience, a survey questionnaire posed four open-ended questions: What three coping strategies, individual and couple, were the most helpful for maintaining the marriage? What circumstances supported your continuing the marriage? What external factors worked against or interfered with staying married? What advice would you give another couple after one of the spouses comes out?

Data gathering took place from 1997 to 1999 through regular mail and e-mail. Questionnaires were sent to spouses I knew from previous contacts to be still married, spouses on Internet mailing lists who responded to an invitation to participate, and leaders of straight spouse support groups in the United States and of bisexual groups here and in Australia. Completed surveys were returned by almost all previously interviewed spouses, about half of Internet list members who requested them, and a handful of support group members. At the final count, more bisexual husbands and wives of bisexual men responded than did gay husbands, lesbian or bisexual wives, or the heterosexual spouses of gay men, lesbians, or bisexual women.

The core group totaled 56 self-identified bisexual husbands and 51 self-identified heterosexual wives of bisexual husbands. Of these, 18 husbands and wives were married to each other, meaning that the two samples together represented 89 enduring bisexual-heterosexual marriages. The gay married men and wives of gay men, who formed the next largest respondent groups, became the comparative samples. These groups consisted of 32 self-identified gay husbands and 28 self-identified heterosexual wives of gay husbands. Twelve husbands and wives were married to each other, resulting in 48 enduring gay-heterosexual marriages in the two spouse samples.

Responses were analyzed in several ways. A content analysis was conducted on responses of each spouse sample to each question to see which, if any, coping strategies, supportive circumstances, and negative factors had been critical to their individual efforts to maintain their marriages.[21] Similar responses to each question were grouped, tallied, and ranked by the number of times mentioned. "Advice to other couples" was also analyzed, and responses were grouped, tallied, and ranked to see which, if any, of the most frequently cited strategies, supports, and deterrents were stressed to couples in similar circumstances.

Two other analyses were conducted: (1) comparisons and contrasts between the responses of the four spouse samples in order to discover what, if any, patterns were distinctive to the bisexual husbands or wives of bisexual men; and (2) analyses of the factors most often mentioned by each sample as a way to identify the significance of different variables for spouses in each type of mixed-orientation marriage and to discern possible patterns of couple interaction unique to marriages of bisexual husbands and heterosexual wives.

THE SAMPLES

Demographics of age, residence, length of marriage, year of marriage, time since disclosure, and children were chosen to describe the spouse samples. While most respondents were between thirty and fifty years old, the ages of all the spouse samples, except for the wives of gay men, ranged from their twenties to their seventies (Table 1), a broader spread than that found in most studies of sexuality. The bisexual husbands and wives of bisexual men

TABLE 1. Ages by Decade
Bisexual Husbands (BH) (N = 56)–Heterosexual Wives of Bisexual Men (WB) (N = 51)
Gay Married Men (GH) (N = 32)–Heterosexual Wives of Gay Men (WG) (N = 28)

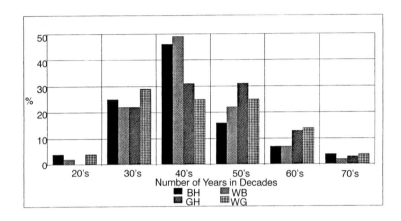

were slightly younger, on average, than their counterpart samples, and nearly half were in their forties. The gay married men and wives of gay men were more evenly grouped among thirty-, forty-, and fifty-year-olds.

Most spouses lived in the United States and resided in small towns, medium-sized cities, metropolitan areas, or suburbs (Table 2). The residences of the bisexual husbands were the most evenly divided among the four types of locale, and the heterosexual wives of bisexual men the least, with the largest cluster living in suburban areas. The gay married men more often resided in small towns or suburbs, while most of the heterosexual wives of gay men were divided among medium-sized cities, small towns, and suburbs.

The length of the marriages at the time of the survey ranged from less than a year to sixty years. The vast majority of the bisexual husbands and wives of bisexual men had been married from a year to thirty years, and more had been married for ten years or less than had the gay husbands and wives of gay men (Table 3a). In general, respondents in the latter sample had been married longer than the spouses in bisexual-heterosexual marriages (Table 3b).

The years in which the spouses married were grouped into time periods that demarcated shifts in societal attitudes toward homosexuality and bisexuality, because these changes affected the decision of many gay and bisexual men to marry. Substantially fewer bisexual husbands and wives of bisexual men, compared to gay husbands and wives of gay men, married before Stonewall, and proportionately twice as many married in the 1990s (Tables 4a and 4b). Among the bisexual husbands and both groups of wives, roughly

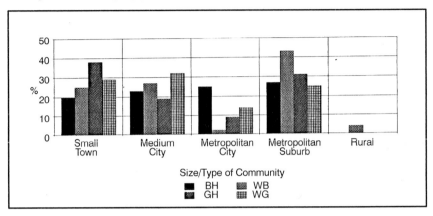

TABLE 2. Residence by Size and Type of Community
Bisexual Husbands (BH) (N = 56)–Heterosexual Wives of Bisexual Men (WB) (N = 51)
Gay Married Men (GH) (N = 32)–Heterosexual Wives of Gay Men (WG) (N = 28)

TABLE 3a. Number of Years Married by Decades
Bisexual Husbands (BH) (N = 56)
Heterosexual Wives of Bisexual Men (WB) (N = 51)

two-fifths had stayed married for at least three years after disclosure of the husband's sexual orientation, the typical turning point for marital dissolution or continuation (Tables 5a and 5b). While more gay husbands remained married at least that long, more bisexual husbands were still married seven or more years after disclosure. Most spouses in every sample were parents, with an average of two children each; proportionately more bisexual husbands and wives of bisexual men had minor children than their counterparts (Table 6).

TABLE 3b. Number of Years Married by Decades
Gay Married Men (GH) (N = 32)
Heterosexual Wives of Gay Men (WG) (N = 28)

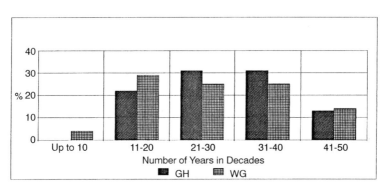

TABLE 4a. Year of Marriage by Time Period
Bisexual Husbands (BH) (N = 56)
Heterosexual Wives of Bisexual Men (WB) (51)

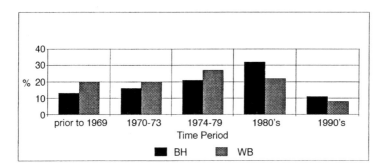

THE FINDINGS

We celebrate the process itself. That has become our relationship.

–the heterosexual wife of a bisexual man

HOW DID SPOUSES MAINTAIN THEIR MARRIAGE?

The spouses' responses paint a vivid picture of how bisexual husbands and wives of bisexual men in 89 marriages rewrote their marriage scripts. Al-

TABLE 4b. Year of Marriage by Time Period
Gay Married Men (GH) (N = 32)
Heterosexual Wives of Gay Men (WG) (N = 28)

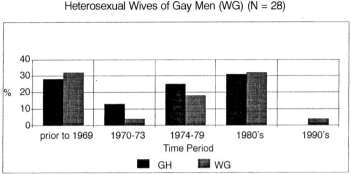

TABLE 5. Time Since Disclosure
Bisexual Husbands (BH) (N = 56)–Heterosexual Wives of Bisexual Men (WB) (N = 51)
Gay Married Men (GH) (N = 32)–Heterosexual Wives of Gay Men (WG) (N = 28)

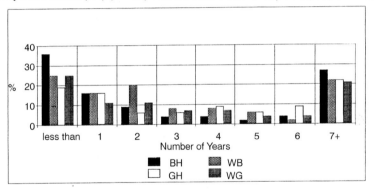

though there is considerable variation, clusters of similar responses illuminate ways in which the redefining process functions in a generally non-supportive context. The findings of this study confirm most previous research
while adding new data and clarifying some differences between marriages of
bisexual and gay men. The import of the self-report data lies in the descriptions of how spouses' dealt with the consequences of the disclosure within
their marriages.

The following sections present the most helpful coping strategies, supportive circumstances, and negative factors reported by the largest numbers of

TABLE 6. Number of Children and Minor Children
Bisexual Husbands (BH) (N = 56)–Heterosexual Wives of Bisexual Men (WB) (N = 51)
Gay Married Men (GH) (N = 32)–Heterosexual Wives of Gay Men (WG) (N = 28)

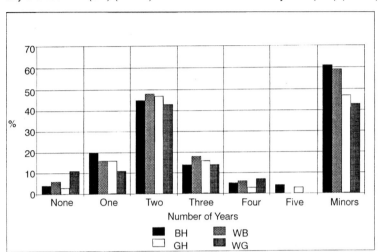

spouses within each sample of bisexual husbands, heterosexual wives of bisexual men, gay husbands, and heterosexual wives of gay men, respectively. In each section, the responses of bisexual husbands and wives of bisexual men are discussed in terms of their individual experiences and their interactions with their partners. The responses of the comparison groups of gay husbands and wives of gay men follow to show similarities and differences between their experiences and those of the spouses in bisexual-heterosexual marriages. In the last section, I describe the overall process by which spouses in each type of marriage redefine their marital relationship and the unique struggle faced by bisexual husbands and wives of bisexual men.

THE MOST HELPFUL COPING STRATEGIES

The survey question asked "What three coping strategies, individual and couple, were the most helpful for maintaining the marriage?" Coping strategies refer to behaviors or capacities that helped the spouses deal with disclosure issues and work out enduring marriages. All of the samples addressed the individual spouse, the relationship, and the redefining process itself. While the survey question asked only for strategies that helped the spouses cope as individuals and as couples, the respondents introduced factors related to the *process* of their work, i.e., behaviors by which one or both spouses kept the couple's redefining work moving toward a mutually acceptable solution. The process factors add a key dimension to our understanding of the post-disclosure experiences of mixed-orientation couples.

Bisexual Husbands and Heterosexual Wives of Bisexual Men

Individual Spouses. The most helpful coping strategies for the bisexual husbands focused on aspects of the couple relationship, rather than individual concerns (Table 7). Communication was mentioned most often, and denoted a two-way, ongoing dialogue through which much of their redefining work was done. "Making time to talk" was part of the process. "We talked for 2-4 hours every day for the first 3 weeks after I came out," one man explained. "We also read a book together, *The Good Marriage*, and discussed it."[22] Another said, "We made sure that we talked no matter how painful it might have been."

Often combined with communication, honesty created a shared foundation for rethinking the marriage together. "By being honest with each other as to what we need and want," one man wrote, "we have developed a stronger bond." Being candid encompassed sharing what it meant to them to be bisexual, such as "feeling free to express the 'feminine' side of me (tenderness and softness)," and informing the wife of gay-related activities. "She knows when I go out and who I am seeing. Always had open communication and that has made this more bearable."

Peer support, primarily through on-line mailing lists but also through face-to-face meetings with other married bisexual and gay men, helped more respondents than did therapy. Interacting with peers was a way to "search for strategies that find common ground solutions that help preserve the marriage and the relationship." Therapy was helpful for fewer of the bisexual men than for any other spouse sample.

Love played a key role for many men, providing the "energy that can fuel couples' renegotiating." In some instances, love was inferred simply by the wife's decision "not to throw me out." A number of men spoke of mutual love; for example, one bisexual husband stated, "We knew that we loved each other, and we took extraordinary steps to make sure that we reinforced our love." Love was also a catalyst for other strategies, like stressing their commitment to the relationship. One man wrote, "I reassure[d] my wife every day of how in love with her I am and am still attracted to her sexually."

TABLE 7. The Most Helpful Post-Disclosure Coping Strategies Ranked by Percentage of Spousal Samples

Response Rank	Bisexual Husbands. N = 56	Wives of Bisexual Men. N = 51	Gay Husbands. N = 32	Wives of Gay Men. N = 28
Most cited response	Communication 17 / 31%	Communication 27 / 53%	Counseling / Therapy 18 / 59%	Therapy 10 / 36%
2nd most cited response	Honesty 15 / 27%	Counseling / Therapy 22 / 42%	Peer Support 17 / 56%	Peer Support 9 / 32%
3rd most cited response	Peer Support 13 / 23%	Honesty 18 / 35%	Honesty 16 / 50%	Reading 9 / 32%
4th most cited response	Reassurance of Wife. 11 / 20%	Peer Support 15 / 29%	Communication 12 / 38%	Honesty 6 / 21%
5th most cited response	Therapy 9 / 16%	Reading 12 / 24%	Love 8 / 25%	Communication 6 / 21%
6th most cited response	Mutual Respect 9 / 16%	Taking Time 9 / 18%	Compromise 5 / 16%	Acceptance 5 / 18%
7th most cited response	Love, & Empathy (tied) 8 / 14%	Flexibility 8 / 15%	4 tied at 4 / 13%: Denial/Secrecy, Religion, Space for Each Other, Monogamy*	Care of Self 5 / 18%

*9% of gay married men cited parenting/family, redefining marriage, taking time, and friendship.

Another spoke of "being tender and loving [as his] straight spouse was going through a lot."

Related to love were empathy and marital sex, strategies that were unique to the bisexual husband sample. The role of marital sex in their coping highlights the dual attraction that distinguishes the bisexual men from their gay counterparts. "All expressions of sexuality are about us," one husband commented, "bringing us together rather than tearing us apart." Another said that sex with his wife had never been better, echoing many other married bisexual men, who describe increased openness of sexual expression after coming out.

Communication, honesty, peer support, therapy, and taking time to work through issues played such key roles in the men's coping that these strategies were reiterated in the advice they offered to other couples facing disclosure.

Compared to the bisexual husbands, more wives of bisexual men found communication, therapy, honesty, peer support, and taking time helpful (Table 7). Like the men, the wives advised these strategies for other spouses. Continuous dialogue marked their coping. One woman wrote soon after her husband came out, "We've made time to talk a lot . . . [and] have tried to share in a non-judgmental way, speaking out of love not fear." Three years later, she reported, "Communication continues to be one of the most important aspects of our relationship. . . . As a result of the deep level of honesty and realness that has evolved through this process, the communication has become more and more easy and something we both cherish and honor."

Honesty was a more important coping strategy for wives than for bisexual husbands. Their husbands' telling the truth about their sexuality helped the women rebuild trust. "Once he opened up and told me what was going on," a wife wrote, "I trusted more." Often linked with communication, honesty also included the wives' ability to express their own needs and pain.

Therapy, peer support (mostly on-line), and, unlike the bisexual husbands, reading helped a number of wives cope with their initial feelings of devastation and confusion and their fears about the implications of the disclosure. Books educated them about bisexuality and mixed-orientation marriages and enabled them to reconnect to their husbands. One wife explained, "I read about bisexuality so I could ask [my] husband how he felt."

Proportionately more wives of bisexual husbands found taking time helpful than did spouses in any other sample, and they alone mentioned flexibility. By going slowly and being willing to stretch their concepts of sexual orientation and marriage, they gradually understood and then accepted their husbands' bisexuality.

Couple Interaction: Focus on the Relationship. Most of the coping tools that were helpful to the bisexual husbands and wives of bisexual men focused on their relationship with their partners. Their communication, honesty, love, empathy (among husbands), and flexibility (among wives) delineate an active engagement with their spouses on many levels: emotional, sexual, verbal, physical, and cognitive. One husband wrote, "We spent many days and nights talking honestly, listening empathetically, touching, making love." Strikingly different from the spouses in gay-heterosexual marriages, few found that parenting or family events helped them cope, even though proportionally more of them had minor children.

Both spouse samples considered honesty, taking time, communication, and peer support to be critical strategies for other couples in a similar position. However, the husbands and wives used these coping tools with their respective spouses in different, but complementary, ways, reflecting where they were in the process of dealing with the disclosure. Husbands explained and reassured; wives raised questions about what bisexuality implied for the husbands, themselves, and their marriages. It helped, one wife said, when her husband "explain[ed] his feelings and interpretation of bisexuality." A bisexual husband reported, "Talking [is] bloody hard, but it always removes problems if handled calmly."[23]

Honesty was often intertwined with communication. Bisexual husbands told their wives about their same-sex desires as candidly as possible and, to some degree, reported any same-sex or gay-related experiences; wives expressed their confusion, hurt, and sexual/intimacy needs. "We pledged full disclosure to each other," one wife wrote, "before anything that threatened monogamy occurred." A bisexual husband explained, "She knows that my hiding being bi from myself and others was my own internal hell. She knows that I am happier admitting to myself that I am bi." Such honest communication reinforced the couple's bond and set a baseline for recreating their marriage.

Love was mentioned by smaller numbers of both the husband and wife samples and functioned differently for each. For bisexual husbands, love often involved expressive, overt actions, whereas for wives, it was frequently more embedded in their perceptions or behaviors. "I felt our love might be able to encompass this new aspect of him," one woman commented. Another spoke of her flexibility as a way to "expand my capacity to be a loving person." A similar coping method was the capacity to tune in to another person's perspective or feelings. Mentioned only by these two spouse samples, this strategy took the form of flexibility for some wives and empathy for some husbands.

Underlying all of these behaviors and capacities was taking time to communicate and to engage in a dialogue. The value that bisexual married men and wives of bisexual men placed on such an exchange was demonstrated by the fact that both spouse samples recommended this strategy much more frequently than did gay married men or wives of gay men.

Gay Married Men and Heterosexual Wives of Gay Men

Individual Spouses. Compared with the coping strategies most helpful to the bisexual husbands and wives of bisexual men, those reported by the gay husbands and wives of gay men addressed individual concerns and family matters, as well as the marital relationship (Table 7). Among the gay married men, many strategies focused on their sexual orientation and indicated varying degrees of conflict between being attracted to men and being married, a struggle that few bisexual husbands reported. An overwhelming proportion, the highest of any sample, found therapy, peer support (mostly on-line), and honesty to be helpful in coping with the difference between their sexual needs and those of their wives, a wider gap than that existing between bisexual husbands and their wives.

To bridge this difference, honesty was used by half of the gay married men to affirm their own integrity and to reestablish the wife's trust, and a larger percent, compared to the bisexual husbands, reported that communication and love helped them cope than did the bisexual married men. In addition, unlike the bisexual husbands, a number of gay married men found parenting and family events and the couple's friendship to be helpful in maintaining their marriage. Unique among all the samples, some also reported strategies that circumscribed or compartmentalized their same-sex desires and activities: denial/secrecy, compromise, religion, and monogamy. Denial was used to avoid hurting the wife or provoking a breakup, and secrecy protected both spouses from outside negativity. Religious faith or prayers helped the men stay committed to the marriage and confirmed their integrity.

Among the wives of gay men, therapy and peer support were considered the most helpful coping strategies, although these figures were significantly less than for the gay married men (Table 7). However, similar to the contrast between the wives of bisexual men and bisexual husbands, more wives of gay men were helped by reading than were gay married men. Unique among all samples, a number of wives saw accepting their husbands' homosexuality and taking care of themselves as important strategies, and more coped through couple or family activities than did any other spouse sample.

Couple Interaction: Focus on the Individual and the Family. Like spouses in bisexual-heterosexual marriages, large numbers of gay married men and heterosexual wives of gay men cited communication as a helpful strategy and advised it for other couples. Yet, different from the other two samples, more of them used strategies that address individual and family needs rather than the couple relationship. They also described aspects of their relationship that grounded the marriage: for some men, friendship as well as love, and for a number of wives, a "good marriage" or "understanding each other."

Three strategies that were unique to one or both of the samples from gay-heterosexual marriages were designed to accommodate the needs of the partner: compromise by husbands, acceptance by wives, and both spouses' making space for each other. To develop and sustain this balance of individual and couple needs, their common advice for coping was to create a support system, communicate, and "take time."

SUPPORTIVE CIRCUMSTANCES

The survey question about supportive circumstances asked "What circumstances supported your continuing the marriage?" Supports were found within the spouses' immediate and extended family, as well as in their social milieu, religion, or therapy (Table 8). Expanding our view of mixed-orientation marriages, couples indicated that the relationship itself was a key support. Its quality served as a rationale for continuing the marriage and, as their relationship developed through jointly working out new parameters for the marriage, became an empowering force in their endeavor. The qualitative aspect of the relationship, denoted by phrases such as "great marriage," differs from couple interaction, the behavioral component of the couple's work.

Several methods that spouses used for coping with the disclosure and its implications became so much a part of couple interactions that they served a supportive function as well, confirming the wisdom of their decision to stay married. Despite a range of personal, relational, familial, and social variables, clusters of responses indicated two major types of supports: those that enabled spouses to create alternatives to their pre-disclosure relationship and those that sustained the delicate balance they had created within the post-disclosure marriage. Few spouses mentioned their jobs or their communities, even though these were examples provided on the survey form.

Bisexual Husbands and Heterosexual Wives of Bisexual Men

Individual Spouses. The factors that supported the largest number of bisexual husbands–love, children, and communication–indicate that they were intensely satisfied with couple interactions and closely involved with or supported by their children (Table 8). The love between them and their wives

TABLE 8. Supportive Circumstances for Maintaining the Marriage Ranked by Percentage of Spousal Samples

Response Rank	Bisexual Husbands. N = 56	Wives of Bisexual Men. N = 51	Gay Husbands. N = 32	Wives of Gay Men. N = 28
Most cited response	Love 22 / 39%	Quality of Relationship 20 / 39%	Quality of Relationship 19 / 59%	Quality of Relationship 15 / 54%
2nd most cited response	Children 15 / 27%	Children 20 / 39%	Children 9 / 28%	Friends 11 / 39%
3rd most cited response	Couple Communication 13 / 23%	Financial Need 20 / 39%	Love 9 / 28%	Children 10 / 36%
4th most cited response	Acceptance 9 / 16%	Love 16 / 31%	Ourselves 9 / 28%	Religion 10 / 36%
5th most cited response	Family 9 / 16%	Friends 12 / 24%	Financial Need 8 / 25%	Peers 9 / 32%
6th most cited response	Peers 8 / 14%	Family 10 / 20%	Lovers 6 / 19%	Love 8 / 28%
7th most cited response	Friends 8 / 14%	Ourselves 10 / 20%*	Friends 5 / 16%	Financial Need 8 / 28%

*10% of wives of bisexual men also cited peers as supportive factors

encouraged the largest number of men to continue working on the marriage, and many noted love's generative power to keep the relationship alive. Many bisexual husbands also considered couple communication to be critical, though it was not mentioned by any other sample. Continuous dialogue helped their wives understand bisexuality, and the wives' acceptance provided another means of support that was unique to the married bisexual men.

Among the wives of bisexual men, many found support through children, financial needs, and the quality of the relationship, particularly its emotional or sexual aspects (Table 8). "We felt a bond I describe as soul mates," one woman wrote. "We didn't want to abandon all of this." Another said, "Physical closeness played a big part in helping me feel wanted and secure during a vulnerable time." Love supported almost as many wives of bisexuals as it did bisexual husbands. "I fell in love again with him after he came out," one wife noted. Another said, "I believ[ed] my spouse's desire to be with me and love me." Unique among the spousal groups, some of the wives felt that marital sex confirmed this love.

Their children and finances, the other most-mentioned supports, were cited by more wives of bisexual men than by spouses in the other samples. A number expressed a strong desire to continue to meet the needs of their minor children in a family setting, while others were supported by adult children. However, only one wife, a university student, said that finances played a major role in continuing the marriage.

Unlike the bisexual husbands, a number of wives reported that therapy offered support, just as it had served as an effective coping strategy. Friends and families of origin also were supportive. One wife's decision to stay married was reinforced by a friend's casual remark, "It's so obvious you love each other."

Couples: Love, Mutuality, and Family of Origin. Circumstances that supported the bisexual husbands and wives of bisexual men, compared with those reported by the spouses in gay-heterosexual marriages, denote more levels of engagement and mutual nurturing in their relationships and fewer instances of insular experiences as couples or parallel activities as individual spouses. Love and children, more often than outside factors, provided support for continuing the marriage. In addition, their families of origin often stood behind them, which was rarely the case for the spouses in gay-heterosexual marriages. All told, most bisexual husbands and wives of bisexual men relied primarily on themselves and their circle of family and friends to develop a solid basis for their relationship to survive and grow.

Gay Married Men and Heterosexual Wives of Gay Men

Individual Spouses. The spouses in gay-heterosexual marriages found supports more often within the marriage itself. The number of gay married men who felt sustained by the quality of their relationship exceeded that of the other three groups, especially the bisexual husbands (39% to 9%). Only gay husbands mentioned "ourselves" as a key support, in about the same proportion as those who noted children, love, and finances (Table 8). Several men, unique among all the samples, also found support from their lovers and a sense of autonomy.

The gay married men's responses generally fell into two sub-groups. For the majority, the quality of the relationship provided the main support for staying married. This quality was comprised of love; the couple's own efforts, typically without support from their families of origin; and a shared history and friendship that had bonded them together so closely that the relationship could not be dissolved easily. For a smaller number of men, some degree of autonomy existed alongside a deep friendship with their wives and their lovers' support of the marriage.

The wives of gay men present a different picture, though it too suggests a solid relationship and parallel sources of support (Table 8). The quality of the relationship supported the largest proportion of any sample and, for a number of wives, love and financial need reinforced their decision to stay married. Beyond the relationship, a support system of friends, children, religion, and peers sustained them.

Couples: Quality of the Relationship. The largest proportion of both the gay married men and wives of gay men were supported by the quality of their relationship, many more than the bisexual husbands and slightly more than the wives of bisexual men. Similar proportions of the husbands and wives in gay-heterosexual marriages found that their love and friendship, and financial needs, bolstered their staying married. While few were applauded by their families of origin and some devised parallel means of support, several spouses in both samples had the support of a singular kind of extended family: the husbands' lovers, who respected the primacy of the wife, their marriage, and the family.

NEGATIVE EXTERNAL FACTORS

The survey question asked "What external factors worked against or interfered with staying married?" Compared to their answers to the other survey questions, many fewer spouses identified external factors that interfered with the marriage. This fact contradicts their comments about obstacles made elsewhere in the survey, as well as responses I have heard from other spouses over the years, and probably reflects the proactive attitude of spouses who are trying to stay married. Once a couple determines to beat the odds, both spouses seek to minimize anything that might shake their faith.

The negative factors that were specified, therefore, are especially significant. Both samples of wives, more recently aware of their husbands' sexuality, reported many more obstacles than did the men (Table 9). All of the samples, husbands and wives alike, spoke of factors within the marriage, even though the survey question specified "external factors." These internal negatives, introduced by the respondents and linked to the husband's sexual

TABLE 9. Negative Factors that Interfered with Maintaining the Marriage Ranked by Percentage of Spousal Samples

Response Rank	Bisexual Husbands. N = 56	Wives of Bisexual Men. N = 51	Gay Husbands. N = 32	Wives of Gay Men. N = 28
Most cited response	None 12 / 21%	None 12 / 24%	None 7 / 22%	Dishonesty 10 / 36%
2nd most cited response	Desire / Need for Homosexual Sex or Relationship 6 / 11%	Traditional Concepts of Marriage 8 / 16%	Fears 4 / 13%	Friends' Negativity 10 / 36%
3rd most cited response	Social, Religious Attitudes Towards Homosexuality / Bisexuality 5 / 9%	Husband's Desire / Need for Homosexual Sex or Relationship 7 / 14%	Dishonesty / Distrust 4 / 13%	Husband's Lovers 9 / 32%
4th most cited response	Friends' Negativity 5 / 9%	Closet / Denial / Isolation 6 / 12%	Closet / Denial 3 / 9%	Husband's Gay Sexual or Social Activity 5 / 18%
5th most cited response		Social, Religious Attitudes towards Homosexuality / Bisexuality 6 / 12%	Internet Activity 3 / 9%	4 tied at 3 / 11%: Husband's Desire / Need for Homo-sexual Sex or Relationship, Husband's Internet Activity, Family Negativity, and Social or Religious Attitudes Towards Homosexuality/ Bisexuality
6th most cited response		Religious Views of Marriage, and Husband's Gay Sexual or Social Activity 5 / 10%		

orientation, offer another insight into the dynamics of post-disclosure marriages. Unlike outside forces that can be withstood within a supportive family environment, these deterrents are ever-present in the family setting itself.

Bisexual Husbands and Heterosexual Wives of Bisexual Men

Individual Spouses. Proportionately fewer bisexual husbands reported factors that interfered with the marriage than spouses in any other sample (Table 9). Their "desire/need for homosexual sex" referred to the feelings themselves or to an internal tug-of-war between this need and a commitment to monogamy. The two negative forces that affected some men were particular gay friends who disparaged their staying married and encounters with homophobia, biphobia, and stereotypes about bisexual persons among friends or church congregations.

The wives of bisexual men encountered the most obstacles of all the samples (Table 9). While they felt the same negatives as the bisexual men, they were affected by an array of other deterrents from outside the marriage. Markedly different from factors that troubled the other spouse samples, they reported the influence of traditional concepts of marriage, including fidelity and monogamy, and personal or religious views about marriage. The religious attitudes of outsiders about bisexuality and marriage also impacted a number of wives. Fellow church members rejected one couple, and a minister/therapist who was lesbian advised another wife to divorce her bisexual husband.

Obstacles within the relationship stemmed from the husband's sexual orientation. Same-sex desire or behavior or gay-related social activities kept the husband from the family, competed with intimate time with his wife, or raised her fear that he would leave. "He's looking for Mr. Right," one woman wrote. Another said, "I worry he'll find someone he likes better than me."

Unique to the wives of bisexual men was social isolation, a byproduct of denial and secrecy about the revealed sexual orientation. Among outsiders who knew of the situation, both gay and heterosexual friends, as well as the men's lovers, were seen as obstacles.

Couples: Same-Sex Desire and Traditional Marriage. Obstacles perceived by both the bisexual husbands and wives of bisexual men were the husband's desire for homosexual sex and the negativity of friends, religions, and social attitudes toward homosexuality or bisexuality.

Gay Married Men and Heterosexual Wives of Gay Married Men

Individual Spouses. The same proportion of gay married men cited negatives as did the bisexual husbands, but the factors that impacted them differed and all were internal to the marriage (Table 9). Fears included their wives' anxieties as well as their own. Their dishonesty, their wives' distrust, self-denial, and being closeted also deterred several gay husbands and reflected personal conflicts that several described in their responses. Being on-line with gay or bisexual men caused conflict within the marriage and family, taking them away from their wives and children.

More wives of gay men encountered negative factors than any other sample, and a greater number of obstacles impacted them (Table 9). Most deterrents to staying married were linked to the husband's same-sex needs or behavior. The husband's dishonesty, friends' negativity, and the husband's lovers impacted the largest number. Some lovers did not support the marriage or the wife, and most took the men away from the home for periods of time.

Couples: Dishonesty, Internet, Friends, and Lovers. The gay married men and wives of gay men experienced more negatives within their respective marriages than from outside. Tension within the relationship was caused most often by the husband's dishonesty and his time spent on the Internet.

Regardless of the type of mixed-orientation marriage, the most striking finding is that these spouses continued to work on their marriages despite external and internal impediments. These same factors cause many spouses in other mixed-orientation marriages to divorce. Inasmuch as the spouses cited past as well as present negatives, it appears that once they moved beyond the initial turmoil of disclosure, they accepted many negatives as "givens" in their endeavor. Learning how to take such hurdles in stride required time, and taking the time needed lay at the heart of their achievement. As time passed, the husbands' sexual needs and activities and the wives' pain and distrust were offset by the quality of the relationship.

Few spouses mentioned a lack of role models, even though this is a common complaint elsewhere. Unlike the deterrents present in their lives, the absence of peer support to stay married was more quickly accepted and transcended. Ultimately, the spouses and their respective partners relied solely on themselves. To get through the reported fears, tears, anger, and agonizing conflict, they demonstrated a high degree of motivation, commitment, and persistence.

The bisexual husbands and wives of bisexual men experienced additional cognitive problems as they tried to fathom bisexuality. Yet the men's dual attraction afforded couples an active, mutually desired sexual relationship, something that only a small number of gay married men and wives of gay men reported. All told, the spouses in bisexual-heterosexual marriages were able to overcome obstacles through multidimensional interaction, which is encapsulated in advice offered by a bisexual husband and his wife, three years after he came out. Husband: "Talk to one another. Hold one another, nurture one another, listen to one another. The straight spouse will need lots and lots of reassurance, and this will not go away for a couple of years." Wife: "Try to address your own needs within the context of your new reality. Things will never be as they were, so try viewing your needs within the framework of a redefined dynamic relationship."

DISCUSSION

There are more things in heaven and earth
Than are dreamt of in your Philosophy.

–Hamlet to Horatio, *Hamlet*, Act I, Scene 5

While the self-selected nature of the samples limits generalizing beyond the data, the spouses represent a sizable group whose experiences need to be recognized. Given the paucity of information about lasting mixed-orientation marriages, and that what we do know indicates that extensive forces work against them, these findings offer insights into an extraordinary achievement. Other samples might present different profiles, yet these spouses echo reports voiced by hundreds of others whose marriages endured after disclosure.

Despite its limitations, the study confirms most previous findings and adds details about the behaviors and capacities that spouses found to be most helpful. Not all characteristics noted in earlier studies were reported by large numbers of spouses or by all samples. Rewriting marriage "rules" and commitment to work on the marriage, though evident, were mentioned by only a few. Compromise and autonomy were reported by gay married men alone. Only wives of gay men and bisexual husbands cited the wife's acceptance. Empathy and flexibility were unique to the bisexual husbands and wives of bisexual men, respectively.

More important, the responses of these spouses serve as snapshots of works in progress, documenting the process of redefining marriages after disclosure. Honesty, communication, peer support, therapy, and taking time helped large numbers in all the samples. These behaviors address the three components of maintaining a marriage: the individual spouses, the couple, and the process of redefining the relationship. Honest communication enabled each spouse to reveal his or her feelings and needs, while individual and couple therapy, as well as peer support, helped both spouses work through problems posed by the mixed-orientation relationship or the wives' plummeting self-esteem and sense of powerlessness.

The factors that the spouses introduced in their self-reports pinpoint key variables of the redefining process: the quality of the relationship, deterrent forces within the marriage, and the passage of time. How the spouses handled these elements was critical. Working with their respective partners, they capitalized on positive parts of their relationship to reconcile the husband's desire for same-sex activities and the wife's fears and sense of isolation. Letting time take its course allowed for continuous dialogue and day-to-day interactions through which to modify parameters of their marriage. Going slowly made it more likely that they could resolve the conceptual and pragmatic problems raised by unexpectedly finding themselves in a mixed-orientation marriage, rather than break up prematurely.

The couple's relationship was the pivot upon which the redefining process revolved. The strength of the couple bond best explains why many marriages endured, despite individual pain and confusion, tensions in the relationship, outsiders' negativity, and non-supportive religious and societal views. While peers helped many cope, few provided support for a lasting marriage. Therapists assisted some spouses. Ultimately, however, the spouses worked through these issues and modified their concepts of marriage and sexuality by themselves. As a result, they created their own supportive context.

Post-disclosure issues faced by spouses in bisexual-heterosexual marriages pose an additional challenge. Besides modifying long-held concepts of marriage and sexual orientation and accommodating each other's feelings and needs, bisexual husbands and wives of bisexual men have to deconstruct dichotomous views of sexual orientation. For spouses in this study and their respective partners, the reported give-and-take needed to reformulate previous concepts of marriage and sexuality fortified their relationship. Several husbands were surprised by their wives' strength and understanding as they tried to resolve the daunting problems that faced them. The very bisexuality that posed many of the problems enabled couples to continue their sex lives and affirm their bond. As their relationship grew stronger, their bond became an anchor on which they could depend when outside forces or inner faults tested the marriage's stability.

The outstanding characteristic of the spouses in bisexual-heterosexual marriages is the multidimensional nature of the couple's interactions: emotional, cognitive, verbal, and behavioral, as well as sexual. Distinct from the spouses in gay-heterosexual marriages, open communication, honesty, and love supported their continuation of the marriage and also helped them cope. Honest communication strengthened the trust level of both spouses and encouraged them to express intimate concerns. The husband's empathy and the wife's flexibility engendered mutual respect for each other's identity and integrity.

Countering the codependency label sometimes ascribed to mixed-orientation couples who stay married, the spouses displayed an interdependence whereby they discerned and expressed their own needs and feelings and had an equal say in decisions. Indeed, understanding each other's needs was advised by the largest number of bisexual husbands and by them alone of all the samples. Both husbands and wives used time as an ally. "We were willing to take time to get used to newfound truths about ourselves separately and what we want as a couple," a wife wrote.

The process is dynamic. The heterosexual wife tries to understand bisexuality and work with her husband to reconcile his new identity with the status of being married. For the bisexual husband, having a wife who is supportive and with whom he continues to enjoy sex offsets a lack of support from gay and heterosexual communities. While he tries to understand his wife's anger and fear, she gradually accepts his bisexual needs, which, in turn, strengthens his sense of integrity. The husband's growing sense of fulfillment promotes his wife's awareness of a need to take care of herself and to tap her own potential, termed by one woman as "Self Discovery." Self-enhancement, reported also by wives of gay men, has the additional potential of sexual expansion.

The task is not easy, and the struggle is marked by painful decisions to change old habits of living and thinking. The experience of these spouses in making that transformation, despite daunting obstacles, reinforces the impression that when bisexual husbands and heterosexual wives work jointly to create an enduring marriage, the odds are tilted toward achieving their goal.

This study, of course, raises further questions: Are bisexual men who disclose before marriage more likely to maintain their marriages than those who come out afterward? Does a husband's bisexual identity become less, more, or equally important as he integrates it into his marriage?

In the meantime, and with a cautionary note that the behaviors and capacities of these husbands and wives do not automatically bring about a lasting marriage, their experiences may serve as role models for other bisexual husbands and their wives trying to construct a marriage that endures. These spouses provide a beacon of possibility and promise rewards for others facing the challenge of disclosure. The script is clear. The wider the chasm, the stronger the bond needed to join the two sides, and the deeper and more integrated the reconstructed marriage.[24] Should the marriage not endure, and some couples find that to preserve their precious relationship they need to separate, the richness of the bond will be more than worth the venture.

NOTES

1. Amity Pierce Buxton, *The Other Side of the Closet: The Coming-Out Crisis for Straight Spouses and Families* (New York: John Wiley and Sons, 1994), and "The Best Interest of Children of Gay and Lesbian Parents," *The Scientific Basis for Custody Decisions*, eds. Robert Galatzer-Levy and Louis Kraus (New York: John Wiley and Sons, 1999), 319-46.

2. This estimate is based on recent surveys and commonly accepted percentages of gay men and lesbians who were once married. See Edward O. Laumann, John H. Gagnon, Robert T. Michael, and Stuart Michaels, eds., *The Social Organization of Sexuality: Sexual Practices in the United States* (Chicago: University of Chicago Press, 1994); Alan P. Bell and Martin S. Weinberg, *Homosexualities: A Study of Diversity Among Men and Women* (New York: Simon and Schuster, 1978). Larger estimates stem from faulty base figures–for example, Kinsey's ten percent number included men who were not exclusively engaged in same-sex behavior. Alfred C. Kinsey, Wardell B. Pomeroy, and Clyde E. Martin, *Sexual Behavior in the Human Male* (Philadelphia: W. B. Saunders Company, 1946).

3. See, for example, Judd Marmor, "Introduction," *The Bisexual Spouse: Different Dimensions in Human Sexuality*, ed. Ivan Hill (New York: Harper and Row, 1989), 253-55, 259-60.

4. Beth A. Firestein, ed., *Bisexuality: The Psychology and Politics of an Invisible Minority* (Thousand Oaks, CA: Sage Publications, 1996); A. P. MacDonald, Jr., "A Little Bit of Lavender Goes a Long Way: A Critique of Research on Sexual Orientation," *Journal of Sex Research* 19, no. 1 (1983): 94-100.

5. Buxton, "The Best Interest of Children of Gay and Lesbian Parents," and *The Other Side of the Closet*.

6. Buxton, *The Other Side of the Closet*.

7. For an overview of the bisexual movement, see Naomi Tucker, ed., *Bisexual Politics: Theories, Queries, and Visions* (Binghamton, NY: Harrington Park Press, 1995).

8. Alan S. Yang, "From Wrongs to Rights: Public Opinion on Gay and Lesbian Americans Moves Toward Equality," report of the NGLTF Policy Institute, 1999; *Reuters*, December, 1998.

9. Lawrence J. Hatterer, *Changing Homosexuality in the Male: Treatment for Men Troubled by Homosexuality* (New York: Dell, 1970); Myra Hatterer, "Problems of Women Married to Homosexual Men," *American Journal of Psychiatry* 131, no. 3

(1974): 275-78; Laud Humphreys, *Tearoom Trade: Impersonal Sex in Public Places* (Chicago: Aldine Publishing Company, 1970); K. Imielinsky, "Homosexuality in Males with Particular Attention to Marriage," *Psychotherapy and Psychosomatics* 17 (1969): 126-32.

10. Buxton, "The Best Interest of Children of Gay and Lesbian Parents," 319-46; J. D. Latham and Geoffrey D. White, "Coping with Homosexual Expression within Heterosexual Marriages: Five Case Studies," *Journal of Sex and Marital Therapy* 4 (1978): 198-212; Brenda Maddox, *Married and Gay: An Intimate Look at a Different Relationship* (New York: Harcourt Brace Jovanovich, 1982); John Malone, *Straight Women/Gay Men: A Special Relationship* (New York: Dial Press, 1980); Brian Miller, "Gay Fathers and Their Children," *Family Coordinator* 28 (1979): 544-52; Rebecca Nahos and Myra Turley, *The New Couple: Women and Gay Men* (New York: Seaview Books, 1979); Charlotte J. Patterson, "Lesbian Mothers, Gay Fathers, and Their Children," *Lesbian, Gay, and Bisexual Identities Over the Lifespan: Psychological Perspectives*, eds. Anthony R. D'Augelli and Charlotte J. Patterson (New York: Oxford University Press, 1995), 262-92; Michael W. Ross, *The Married Homosexual Male: A Psychological Study* (Boston: Routledge and Kegan Paul, 1983). Studies of integrating homosexual identity with fatherhood continue. See, for example, Gerd Buntzly, "Gay Fathers in Straight Marriages," *If You Seduce a Straight Person Can You Make Them Gay?: Issues in Biological Essentialism Versus Social Constructionism in Gay and Lesbian Identities*, eds. John P. De Cecco and John P. Elia (New York: The Haworth Press, Inc., 1993), 107-14.

11. John J. Brownfain, "A Study of the Married Bisexual Male: Paradox and Resolution," *Journal of Homosexuality* 11 (1985): 173-88; Eli Coleman, "Bisexual and Gay Men in Heterosexual Marriages: Conflicts and Resolutions in Therapy," *Journal of Homosexuality* 7 (1981/1982): 93-103, and "Integration of Male Bisexuality and Marriage," *Journal of Homosexuality* 11 (1985): 189-208; Dwight Dixon, "Perceived Sexual Satisfaction and Marital Happiness of Bisexual and Heterosexual Swinging Husbands," *Journal of Homosexuality* 11 (1985): 209-22; Joan Dixon, "Sexuality and Relationship Changes in Married Females Following the Commencement of Bisexual Activity," *Journal of Homosexuality* 11 (1985): 115-33; Fritz Klein, *The Bisexual Option: A Concept of One-Hundred Percent Intimacy* (New York: Arbor House, 1978); Barry Kohn and Alice Matusow, *Barry and Alice: Portrait of a Bisexual Marriage* (Englewood Cliffs, NJ: Prentice Hall, 1980); David R. Matteson, "Bisexual Men in Marriage: Is a Positive Homosexual Identity and Stable Marriage Possible?" *Journal of Homosexuality* 11 (1985): 149-73; Regina U. Reinhardt, "Bisexual Women in Heterosexual Relationships: A Study of Psychological and Sociological Patterns," dissertation, Professional School of Psychological Studies, 1985; Jennifer Schneider and Burt Schneider, *Sex, Lies, and Forgiveness: Couples Speaking Out About Sexual Addiction* (Hazelton Foundation, 1991): 183-222; Timothy J. Wolf, "Selected Psychological and Sociological Aspects of Male Homosexual Behavior in Marriage," dissertation, United States International University, 1982, and "Marriages of Bisexual Men," *Journal of Homosexuality* 11 (1985): 135-48.

12. Sandra Auerback and Charles Moser, "Groups for the Wives of Gays and Bisexual Men," *Social Work* (July-August 1989): 321-25; Buxton, *The Other Side of*

the Closet, 1991 and 1994; George Deabill, "An Investigation of Sexual Behaviors in Mixed Sexual Orientation Couples: Gay Husbands and Straight Wives," dissertation, Institute for the Advanced Study of Human Sexuality, 1987; Jean S. Gochros, *When Husbands Come Out of the Closet* (Binghamton, NY: Harrington Park Press, 1989); Dorothea Hays and Aurele Samuels, "Heterosexual Women's Perceptions of Their Marriages to Homosexual or Bisexual Men," *Journal of Homosexuality* 17 (1989): 81-100; Hill, *The Bisexual Spouse*; David Matteson, "Married and Gay," *Changing Men* (Spring-Summer 1988): 14-16; Hans Van der Geest, "Homosexuality and Marriage," *If You Seduce A Straight Person Can You Make Them Gay?* 115-24; Catherine Whitney, *Uncommon Lives: Gay Men and Straight Women* (New York: New American Library, 1990).

    13. Deborah Abbott and Ellen Farmer, *From Wedded Wife to Lesbian Life: Stories of Transformation* (Santa Cruz, CA: Crossing Press, 1995); Aileen H. Atwood, *Husbands Who Love Men: Deceit, Disease, Despair* (Providence, UT: AMI Publications, 1998); Martha B. Barrett, *Invisible Lives: The Truth About Millions of Women Loving Women* (New York: William Morrow, 1989); Robert Bauman, *Gentleman from Maryland: The Conscience of a Gay Conservative* (New York: William Morrow, 1986); Terry Norman, *Just Tell the Truth: Questions Families Ask When Gay Married Men Come Out* (Kansas City, MO: Prehension Publications, 1998); Carol Lynn Pearson, *Good-Bye, I Love You* (New York: Jove, 1989); Carren Strock, *Married Women Who Love Women* (New York: Doubleday, 1998); Mel White, *Stranger at the Gate: To Be Gay and Christian in America* (New York: Simon and Schuster, 1994); Sally L. Whitehead, *The Truth Shall Set You Free: A Memoir* (San Francisco: HarperSanFrancisco, 1997).

    14. Despite demographic diversity, the majority were white middle-class U.S. residents, from 30-60 years old, educated through at least the first year of college. The samples were also limited to those who made themselves known through seeking support or information or by participating in gay, lesbian, or bisexual organizations.

    15. Fritz Klein, Barry Sepekoff, and Timothy J. Wolf, "Sexual Orientation: A Multivariable Dynamic Process," *Journal of Homosexuality* 11 (1985): 35-49. See also Anthony R. D'Augelli and Charlotte J. Patterson, eds., *Lesbian, Gay, and Bisexual Identities Over the Lifespan: Psychological Perspectives* (New York: Oxford University Press, 1995).

    16. Ronald C. Fox, "Bisexual Identities," *Lesbian, Gay, and Bisexual Identities Over the Lifespan*, 48-86; Janet Lever, David E. Kahouse, William H. Rogers, Sally Carson, and Rosanna Hertz, "Behavior Patterns and Sexual Identity of Bisexual Males," *Journal of Sexual Research* 29 (1992): 141-62; Michael W. Rossand and Jay P. Paul, "Beyond Gender: The Basis of Sexual Attraction in Bisexual Men and Women," *Psychological Reports* 71 (1992): 1283-90; Martin S. Weinberg, Colin J. Williams, and Douglas W. Pryor, *Dual Attraction: Understanding Bisexuality* (New York: Oxford University Press, 1994).

    17. John H. Gagnon, "Gender Preferences in Erotic Relations: The Kinsey Scale and Sexual Scripts," *Homosexuality/Heterosexuality: Concepts of Sexual Orientation*, eds. David S. McWhirter, Suzanne A. Sanders, and June M. Reinisch (New York: Oxford University Press, 1990), 177-297; Kinsey et al., *Sexual Behavior in the Human Male*; Fritz Klein, *The Bisexual Option*, second edition (Binghamton, NY:

Harrington Park Press, 1993), 12-28; Richard G. Parker and John Gagnon, eds., *Conceiving Sexuality: Approaches to Sex Research in a Postmodern World* (New York: Routledge, 1995).

18. Buxton, *The Other Side of the Closet*, 1994; Coleman, "Integration of Male Bisexuality and Marriage"; Gochros, *When Husbands Come Out of the Closet*; Latham and White, "Coping with Homosexual Expression within Heterosexual Marriages," 34; Matteson, "Bisexual Men in Marriage"; Whitney, *Uncommon Lives*; Wolf, "Marriages of Bisexual Men," and "Selected Psychological and Sociological Aspects of Male Homosexual Behavior in Marriage."

19. The countries included were Australia, Canada, China, England, Estonia, France, Germany, India, Ireland, Israel, Italy, Mexico, New Zealand, Puerto Rico, and Singapore.

20. Maurice Merleau-Ponty, *Phenomenology of Perception*, trans. C. Smith (London: Routledge and Kegan Paul, 1962).

21. Only the factors mentioned by more than 10% of each sample are considered in the study.

22. Judith S. Wallerstein and Sandra Blakeslee, *The Good Marriage: How and Why Love Lasts* (Boston: Houghton Mifflin, 1995).

23. Gender differences may also play a part here. See Philip Blumstein and Pepper Schwartz, *American Couples: Money, Work, Sex* (New York: William Morrow, 1984); Deborah Tannen, *You Just Don't Understand: Women and Men in Conversation* (New York: Ballantine Books, 1990).

24. See Thomas P. Malone and Patrick T. Malone, *The Art of Intimacy* (New York: Prentice Hall, 1987).

The
Married Man
On-Line

Larry W. Peterson

[Haworth co-indexing entry note]: "The Married Man On-Line." Peterson, Larry W. Co-published simultaneously in *Journal of Bisexuality* (Harrington Park Press, an imprint of The Haworth Press, Inc.) Vol. 1, No. 2/3, 2001, pp. 191-209; and: *Bisexuality in the Lives of Men: Facts and Fictions* (ed: Brett Beemyn and Erich Steinman) Harrington Park Press, an imprint of The Haworth Press, Inc., 2001, pp. 191-209. Single or multiple copies of this article are available for a fee from The Haworth Document Delivery Service [1-800-342-9678, 9:00 a.m. - 5:00 p.m. (EST). E-mail address: getinfo@haworthpressinc.com].

SUMMARY. This article explores the impact of the Internet upon married bisexual and gay men, including the importance they attach to being on-line. What do the men talk about? What issues are most significant to them? What do they gain from the experience of being on-line? Quotations from many on-line posts are included. The information was collected from 1,420 posts written by approximately 350 men from a list administered by the author. In addition, the author includes insights gained from reading posts on nine other lists that include bisexual/gay married men. *[Article copies available for a fee from The Haworth Document Delivery Service: 1-800-342-9678. E-mail address: <getinfo@haworthpressinc. com> Website: <http://www.HaworthPress.com>]*

KEYWORDS. Bisexual men, bisexuality, gay, married men, men's support, on-line

During the three and a half years that I administered an on-line support group for bisexual/gay men who are out to their wives, I was struck by the tremendous impact of the Internet upon myself and the other married bisexual and gay men. For many of us, access to electronic mailing lists has dramatically changed how we perceive our sexuality in ways that are unlike any previous influences upon our lives. Yet, these experiences have been almost entirely ignored by researchers.[1] In this article, I plan to consider what is important about married bisexual and gay men being on-line and, after explaining how this information was obtained and developed, discuss the impact that these lists have had on their subscribers. What do the men talk about? What issues are most significant to them? What do they gain from the experience? I will quote from many on-line posts to provide a sense of both the quality and the nature of the comments.[2]

The information for this article resulted from my reading of 1,420 messages[3] that were posted by approximately 350 men to the list for bisexual/gay married men that I oversaw.[4] In addition, I gained insight from reading posts on nine other lists that included bisexual/gay married men.[5] The list that I managed for married men averaged from 150 to 200 subscribers most of the time over the last three years, and another list for married men that I was involved with for two years consisted of slightly more than 200 subscribers at any given time. Besides managing one list for men and another for these men and their wives, I facilitated four national conferences for bisexual/gay married men and, with my wife, hosted four gatherings for these men and their wives. At each of the conferences, we discussed some of the topics included in this article. However, every quotation that follows appeared on-line. Part of the goal of this article is summed up nicely by one man's post:

But how do we struggle for our place in the sun? The sun doesn't shine in the closet. Demanding to be considered equal to my brothers endangers my family and makes us all outcasts. Lucky are we to have each other through AOL and face to face support groups. All of us in this complicated world struggle with one thing or another. It's just that doing it in the closet makes it seem we are very different. But I don't think we are. It just seems that way.

To illustrate the relative importance of different topics for the men on the list, I include the number of times that a particular issue was raised within the 1,420 posts. The topics that I identify are not always the main subject per se of the post, but they do represent an important concern or item shared. In regard to the accuracy or truthfulness of the comments that were sent to the lists used for this study, I have never had the impression that anything said was untrue or intentionally deceptive. Nor, in my experience, do such support lists provide an avenue for a person to try out a new identity or gender. Having met many of the men face-to-face at various list-member gatherings, I believe that what they say within the confidential confines of a support list can generally be accepted as honest and reliable. In this respect, these lists differ dramatically from other kinds of on-line interactions. For example, the conventional wisdom among list members is that men who place Internet personal ads often lie about their age, appearance, or sexual experience.

AN OVERVIEW OF THE MEN ON-LINE

From both the posts to the lists and personal interactions with these men over the past four years, I have been able to make seven general observations about married bisexual and gay men on-line. These characterizations are ones that largely define the men within the lists and indicate their priorities for discussion. My first observation relates to when the men acknowledged their sexuality to themselves. Some of the men have only recently admitted that they are bisexual or gay. For these men, it is not uncommon that the catalyst was the death of a father or father-in-law (for me, it was the latter). If not a death, then something else caused these men to ask themselves whether they wished to live the rest of their lives refusing to acknowledge their same-sex desire. Other men were out to themselves before they decided to marry. Some thought that marriage would make them heterosexual, even though they recognized that they had been attracted to men since childhood. Others married with the full knowledge that they were bisexual or gay and did not expect their marriage to change their sexuality; they loved their wives enough to marry anyway. As one man wrote,

> I chose heterosexual marriage because I loved my wife, felt we had more going for us than I had ever had with a guy. I wanted the challenge and surprise of heterosexuality after years of homosexual relationships which for me were great but also predictable in a way.

Another man, who was out to his wife when they married, commented,

> For us the issue was negotiating how I would express those feelings. I do think that there must be others, like us, for whom the crucial issues don't revolve around some competition between hetero- and homosexual feelings, but around how homoerotic feelings are integrated in a healthy marriage.

Many of the men who were out to their wives before marriage now admit, however, that neither they nor their wives knew what his sexuality meant for their marriage and what challenges were ahead.

My second observation relates to the extent to which the men are out. Later in the article, the topic of "coming out" will be explored further, but here it is important to note that there is great variation in the degree to which the men are out to their wives, kids, parents, co-workers, friends, and in the community where they live. In fact, many married bisexual and gay men on-line are not out even to their wives. They use the Internet, especially chat rooms and lists, to find men who live in the vicinity, or in areas where they travel, for conversation and/or sex. The men who are not out to their spouses discuss some of the same topics on-line as those who are out to their wives, such as details of male friendships, safer sex, providing on-line support, and opportunities to connect with others, but usually they are not interested in discussing any of the complexities of coming out to others or the challenges that relate to communication with their wives. Unlike their friends who are out to their wives, these men may prefer to talk on-line about where they hide their pornographic materials or how they protect their e-mail or other confidential computer files.

My third observation relates to the level of intimacy the men have with their wives. Some married men identify as gay and no longer wish to be intimate with their wives, while others continue to do so. Some men seek ways to be intimate with their wives short of intercourse, and some do not. This issue will be explored further below.

My fourth observation relates to how the men identify themselves. Discussions related to the terms "gay" and "bisexual" periodically constitute on-line "threads."[6] Whether they are gay or bisexual appears to be very important to some men. Others do not care to identify themselves any more specifically than "not straight." Nor do most subscribers seem interested in how these terms are defined. Bisexuality, for example, simply means being attracted to both women and men; the fact that its meaning is often contested within sex research is probably unknown to most of these men and would not matter in any case. What does interest them is whether subscribers identify as bisexual, gay, or "not straight." This topic will be explored in greater detail in the section about self-image.

My fifth observation relates to the sexual activities outside of the marriage. This is what I call the Fidelity Factor. Here it may be helpful to think in terms of a continuum similar to the Kinsey Scale, with total monogamy at one end and an open marriage for both spouses at the other. In between these extremes lie several options well represented within the lists: a husband with only one male sexual partner/a wife with no others, a husband with multiple male partners/a wife with no others, and a ménage a trois, perhaps with the second man living with them.

Monogamy is a major issue for both wives and the men on-line, many of whom wrestle with this issue or seek to re-negotiate this aspect of the marriage. One man who is monogamous comments that

> We are presently in counseling and have chosen to not have an "open" marriage now or at any time in the future. To us, that seems to be a violation of the marriage vows we originally took and, from a spiritual viewpoint, would be considered adultery . . . however, please realize that is our opinion for ourselves and we respect each individual to do what works for their own marriage, providing both partners are in total agreement.

But, in other marriages, the husband and wife agree to remain married and allow the man to have some sexual involvement with other men.

> I for one cannot stay in a marriage and be monogamous, because that would be denying who/what I am. Both my wife and I feel that the easier road would be divorce, but because of the love we share we are both prepared to take the more difficult journey, and in our case that means that I'm allowed to have relationships with other men. I know it causes my wife pain, and at times I've been depressed about that–but she says she'd rather deal with the few "down" days she has than go our separate ways.

In some cases, the wife chooses to have sexual relationships with men other than her husband. In other cases, the man and his wife seek another man who will interact sexually with both of them. Sometimes a man will seek only one male sexual partner–often another married man–who accepts that the husband's first priority is his wife and family. Some wives feel more comfortable with their husbands seeing only one other man, believing that it reduces any potential health risk and is easier logistically. It is not uncommon for the wife in this situation to wish to meet the man with whom her husband is sexually involved. In contrast, some wives prefer that their husbands avoid an ongoing relationship with only one other man because they feel that there is less chance that way of their husbands leaving them for another man. As a result, these men are more likely to have multiple male partners. Within my own list, there are also at least two cases in which two men and a woman live together in the same house as a family unit. In both instances, the wife interacts sexually with her husband but not with his male partner.

My sixth observation relates to how much communication exists between the husband and wife about his sexuality. Obviously this observation is not relevant for the men who are not out to their wives. But those who are open may talk to their wives about their fears, desires, and actions. One man shared with me that his wife once told him that she trusted him never to embarrass her or their immediate family and expected him to practice safer sex and to be home at night in bed with her. Otherwise, she did not want to talk about the subject ever again or know anything about what he did with other men during the day. Other husbands ultimately have ongoing discussions with their wives about their sexuality and the implications for their marriage. Many of these men tell their wives when they are meeting other men so that their spouses know their whereabouts.

My last observation concerns whether the man is married or divorced. Many divorced bisexual and gay men remain on lists designed for married men for a variety of reasons: some of the topics discussed are still relevant to them, they have strong friendships with other men on-line and feel loyal to them and the list, and they want to offer help and support to other married men who may decide to separate or divorce.

THE BACKGROUND OF THE MEN

The men in my sample are a privileged group and do not represent the full range of married bisexual/gay men. From personal experience, I know that many men are not on-line. For example, when I attended meetings of the

Wilmington, Delaware chapter of GAMMA (Gay Married Men of America), I was the only one of the seven members who was on-line; among the 46 men in the Philadelphia chapter, just two of us were active on the Internet.[7] The men who belong to the lists I used for my research are well-educated–graduate degrees are not uncommon–and many are professionals, working as doctors, lawyers, educators, computer specialists, corporate managers, union leaders, therapists, nurses, salesmen, accountants, engineers, ministers, visual artists, and musicians. Most of the men have one or more children, love them dearly, and enjoy the challenges of fatherhood. Maintaining a loving relationship with their children is one of the most common topics on my list and one of the main reasons why many men continue to have a close relationship with their spouse (or former spouse).

The men who posted to my list over the past four years come from almost every state in the U.S. (only Alaska, Mississippi, North Dakota, and South Dakota were not represented). At any one time, less than two dozen men resided in Canada, and only one man lived in each of the following countries: Ireland, Denmark, Italy, Brazil, Australia, New Zealand, Thailand, England, and Israel. The large majority of the men are white; most are in their 40s or 50s (40% and 33% respectively). But there are men in their 20s (2%), 30s (20%), 60s (4%), and 70s (1%). These percentages reflect the membership of one list at the time the article was written. Memberships on lists fluctuate daily as people subscribe and unsubscribe. As a group, the most transient members are the men in their 20s or early 30s. They do not remain very long on a list for married men because they typically divorce within a year of joining and then put that part of their lives behind them.

THE IMPORTANCE OF THE INTERNET

To illustrate why married men join one of these on-line lists, I have selected quotes from two men. I could easily provide several hundred similar examples.

> Many of you have mentioned in recent posts about the value our list has to you. I for one don't know what I would do without it. As one other mentioned, I too check mail a couple of times a day. This list more than anything else has helped me to cope with myself, with coming out, and more importantly to see a bright light at the end of the tunnel that gives strong indication that my marriage will hang together, not for the sake of our kids, friends or neighbors, but for the sake of my wife and I who

both place strong value on the togetherness we have had for many years.

> . . . eye contact seems to make me self-conscious. On the Net, I can be completely open with people in ways that would be intimidating if eye-to-eye. . . . I would be the last to condemn the Net as a way to avoid intimacy or human contact. It certainly has advantages over the "bar scene" for realism and honest connection.

It is interesting to note how much time these men spend on the Internet. Seventy-three men responded to my request to estimate how much personal time they spend on-line. As a group, they average from 12 to 15 hours a week. The lowest response I received was an hour and the highest was an incredible 90 hours per week. One important variable in how much time these men spend on-line is when they first came out. Typically, men devote much more time to the lists in their first year after coming out, then their involvement drops off, often dramatically. But, for many married bisexual and gay men, this on-line period is critical. As the previous quotes demonstrate, they develop a sense of community through receiving support from dozens of other men like themselves and no longer feel that their situation is unique. The men often share very intimate details of their lives and inner thoughts, which for some is a new experience. Many also establish close friendships with other men for the first time in their lives.

Through the Internet, they can arrange to meet other men who live within easy driving distance or in other cities. Many of the men on-line travel as part of their jobs, so it is not uncommon for them to try to meet other men when they visit a particular city. These meetings may be for conversation only or may include sex. Many men date others whom they met initially via the Internet, and it is not uncommon for men to fall in love with someone they met on-line. In some cases (including my own), men experience a high level of intimacy without having personally met the other man.

Lists are also used by many bisexual and gay men to develop friendships and relationships that constitute what Stanley Siegel and Ed Lowe, Jr. call a "male family."[8] My own experiences, as well as those of others on these lists, demonstrate that men often create "cyber-families" with other men whom they have come to love and respect and whom they know will "be there" when needed. Significantly, many of these men feel that they never would have come out to themselves or others had they not found the Internet. It was through chat rooms and/or lists for bisexual/gay men that they finally realized or admitted that they were not heterosexual. And this momentous admission started many of them on a new path of discovery that continued to be directly tied to the Internet.

Being able to establish an on-line network of friends and acquaintances who are facing similar challenges, these men feel exhilarated and validated, and no longer feel so isolated and alone. They excitedly share their fantasies and joys, and even their experiences meeting or dating other men. They also seek advice about coming out to their wives, children, and co-workers, and may ask questions about how to find a sympathetic therapist or information on HIV, AIDS, and STDs. Friendships that begin on-line often move off-line through face-to-face meetings or phone conversations. Since there are few if any affirming examples for married bisexual and gay men in our culture, these men often look to on-line colleagues to be role models and are able to develop a more positive self-image and self-assurance through learning about other men's experiences and the attitudes and decisions they have in common.

TOPICS DISCUSSED IN POSTS

To identify the specific topics that men discussed and how often each topic was explored, I began by tabulating the total number of times that a topic appeared in the 1,420 posts. By far, the most common type of comment involved a man sharing information about himself and his situation (approximately 1,277 times). These comments may be as simple as "what I did last night" or relate to his conception of identity labels, coming out, relationships with other men, marriage, and opinions about a wide variety of other topics. The most frequently mentioned personal issue was self-image or factors that contribute to self-image.

Self-Image

Married men who are bisexual or gay, like many other bisexual and gay men, frequently struggle to develop a positive concept of themselves. For those who have Net access, the change in self-image is readily apparent.

> Just acknowledging that one is homosexual is enough to incur approbation, even without any act being committed. So, we must be gentle with ourselves and all the things I wrote in my post to "Henry." The payoff, as I am experiencing now, is to feel integrated, whole, wholesome, and deliciously alive! It is worth all the doubt and anguish. It is a feeling that I would not want to die without knowing.

My liberation is that, as I came to the threshold of losing everything because of whom I am intrinsically, I had this surreal experience of discovering that I was not losing much, except the internalized homophobia and subliminal messages of self-hate that I have been so thoroughly immersed in as an American man. What I find I am losing is my vulnerability to those missiles of venom that pack the hate letters in the media and the ridicule of the stereotypical characters of queers in films. I see the affronts, I find them stupid and destructive and take what action I can to counter them, and then I realize that my attention is much more easily focused on the fine people around me, and the fine man inside me.

These quotations reveal some of the significant ways that the Internet has a very positive effect on these men. As shown by their comments over several years, receiving validation and support helps build their self-esteem on a long-term basis.

One aspect of self-image that is the subject of frequent posts is the use of the terms "gay" and "bisexual." Using the Klein Sexual Orientation Grid, most of the men on the lists would be considered bisexual, for one of Klein's criteria for bisexuality is way of life.[9] Some of the men do, in fact, call themselves bisexual and state that they are attracted to both women and men. Moreover, a number of the men have commented that if their wives die or seek a divorce, they would eventually hope to remarry. But even though most of the men on the lists are married, a significant number still feel very strongly that the word "gay" identifies them best. While Klein's Grid attempts to account for sexual complexity through its consideration of past, present, and future behavior and preferences, most men, in my experience, use the single criterion of present sexual attraction to decide if they are gay or bisexual. Here, whether they have intercourse with their wives is often the determining factor. Other men do not concern themselves with terminology and usually do not participate in the discussions or threads that consider what it means to be gay versus bisexual. Some simply observe that they are "not straight" and leave it at that.

Labels are just that . . . they are NOT who we are but rather generalizations. . . . I label myself bi for want of anything more expressive. . . . I am a man that is drawn to sex with other men, I am married . . . happily and we chose to stay married though it is not easy . . . the best lovemaking that I have or make is with my wife, yet I am drawn to men . . . so I am bi, but then there are those times when I am decidedly attracted to women both emotionally and physically. . . . I am a man and I respond to people . . . men and women . . . and am capable of responding emotionally and physically to all if the conditions are right. . . . Gay? No. . . . Bi? . . . I suppose so. Straight? What does that label mean?

Within the posts discussing sexual identity terms, 29 involved a man describing what label best fits him, and another 67 specifically included thoughts about being bisexual.

Coming Out

Coming out–both coming out to oneself and the timing and nature of coming out to others–is also an important concern for the men in the sample. Sometimes the issue is discussed in terms of how it impacts the man himself.

> I feel quite differently about the effect that coming out has on the balance of power between myself and those to whom I reveal myself. Rather than giving the "outee" a tactical advantage over me, I see it as taking back the power that is rightfully mine. I feel that the person who keeps a secret, especially a shame based secret, is living in the constant fear of being discovered. Therefore, those who may stumble upon the secret know that it is within their power to deny the subject of that knowledge the thing they value most, their need for acceptance and love (and, in the old days, their liberty or even life). When you owe your happiness or success to withholding the truth, the truth doesn't set you free, it imprisons you.

Many men have shared very moving stories on-line about coming out to their children, often relating in great detail what they and their children said and how they felt about the experience. For example, one man, who had come out to his eleven-year-old son, wrote:

> To let you know how good things have gone for me and my son, this is what he wrote in my birthday card: "Even though you are gay, I still will love you for the rest of my life. For that's what friendship is for (or in this case Father-son-hood)." I started to read this out loud and couldn't finish as I got so choked up.

The men on the lists frequently advise and provide support to one another about coming out to their children, as well as to their parents, wives, and doctors. Since coming out is often a complex and never-ending process, this topic is discussed repeatedly; in the posts read for this article, it appears 120 times.

Wives

For the men on the lists who are out to their wives, another frequent topic is the nature of their marriage. These men are concerned about how they can maintain a sex life with their wives, or how they can be "intimate" with them if intercourse is not an option; whether they should stay married, and if so, whether they should remain monogamous; and how they can better communicate with, or understand, their spouses.

> My experience when it gets right down to the bone is that what our wives ARE always talking about are things like . . . do you really love me? . . does my opinion count with you? . . . I . . can I depend on you? . . . Underneath much of our huffing and puffing, these are the real messages that are often being expressed.

> When I examine why the "successful in surviving" marriages of my list brothers do so well, the common factor I note is a wife who deeply loves her husband FOR WHO HE IS DESPITE his sexuality. Those wives are courageous and creative about supporting what is healthy for their husbands, while being assertive about the limits and accommodations they need to maintain their flexibility.

Being in a mixed-orientation marriage (i.e., one spouse straight and one bisexual or gay) can be a lifelong challenge, and for the men who are out, relating to their wives is a constant concern. Many men note that their marriage takes a cyclic pattern, alternating between emotionally high and low periods. Among the difficulties often cited is the difference between a wife accepting her husband's sexuality intellectually and accepting it emotionally as a lived reality. Intimacy with one's wife is another delicate topic. If sexual intercourse itself is not an option, some men turn to alternatives (for example, sex toys or oral sex) to maintain an intimate relationship, as well as to respond to her sexual needs. Regarding these and other issues, men who have been out to their wives for several years often share their experiences to educate and support men who have recently revealed their sexuality to their spouses.

Other Men

Men also regularly discuss their relationships with other men. The most frequent questions raised here include: where do you meet men?; how can you tell when a man at a bar is interested in you?; what is the "hanky code"?; should I remain monogamous to a male partner?; what are the differences between a purely sexual relationship and one that includes emotional ties, perhaps including love?; do I really need intimacy with another man?; and how do I avoid falling in love with another man? The following two quotes reflect some of these concerns and illustrate how an acceptance of their desire for other men can have a tremendous impact on the lives and identities of list members.

> As I work through all the changes since coming out three years ago and having to re-examine my values and belief system in the new context, I am realizing slowly that I accept [certain things] without question. One of them is that I trust totally my need for M2M (male-to-male) intimacy. I cannot go back in the closet, I do not feel whole as a married man monogamous to my wife, and I am willing to risk my marriage–as wonderful as my wife is–to seek wholeness. My spiritual and religious beliefs now are vital again, but with many new variations, but the core is still there intact and firm.

> In all of your posts I can "hear" that this relationship with this boy-friend has you feeling out of alignment with your core values. That is always disconcerting . . . and I believe that's for a good reason. I think it is this feeling that, if we are "listening," helps guide us, helps us to find OUR OWN way. Follow your instincts "Harry," Alignment, Integra-tion, Values, Authenticity . . . these are important elements of peace. Going in the direction of these can never be wrong in my opinion. Peace to you Harry . . . and all of our on-line family.

Support

As the last quote demonstrates, the men often readily provide support to others in need. In the posts used for this study, supportive statements ap-peared more than one hundred times. Men sent moving messages to one man when his daughter committed suicide, to another when his wife died, to another when his son was killed in a hit-and-run accident, and to yet another when he continually wrote about his despair. Phone calls were also common-ly made to men who expressed sadness or despondency. Again and again, many of the men demonstrate how much they care. An important aspect of this support involves exchanging information. Frequently, a man will tell other list members if he is aware that someone else needs attention and comfort. Men also often exchange opinions about books that they have read, and several essays written by Amity Pierce Buxton, the author of *The Other Side of the Closet: The Coming-Out Crisis for Straight Spouses and Families,* were mailed without charge to any man on the list requesting copies.[10] Other articles; excerpts from books, speeches, reports, and newspaper accounts; previously private e-mail messages; and postings from other lists are likewise shared, in part to stimulate discussion. One final aspect of support that I wish to mention here relates to "advice." Given the sensitivity of many of the issues that married bisexual and gay men face, most list members hesitate to give advice per se. Rather, many men prefer to describe what has or has not worked for them. They do not advise someone to follow their lead because they feel that each man must make these decisions for himself.

Marriage

Another topic of concern for many men is the nature or functioning of a mixed-orientation marriage. As some of the previous quotations and topics indicate, the subject of marriage arises frequently (93 times), including the issue of whether to stay married (an additional 55 times). Men who have decided to remain in their marriage often discuss the boundaries that they and their wives have agreed upon since his coming out and the new vows that they have developed together. Other men describe their separation and divorce. The following quotes help illustrate the kind of dialogue that occurs around this topic:

> I have also noticed a preponderance of messages lately from men who are divorcing, separating, or otherwise ending the marriage to pursue life as a single gay or bi men. I applaud them for their courage, for I have followed their struggles posted here, as they tried to "make it work" but for various reasons have found it necessary to move on and away from marriage. That is an honorable choice for them. But I want to remind other observers that there are many of us out here who are choosing to stay in our marriages because, for us, at this time, this is an honorable choice for us. We love our spouses and they love us. We are doing the work of integrating our "other" sexuality into our relationships with our wives.

> I was reminded that I need to remain focused on several things which really help me through the many challenges that my wife and I face . . . to remember why I wish to be married. My love for and my bond with my wife is so strong that I need to remind myself of this at times. Also, as "Harry" shared, I seek only one spouse . . . my wife . . . and my male

relationships thus fall into a secondary role. I will never be loved, cherished, cared for, and supported as I am by my wife and I try to return that gift back to her.

Religion and Spirituality

Spirituality, organized religion, and personal religious beliefs and experiences are likewise the subject of frequent posts (referred to 69 times). Among the concerns commonly addressed are feelings of guilt and shame over their sexuality, the ramifications of coming out at church, and the process of finding a church, denomination, or denominational group (for example, Dignity for Roman Catholics, Integrity for Episcopalians, or More Light congregations for Presbyterians) that is supportive of gays. Several pastors on these lists have graciously shared sermons, hymns of their own composition, poetry, and other commentaries to assist subscribers in understanding themselves within a spiritual framework. Men also recommend and sometimes offer detailed reviews of religious and spiritual books, like Chris Glaser's *Coming Out as Sacrament* (which includes specific rituals for a coming out service) and Mark Thompson's *Gay Soul: Finding the Heart of Gay Spirit and Nature* (which contains 16 essays that explore spirituality within the context of sexuality).[11]

Counseling

Counseling is occasionally the subject of on-line discussions and has especially been an important issue at several of the national gatherings held for the men on one of my lists. As in the case of on-line clergy members, it has been helpful that a number of professional therapists subscribe to the lists and are able to answer the men's questions, such as what to ask to determine if a potential counselor is sympathetic, what are appropriate responses from a counselor, and does the counselor's own sexual orientation make a difference. At times, a man has been advised to seek another therapist after sharing something his counselor said. For example, one man was informed by a therapist that he should divorce his wife because, supposedly, mixed-orientation marriages inevitably fail. Other men were told that their bisexual or gay identity was a phase, or that they could choose to convert to heterosexuality.

Miscellaneous Topics

Finally, a number of topics deserve brief mention because they demonstrate the diversity of on-line conversation. Humor frequently appears in the form of jokes or personal anecdotes. For many men, a sense of humor is essential for surviving the challenges of mixed-orientation marriages. Health threads include discussions of safer sex, depression, and erection and prostate problems. Honesty is a topic in 37 posts. Other concerns include the prejudice against gay and bisexual men, anger, dreams, morality, poetry (some written by the men themselves), suggested sexual techniques, political correctness, political action on gay-related legislation, the importance of communication, the perception of being "trapped," and how age affects their situation. One topic that I would especially like to highlight relates to feelings. For many men who first came out to themselves in mid-life, experiencing feelings is a new phenomenon. Having denied their sexuality for most of their lives, they also lost the ability to "feel," except perhaps through movies and books. After coming out, they suddenly find that they can express their feelings, and for the first time, some of them cry and love easily.

CONCLUSION

Lists such as the ones used for this study have dramatically changed the lives of the married bisexual and gay men who have access to them. They now have a ready mechanism to receive information; establish networks, friendships, and male families; seek dates; and even find love. Some married men who had denied their sexual identities were curious enough to explore bisexual and gay chat rooms and lists, which helped them to accept themselves and, in time, to come out.

For men who live outside of urban areas or who wish to keep their sexuality confidential, the Internet provides opportunities to meet other men with similar experiences that would be unavailable or inconvenient otherwise. As one list member commented, "I have had more 'real' communication in the past couple of weeks reading the posts on this list than I've had (total) in the past ten years." Interaction on the Net allows men to feel good about themselves and to develop mentors, models, and often close friendships with other men for the first time. Some of the men consider one or two others whom they have met on-line to be the brother(s) they never had before. Thus, through the Internet, men can find the love and respect that they have long desired from other men.

My own story is typical: after interacting with other men on-line, I came out to myself, then to my wife, and later to my children, some co-workers, and other members of the community. In creating a male "family" for support and nurture, I established strong male friendships for the first time in my life and discovered the love of other men. For me, this was revolutionary, radically transforming how I viewed myself and the world. Other men whom I have met on-line have likewise discussed how the Net has dramatically affected their lives. In the words of one man, "I kept it all bottled up, hid it away from myself, then we bought a computer. . . ." Or, as another man exclaimed when referring to himself and the other married bisexual and gay men on-line, "We are indeed pioneers." When I told the men on the list that I founded that I was using the word "revolution" to describe the changes in my life, one man responded:

> The use of revolution is perfect, not only because of its definition, but because of its etymology. Its root meaning is to "turn again." The Internet and technology have allowed us to turn again, planets make a revolution around the sun, turning again, and societies foment uprisings as they turn again. While the turning always returns, it is never back to exactly the same place. These are revolutions. . . . And that is what we are each and collectively about.

Through the Internet, married bisexual and gay men have been able to create families, find brothers, and discover mentors who can help them cope with similar challenges. To use the nomenclature of the Net, men now speak in terms of cyber-friendships, cyber-families, and "virtual" communities, all of which serve a critical function for men who had previously felt isolated and "weird." The research that I have shared within this article just scratches the surface of bisexual and gay married men's on-line conversations, but I hope that the brief glimpse that I have been able to offer here demonstrates the richness of this material and will spark further studies.

NOTES

1. The only previous work on married bisexual/gay men on-line that I am aware of is Amity Buxton's "Impact of Disclosure of Bisexuality on a Marriage," an unpublished study that uses two of the same Internet lists that I relied on for this essay. Buxton's purpose, in part, was to examine "coping strategies, supportive circumstances, and inhibiting external factors reported by 36 bisexual husbands and 23 heterosexual wives of self-identified bisexual men who attempted to stay married after the men had disclosed their bisexuality." She compared their reported experiences with 30 self-identified gay married men and 31 heterosexual wives of gay husbands. Amity Pierce Buxton, "Impact of Disclosure of Bisexuality on a Marriage," unpublished paper presented at the 105th Annual Convention of the American Psychological Association, Chicago, Illinois, August 16, 1997.

2. Confidentiality is crucial for men to share their innermost thoughts on-line. To protect the privacy of list members, I am not identifying the names of the lists or using the real names of subscribers (the names that appear within the men's quotes were changed from the ones in the original posts). I also keep most quotations brief in order to avoid revealing personal information that might divulge an individual's identity.

3. I owe a tremendous debt to Tom Schwartz of Seattle, Washington, who selected the posts that I read for this article from the archives of the list. All posts, with four exceptions, date from October 1997 to May 1999, and comprise about one half of the total posts to the list during this time. I ignored administrative material, "me too" posts (i.e., messages in which all the person writes is that he agrees with what was said in a post), welcoming messages to new members, posts that simply suggested a Web site to visit or involved a man making arrangements to meet others, and private posts that had been shared publicly.

4. Most of these 1,420 posts will appear in their complete form in a book that Fritz Klein and Tom Schwartz are preparing for publication in the spring of 2000.

5. I use the term "bisexual" to refer to men who self-identity as bisexual. I will examine the different meanings of "bisexual" later in the article.

6. The term "thread" refers to a topic that appears on the subject line for multiple posts. By keeping the subject line the same as the one for the original post, all readers know immediately that this post is a response to a previous one. The "labels" thread (using "bisexual" versus "gay") appears several times a year on the list that I administer.

7. Since I no longer attend GAMMA meetings, I contacted a current member to verify if this is still true. He confirmed that even now, in the summer of 1999, many of the men are not on-line.

8. Stanley Siegel and Ed Lowe, Jr., *Understanding the Life Passages of Gay Men* (New York: Plume, 1994).

9. Fritz Klein, Barry Sepekoff, and Timothy J. Wolf, "Sexual Orientation: A Multivariable Dynamic Process," *Journal of Homosexuality* 11 (1985): 35-49.

10. Amity Pierce Buxton, *The Other Side of the Closet: The Coming-Out Crisis for Straight Spouses and Families* (New York: John Wiley and Sons, 1991).

11. Chris Glaser, *Coming Out as Sacrament* (Knoxville, KY: John Knox Press, 1998) and Mark Thompson, ed., *Gay Soul: Finding the Heart of Gay Spirit and Nature* (San Francisco: HarperCollins, 1990).

Index